THE
GENESIS PRINCIPLE

THE
GENESIS PRINCIPLE

A Journey into the Source of Creativity and Leadership

Hal Isen and Peter Kline

GREAT OCEAN PUBLISHERS
ARLINGTON, VIRGINIA

For information contact:
>Great Ocean Publishers
1823 North Lincoln Street
Arlington, VA 22207

Library of CongressCataloging in Publication Data
Isen,Harold
    The genesis principle : a journey into the source of creativity and leadership /
Hal Isen and Peter Kline
    p.   cm.
    ISBN 0-915556-34-0 (alk. paper)
    I. Kline, Peter, 1936-   . II. Title
PS3559.S42G46   1999
813'.54--dc21   99-19245
                                                          CIP

Printed in the United States of America

In The Valley Of The Shadow

Exodus

Transmutation

To Anita and Stecia

and

To Stephanie, Maureen and Wendy

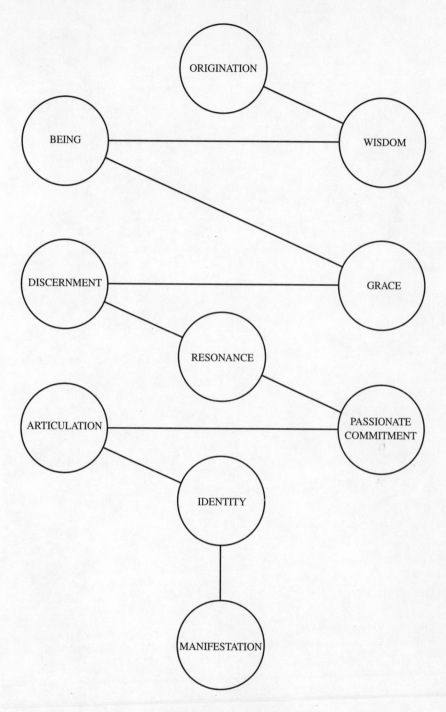

The Tree of Life

ONE

THE LEAVES OF OCTOBER

Man himself is the source of all his troubles,
for the light of God pours over him eternally.
But through his all-too-bodily existence
man comes to cast a shadow,
so that the light cannot reach him.
— Hasidic saying

"You can touch the top of your head now, Mr. Carey."

I glance at the small, rectangular speaker above me; waiting four full heartbeats for further instructions.

Nothing.

I sit up, fully awake now, my fingers feeling their way cautiously across the enormous extension the surgeon has built to contain the additional dendrites he's implanted in my brain. I slide out of bed.

I'm wearing a pair of red, white and blue striped boxing shorts. Glittering red cross-trainers direct my legs towards a corridor lit by cold, flickering, blue lights. Hundreds of people are lining the walls gaping and gesticulating in my direction, expressions of joy and adulation on their faces. Their voices meld into a babbling, indistinguishable hum, from which my name, like a dolphin leaping in the air, keeps repeatedly surfacing and submerging in a sea of sound.

"Dave.... Dave.... Dave."

The current chess champion of the world steps forward and asks for my autograph, his pen expectantly poised above a copy of Chess Masters' Tribune. I pause, give him a knowing wink, and with a sweeping gesture of my hand, scrawl my signature across his paper.

The hallway ends at two massive gray doors. As if on cue, they roll back, and I bound across the threshold into a stark and cavernous stadium, dimly lit except for its center. There, under the glare of giant klieg lights, is a boxing ring, its square surface pristine white. I jump onto the platform and pirouette over the ropes. The crowd roars. I raise my fists acknowledging the ovation.

1

Suddenly there's a new round of commotion, then stunned silence, the thick, no-sound of ten thousand people holding their breath. My opponent has been wheeled into the ring. There it stands, a vertical, black, steel monolith on a dark blue base. I am the human answer to the Deep Blue Menace. I now have a brain that can assess a billion moves a second.

"Clang!"

The first round begins.

Only now do I notice the message flickering on my opponent's monitor. "I am Chess Master 6.0. I can assess a hundred billion moves a second."

I feel as if a leather cinch is being tightened around my chest. The cheers of a moment before have become mocking, derisive laughter. The sounds are no longer human; they are mechanical, metallic. The pungent smell of the massed bodies is replaced by an overpowering, acrid odor I instantly recognize as the smell of the overheated transformer that ran my old Lionel train.

I stumble through the ropes, gasping for air, momentarily blinded by sweat, and the glare of the spotlights.

I'm falling in darkness down a bottomless shaft. In the blackness below, a point of crimson light grows quickly in size. It's a neon sign. I plunge toward it, my arms and legs thrashing helplessly. The letters become legible.

"Delete."

In the darkness, I faintly heard the sound of the ringside bell.

"Dave, are you getting up? Are you going to turn off the alarm, or do you want me to do it?"

It was Janet. I felt the movement of the mattress as her body shifted in bed. The ringing stopped.

I lay there, clinging to sleep; my skin wet and clammy with sweat. In that crossover point from dreaming to waking, I didn't know where I would find myself.

I opened my eyes. The bedroom had a reassuring familiarity. Janet, wrapped in her pink robe, was framed in the bathroom doorway. She tilted her head in that quizzical way she has and shot me a bemused, brittle smile from across the room as she closed the door.

I lay there listening to the muffled sound of the shower splashing on her flesh. For a moment I imagined the water running down her body in little rivulets, following it in my mind along the undulations of her pale skin into the crevices and valleys that I used to long for, that I used to search out and kiss so passionately.

But that was long ago. It was a thought weighted with resignation.

I stared up at the pale yellow ceiling, noting the texture and minute

cracks in the plaster, and replayed the dream. I knew what it was about —
my terror of losing control in the one area that still afforded a semblance of
certainty in my life — technology. Everything else in my personal and professional life seemed to be coming apart like Humpty Dumpty, and nothing
I'd learned in my fifty odd years could patch it all back together again.

My marriage had ceased to exist in all but its outer form. Intimacy lived
only as a faded memory in a grimy mental scrapbook, something I could now
view only through a lens darkened by time, pain, sadness and layers of disappointment as thick as attic dust.

Janet and I lived in the same house. We were civil and polite with each
other. We'd talk intelligently about our finances and our grown-up kids. We'd
plan social functions together. But we were going through the motions. The
lines were spoken, the moves choreographed and performed on cue; but the
whole thing was completely hollow. There was no heart in any of it. Our relationship was as dried out as the leaves of October. I couldn't remember the
last erotic kiss we'd had. There was only photographic evidence that we'd
once felt real passion for one another.

Perhaps from the beginning I'd been too much in love with my work.
My career had placed great demands on the family. I could sympathize with
Janet's frustrations. What percentage of the meals Janet had prepared for my
dinner had to be reheated and wolfed down at midnight before I collapsed into
bed next to an already sleeping wife? Had I at any time in my married life
averaged more than a once a week attendance at family dinners? From how
many of my kids' school games, music and ballet recitals, parent-teacher
meetings and other milestones in their lives had I been AWOL? I had to
admit, it was a pretty shabby record. But, that didn't mean I didn't love them.
I cared a lot about them.

Janet didn't think so. She caricatured my relations as "managed care,"
saying I was motivated solely to get both my family and my work teams performing better. I could see, given my priorities, that it might look that way.
When I focused on relationships, I could never bring myself simply to be with
a person without having some purpose or activity in mind. If I'd told the truth
about it, relationships were of value to me first and foremost for solving problems and achieving goals. Otherwise why bother, what was the point?

My relationship with Janet may also have been shaped by my drive to succeed, but it wasn't all for me. Wasn't I pursuing my career for the benefit of all
of us? We had a beautiful home and more than enough money. The kids went
to the best private schools. Stephen was about to complete his graduate studies
in architecture, and my daughter Sarah's wedding had turned into a thirty-five
thousand dollar bash, on top of my still paying for her medical school tuition.

3

Recently, relations with Janet had come to a head. The specifics weren't important. The weight of resentment between us had piled up so gradually and painfully that we had finally reached a point where the pretense could no longer be held in place with mere manners and rituals. There was too much hostility. We avoided one another and barely spoke.

I tried to hide publicly what was happening to my marriage. I put on a front at work and at the club. I didn't really have any close friends, any that I felt I could confide in. Everyone I knew was too busy keeping their social mask in place, holding it together, guiding conversations into safe shallows that avoided the turbulent waters of the truth.

I made sure not to exhibit any behavior that would suggest I wasn't totally in control, but I was disgusted with myself. Still, my level of disgust was only about a two on a scale of ten — just enough to feel bad, but not enough to make me quit my own bullshitting. On the scale of looking good to others, I still gave myself a nine point five.

My staff wasn't stupid. They could spot the b.s. ten miles away. They knew something was up. But I was so dense, so deluded, that I believed I was fooling everyone. I had to. As the state of my personal relationships faded, I counted more and more on my career to pull me through.

To pull me through for what?

That question I didn't ask myself.

TWO

IN LIMBO

Security is mostly a superstition.
It does not exist in nature,
nor do the children of men
as a whole experience it.
Avoiding danger is no safer
in the long run than outright exposure.
Life is either a daring adventure or nothing.
— *Helen Keller*

In the past, no matter how bad things had gotten at home, I'd always felt competent at work. My career had been a steady rise to the top from among the ranks of technical experts in my field. Self-doubt had only recently taken up residence in my office.

Last year my company, Allied Technologies, was bought out by Henderson-Richmond International, a multi-national conglomerate under the control of billionaire Roger Henderson. I had been promoted to Chief Operations Officer. Soon after, I'd had to contend with downsizing a thousand employees. It was a project demanded by Henderson, who had a dogged determination to drive up the value of Allied's stock.

I'd quickly complied, but one thousand firings wasn't enough for Henderson. Next he'd demanded a total restructuring of our company, a final filing down of our human resources into a fragment of what they had been. Upper management fought hard to resist him, but in the end, Henderson prevailed. I tried to put the personal suffering of the employees that we let go out of my mind. I was surprised at how successful I was at doing that. Maybe Janet had been right. I could numb myself to anything.

A deep sullenness had descended on nearly everyone. A social compact had been broken, an unspoken agreement that had always been based on a balance between the lean times when workers had to be laid off, and the times of prosperity when everyone could expect to share in the profits.

I was certain, given his track record with other companies, that Henderson would stop at nothing to increase shareholder value, even if it meant the demise of our entire organization. After all, if we failed to meet his standards, he could simply dismantle Allied and sell us off piecemeal. There would still be a dozen other subsidiaries of Henderson-Richmond left to feed his ego. In a flash, we could be gone. And I would be the COO who had ushered us out of existence.

I'd devoted my life to the company. Now, during the days that ought to have been the crowning glory of my career, I found myself uncertain and desperate, with a situation that threatened any minute to explode in my face.

While it was my job as chief of operations to keep things running smoothly through the downsizing, it was Diane Foster, the president of Allied Technologies, who bore the ultimate responsibility for the firings. Though just over five feet tall and quite slender, Diane exuded confidence and power. Her deep, gravelly contralto exaggerated the consonants, so no word she spoke was ever in doubt. We got along well. I understood the mess she had to deal with.

When I arrived at my office that morning, Michele, my assistant, handed me a sealed message from Diane, marked "urgent." Diane wanted a conference with me as soon as I got in.

"Take a seat, Dave," she said as I entered the room. Her expression was more serious than usual. I planted myself in the large, dark leather chair in front of her desk, trying to appear efficient and on top of things.

"Lay it on me, Diane," I said, gritting my teeth in a half-humorous smile. "I can take anything."

"Maybe not this," said Diane. "We could both be out of a job this afternoon."

"What's going on?"

"Henderson had one of his temper tantrums in here at seven o'clock this morning. Nobody can figure out how to handle the guy, you know that."

"So what's our game plan?"

"Nothing for you to do now except wait and see." I noticed that she had said "you."

"What's he after this time?"

"To speak frankly, he wants you and me out of the company."

"Sure," I said. I couldn't help it, I slumped in my chair.

"Okay. What does that buy him?" I asked.

"Control. Nothing more. He's got this idea that we're in his way, that without us he could make this company profitable, especially if that means dismantling it — you know, the old 'the operation was a success, but the patient died' strategy.

"To tell you the truth, Henderson is probably reading you and me pretty accurately. You may not like him and his tactics, but he's damn sharp. He knows that I still feel responsible to our workers. We have good people here. Good enough to turn this company around. Henderson doesn't know that, but I do. I say we're creative enough to save Allied —and make it a great investment, good enough to satisfy even Henderson."

I was surprised to see Diane express such feeling.

"I know that you scheduled some vacation time next week..." she began.

"I'll cancel it if you think that would help," I interrupted.

She looked me right in the eye. "No, quite the opposite. Don't cancel it, Dave. I want you to take it, and I want you to take it now. The timing couldn't be better. I need you out of the way for a while, because I don't want Henderson getting excited about anything else you might do in the next few days. I don't want him in here kicking my ass because of what you do."

I noted the hint of disapproval in her last remark. "Why does he dislike me so much?" I asked.

"Don't take it personally, Dave, because Henderson sure doesn't. He doesn't understand that the days of the sweatshop are over, and quite frankly he doesn't like what he calls, 'your touchy-feely style.'"

"Me, touchy-feely?" I said incredulously. "What do you think would give him that impression?"

"He thinks you're a wimp because at the last stock-holders meeting you objected to dropping our bonus program."

I shook my head. "Okay, I get it that he doesn't like me. But what's his problem with you?"

"Like I said, he knows I won't go along quietly if he tries to dismantle the company, and..."

"...and what?"

"Maybe he's got a problem relating to powerful women," she said with a wicked grin.

She was silent for a moment, then continued more pensively. "You know he's the mergers king. He's looked at plenty of companies like ours as more profitable dead than alive."

"Is that how he sees us?"

"Not yet, I think, but I'm not sure."

"What do you want me to do?"

"Like I said before, nothing. Make yourself scarce. Take the week off. Think things over. Let him see what happens when you're not around to keep the rest of us under control."

I laughed weakly. "You think he'll even notice?"

She ignored my comment. "Actually, I *do* have a strategy. It's a pretty good one, too."

"Can you let me in on it?"

"Sure, you've got to know anyway. I've had the accountants draw up two sets of financial reports. One is a forecast based on the way things are going right now. The other is a strategic plan that I've thrown together myself. The way we're going now we're essentially out of business in six months. The other way, I predict we can regroup, build our strengths and regain most of our profitability over the next two quarters. In addition, we may be able to move into some previously undeveloped territory that I'm not going to whisper about even to you.

"What I'm really hoping is that we can successfully pitch this to Henderson and garner support from our Board of Directors and some of our big investors. Some of them still believe in us, I think."

"Sounds risky."

"Dave, at this point, anything is risky, including doing nothing. It's my crazy dream that by next week Henderson will have agreed to hear our proposal even if only grudgingly. That will buy us the time we need to seriously turn this thing around. I'm tired of working the slaughterhouse approach, I want us to produce something original that will lock in our market share. I believe we can manage that."

She stood up and came around her desk, placing her hand on my shoulder. "And you, my friend" she added soothingly, "you use this next week to get some R&R, because if I'm successful with Henderson, I'm going to need you time and a half beyond what I need you now. So stock up on sleep while you have the chance!"

Back in my own office, I closed the door, sat down, closed my eyes and caught my breath. Leave for a week? Temporarily, she'd said, but how did I know that? I had a week to... What?

I was glad Diane had a plan, because I sure didn't. We needed to come up with something—something new, something that would make us so profitable that Roger Henderson wouldn't dream of interfering.

I thought of the last words Diane had uttered as I exited her office.

"Trust me," she had said.

I had no choice.

THREE
EMBRACING THE SHADOW

No age has known so much,
so many different things,
about human beings;
no age has known less than ours
what a human being is.
— *Heidegger*

I switched on the light over the desk in my home office. Everything looked peaceful and unruffled, in stark contrast to my emotional state. Long ago, I had learned the wisdom of clearing my desk when I'd finished a day's work. I kept my things in such immaculate condition that the housekeeper seldom needed to enter the room, except perhaps, to dust and empty the trash.

I'd waited all day for the phone to ring and bring me the news that my job and Allied Technologies were history, but the call had not come. Diane had managed to stave off disaster for a day, at least. It was a small scrap under the table for a starving dog, but it didn't set my mind at ease.

I turned and regarded my computer. It looked perfectly harmless, with none of the menace I had felt in my dream the night before. It appeared to be a quiet, loyal servant with no thought of displacing or humiliating me. At the moment, its screen cover was doing a jump rope ballet with stick figures — innocent enough. But then again, I thought, wasn't that figure on the screen like me, jumping around incessantly at the bidding of technology? Something had gone very, very wrong.

It was a crisis of faith. Last night's dream had tolled the death knell for my unwavering trust in technology. I'd been indoctrinated since childhood with a belief in its ultimate magic, seduced by its promises of progress and prosperity soon to come. With staggering naiveté I'd signed on. Our country was a consumer's paradise, and technology would deliver a perpetual enhancement of the quality of life. Continuous progress was our most important product. It seemed to be the answer to everything — the Holy Grail.

Yet with each passing year, as my responsibilities multiplied, I became more and more concerned about the ever increasing pace and demand the company imposed on its employees. The burgeoning necessity to work longer and harder was dictated by changing conditions in the marketplace. We were reacting to every demand as if in a state of emergency. More and more, our actions were determined solely by the crisis of the day.

After a while I felt I was living out a scene from the German silent film *Metropolis*, where the workers are whipped to shovel more and more coal into the giant furnace fueling the immense machines that run the mythical city — all in the name of Progress.

I remembered the day I began to have serious doubts about my indoctrination. It was the day the first blow was delivered to the world's reigning chess master by a technologically designed adversary — a mute and blind supercomputer and its team of programmers, feeders and handlers. The news of his unprecedented defeat depressed me. I knew that as machines got smarter, people had to follow suit. But the accelerating pace of automation was upping the ante too rapidly.

Clearly, there was a lot of fat to be trimmed from the system. The trouble was, the people trimming the fat didn't understand that there had to be new rules for the playing field of business.

Technology and humanity: which was in the service of which? It's a question that's probably been around since before the first plows, and the balance keeps shifting back and forth with every new technological breakthrough that we humans introduce. Every time we're seduced and hypnotized by our own creations — and the temptation to do so is there as long as we are swayed by our own pride and arrogance — we are in danger of abdicating our role as the creator to become merely the servant, and ultimately the victim, of what we've wrought.

I stared at my computer. I had been blind and deaf to the obvious, entranced by the vision of freedom that innovation promised, only to find myself shackled instead.

But if technology wasn't salvation, what was? How could I assemble on the spot a whole new and different value system? I felt like a pilot trying to do complex computations while the engines on my wings were burning up and the plane was in a nose dive. Maybe I could pull out and recover, but success wasn't predictable.

Over the years I'd groped for new understandings, and I'd kept up with developments in management theory. Like every other company we'd had our bouts of re-engineering, ISO 9000, TQM and so many other "promising" new systems.

I picked up the new book that I'd begun reading the week before. It was about the implications the science of complexity has for organizations. Not bad. Here was the newest theory scratching at the organizational door. I leafed through it perfunctorily, hoping it might hold the secret I was looking for — the key that would help me turn my company around.

After a few minutes, I slammed the book closed and pushed it away. Certainly the ideas were provocative, but there was something missing from this whole continuous search of mine, and I couldn't grasp what it was. All I knew was that without this missing key all the latest information, theories, and techniques were impotent. For the first time in many years I had to acknowledge that I honestly didn't have an answer. I didn't even know if there was an answer.

That night I lay in bed motionless, trying not to disturb Janet, trying to force myself into sleep. I yearned to be unconscious, to shut off my ceaseless self-blaming, and my desperate fear of losing my job. I had reached the bottom of my bag of moves, feints and tricks. Each strategy I auditioned came up short. I'd exhausted all my formulas, and was simply recycling them — same solutions, same results. I knew the problem was with me, who I *was*.

I was on the brink of abyss in every area of my life, and could see no rescue. Finally, in desperation, I tried something I hadn't even thought about since childhood. I decided to pray.

I tried to recall some prayers from my youth, but remembered only fragments of verses and partial phrases. It seemed awkward, phony, like I was kidding myself, going through some futile exercise in self-deception. An inner voice mocked me — *this is stupid, snap out of it, come to your senses.*

I stopped. It was taking me nowhere.

With bone-chilling clarity I realized I was spiritually bankrupt, and nothing in my intellect could compensate for that void. My life had amounted to nothing, and if it meant nothing to me, it surely meant nothing to anyone else.

I was gripped by grief more suffocating than I had ever known. My face was wet with tears. I heard myself mouthing, almost pleading, the only words that would come, "Please.... Please....," to I knew not what.

I stumbled out of bed by sheer force of will, and made my way to the office. I choked back the sobs which pressed themselves against the back of my throat. I found the light switch, closed the door, and sank into an armchair. Gradually, my breathing quieted. Again I uttered in a whisper gone hoarse: "Please.....! Please....!"

But something had changed. This time the words came from a new place, an authentic place. There was no embarrassment, no pride in my plea, no holding back. Instead was a raw, deep yearning. A yearning for...? What...? I didn't know.

Gradually, I felt a calmness spread throughout my body. For once, my mind was silent as if all time had stopped. A line from a psalm emerged from the depths. *"Yea, though I walk through the valley of the shadow of death, I will fear no evil, for THOU art with me."*

Like the intimate whisper of a lover to his beloved, the words lingered inside me, restoring my hope.

I got up quietly and returned to the bedroom. I paused at the doorway for a moment and watched Janet, still asleep. A feeling of tenderness arose in me that I had not known in years. I slipped quietly under the covers, and moored myself gently against her sleeping body. Within moments I was asleep.

FOUR

THE ULTIMATE ANSWER

Things are in the saddle and ride mankind.
— Henry David Thoreau

Early the next morning, I sat in my home office, absent-mindedly shuffling through the contents of my briefcase. My deeply felt experience of the night before had faded like a dream, but I was aware of a vague expectancy that I could not pinpoint.

It had been a long time since I had sorted through my own mail without the benefit of Michele's winnowing hand. A well designed promotion piece caught my eye. I was intrigued by its title, "The John Henry Syndrome". As I read it, I had the sense that it had not reached me by accident.

Do you recall the Legend of John Henry?

He was a champion rail spike driver, "a steel drivin' man." With his combination of intelligence and strength he could not be bested in the speed and accuracy with which he drove spikes.

Then one day an innovative change, a new technology, was introduced — the automatic steam drill. With the survival of manual rail spike driving at stake, John Henry challenged the steam drill to a race. As the race began, John Henry brought to bear all of the principles and practices he had learned over the years that had made him the acknowledged best. He swung his hammer harder and faster than he had ever done before.

He beat the steam drill — he won the race. Then with the cheers of his fellow workers still ringing in his ears, "he lay down his hammer and died," effectively ending his future employment.

Sound familiar? In the midst of unprecedented and accelerating tech-nologic, economic, and social change, many individuals and compa-nies find themselves facing John Henry's predicament. Operating from "tried and true" practices they find that the formulas that worked in

13

the past no longer do.

Our past models for leadership, teamwork and communication can be rendered obsolete by our own successes. Reacting to these changes from our present level of competence leaves us working longer and harder at what we already know — "The John Henry Syndrome."

I stopped reading. My company had "The John Henry Syndrome," I had no doubt of it. The writer had captured in practical terms the essence of our dilemma.

I looked at another section of the brochure.

The Six Levels of Change
Individuals and organizations respond to change in one or more of five different ways:
ignore it, resist it, react to it, accept it or embrace it.
We provide you with a powerful sixth way: Create change.

As excited as I had been a moment before, I found myself turned off by this last sentence. Create change? The expression sounded like just another catch phrase that could only lead to working harder and faster.

I looked at the top of the cover letter with its salutation, "Dear Dave." I got angry.

"More bullshit," I thought, heading for the wastebasket. "Phony familiarity by someone who wouldn't know me from..."

The signature caught my eye. I paused and did a slow double-take. I knew this guy! A memory surfaced that took me all the way back to high school.

My friend Adam once gave a report in science class about our everyday assumptions — how our unexamined beliefs dupe us into thinking we know things. He had used me as a willing guinea pig for his demonstration.

Adam had a mind that was always at play, that was always setting things up to see what would happen next; whether, for example, his setups would irritate people or tickle them or challenge them to a mental duel, or perhaps do something to their thinking that no one would have predicted.

But he wasn't angry or confrontational. His light brown eyes would look into yours intently but not intensely — not trying to do anything with or to you, but just being there with you. It was kind of odd, given the way his mind behaved. Still, on occasion he liked to play with whoever or whatever was around to play with. In that particular science class he'd toyed with me.

"I want to show you something quite remarkable," he said to the class that day. "Who would like to do a little experiment with me?"

14

I volunteered.

"Okay," said Adam. "Tell me something that you know how to do."

"I know how to write," I said grinning.

"Okay. If you do know how to write, tell me how to do it."

"Sure, pick up the pen, and draw the letters on the paper, like this!" I demonstrated by writing my name in a bold flourish across the paper.

"I didn't question whether you can write," said Adam quietly. "I'm questioning whether you know how. Tell me how to write."

"First, I pick up the pen," I began.

"How do you pick up the pen?"

"Well, I grasp it between my fingers..."

"How do you grasp it between your fingers?"

"Just by bringing my fingers together!" I said, getting exasperated.

"How do you bring your fingers together?" Adam said evenly.

"By constricting the muscles in my fingers to come together," I replied.

"How do you constrict the muscles of your fingers to come together?" he persisted with maddening equanimity.

"By sending a signal in my brain to do it!"

"How do you send a signal in your brain to do it?"

"Well, I just think it!"

"How do you just think it?"

"My brain knows how to do it," I said, shakily, my self confidence a shambles now as I realized where this conversation was going to end up.

"And how does your brain know how to think?" asked Adam, delivering the coup de grace.

"I don't know," I said, giving up the ghost of the struggle.

"You do write, but you don't know how, and neither does anyone else in the room," Adam said with understated triumph. "When you finally get through all the levels of explanation, what you and I are finally left with is 'I don't know'. You and I don't really know 'how' to do anything, but we believe we do, when all we really have is a pile of explanations that are intellectual hand-me-downs from some so-called experts."

I looked over at Mr. Phelps, our science teacher. His brows were knitted together, his jaws clenched, and he was hunched over with his arms crossed, leaning against the blackboard. It occurred to me that Adam's demonstration might have been a little threatening for him also.

"Well," I said, "I guess I don't know. I always just took it on faith."

"You see?" Adam said to the class, "What this case demonstrates is a general principle. Nobody knows 'how' to do anything, and they don't even know that they don't know, or why they don't know. We mis-identify explanations, and call them 'knowing'. It may be that the difference between you and a so-called 'expert' is the number of explanations you can come up with before you finally get to 'I don't know!'

"We've mentally gone to sleep, giving up the opportunity to observe the world directly for ourselves. As human beings, we've been given this great gift: to wonder and to question, and we've traded it in for what? For the tranquilized safety of inherited knowledge!"

Adam issued this last statement dramatically, his voice rising, and his arms waving, ending with his right index finger pointing at the ceiling with a flourish, as if nailing his point home. The class, loving Adam's outrageousness, erupted with clapping and cheers. Mr. Phelps clapped too, out of politeness no doubt, but his enthusiasm was considerably more subdued.

Years later, I happened to be reading anthropologist Gregory Bateson's book, *Steps Toward an Ecology of Mind*, and came upon his term: "explanatory principle." It refers to the final explanation that scientists retreat to when they are up against the wall of "I don't know." That was what Adam had been pointing to that day in science class.

After that class demonstration, I practiced being curious and skeptical about everything. From that moment on I no longer believed something just because some expert or authority had declared it to be true. I developed the habit of weighing an idea or purported "fact" as just one plausible interpretation, without feeling the need to believe it unquestioningly. I was careful not to accept instant conclusions about things I had not experienced directly.

In the end, I guess, this balance of skepticism and curiosity had paid off. Adam had instilled it in me with that one little demonstration at my expense. My moment of foolishness in front of the class had reaped long-term dividends for me, awakening a critical thinking faculty that had been dormant and in danger of atrophying in an environment that rewarded right answers far more than authentic inquiry.

I'd seen Adam only once after we'd graduated — quite recently at a class reunion. He was a successful artist, exhibiting his paintings regularly. We'd exchanged phone numbers.

He'd mentioned something about teaching people the principles of creating, but I hadn't paid much attention to him, since it didn't seem relevant at the time. Looking at the brochure he'd sent, I realized that there might be some value there for my business — or more to the point, for me.

Since seeing him after all those years, I'd often thought about Adam. He'd certainly gotten what he wanted out of life, and in a field that allowed him complete self-expression. This was a side of life I'd abolished for myself midway through my second year of college. Since then, everything had always been practical for me. I'd spent my first year and a half in college as an English major. I'd loved it, but not nearly enough to continue, it seemed.

Though I'd had thoughts of becoming a writer, all of that was put aside during a memorable talk I had with my father during the Christmas break of my sophomore year, when he told me he would continue to pay for my education only if I switched my major to business. He considered business to be the only intelligent way to invest money in his son's future.

I knew I could make it in the business world. I'd always enjoyed initiating things, conceiving ideas and making them happen. In high school, I discovered that I had a natural leadership ability. I could manage a group of students and accomplish good results. But I'd also loved writing.

"Look," my father said, "you'll have the best of both worlds. You've had your fun for a year and a half, it's been a good background that will probably make you more interesting when you talk with people. After all, if you want to, you can always write on the weekends."

He assured me that he knew what was best for me, and that he had only my interests at heart. I listened. In my mind's eye I saw my Muse — watching me, beckoning to me. And I saw that both Fear and Uncertainty were standing right beside her, grinning.

I blinked. She was gone. At the end of the conversation I shook my father's hand, sealing our pact. I went for predictability and financial security, and it all boiled down to the brass ring called business. I never looked back. I spent my life climbing the ladder, worrying always about what I did, what other people did, and how it affected our company's profitability. Even when I went as far away as Hawaii for a vacation, I found myself endlessly thinking about situations back at work. Talking to Adam, the only person among all those I'd gone to high school with who seemed interesting to me now, I felt a little envious. He had unlimited creative freedom. I, by contrast, had almost always felt thwarted in my work. Now, the crisis in my career was producing more than just an occasional nightmare. The dreams that had troubled me lately had simply underscored my frustration and disillusionment.

I needed a chance to think — to sort out both my inner and my outer life. I had plenty of time — a whole week of vacation with nothing to do. Janet wasn't planning to stick around, she had tickets to spend the week with her mother in Boston. The idea of a week at home together with no planned diversions had seemed unendurable to both of us.

My only plan was to hang around the house and catch my breath, hopefully muddling through to some direction for my future.

Perhaps calling Adam would help, I thought. Communication was about all I had to fall back on.

FIVE

ENDURING, STRIVING, CREATING

To understand everything except yourself is very comical.
— Kierkegaard

I took a deep breath, cleared my throat and dialed Adam.

An assistant answered — a real person, not a recording. A recording would not have been Adam's style.

I gave my name. Within fifteen seconds I heard the distinct timbre of Adam's voice.

"Dave, how great to hear from you! How have you been?"

"Not bad," I lied, hurrying to get through the customary social grease. "How about yourself?"

"Very well, thanks. It's really good to hear from you, Dave. I was thinking just the other day about how we used to do our Latin homework over the phone together. Remember how we egged each other on to get the translation exactly right? You always had a gift for the right turn of phrase, you know. I admired that in you. You could have been a writer."

"Thanks."

"It's a shame you didn't develop your talent. With your career, I'd be surprised if you had time to wipe your ass, much less develop your writing."

I felt a twinge at that. Adam had always been unabashed in his comments.

"You got the letter and brochure I sent you?"

Odd, after what he'd just said. I stifled a laugh.

"Funny you would send me something like that after what you just said about my career," I said.

"Not at all," said Adam. "I see that a hell of a lot of people feel thwarted in their attempt to be creative in the business world, and I'd like to do something to help."

"What makes you think you can?" I asked peremptorily. But my tone didn't faze him.

"If you and the folks you work with can look beyond the next quarter,

18

maybe to the next decade, you have it all over the guys who run Wall Street," he said.

"Really?" I paused. "Maybe you know something I don't." There was hope mixed with anguish in this remark. "As a matter of fact, it was your brochure that prompted me to call you. Unfortunately, your 'John Henry Syndrome' sounded like the present state of my company."

"Interesting. Want to tell me more?"

I purposely avoided answering him. I had some questions of my own that I needed to deal with first.

"Say, how long have you been in the business consulting field?" I asked, shifting the subject.

"Interesting turn of events, isn't it? It's all pretty new, particularly the organizational stuff. Its been happening gradually, to tell you the truth."

"What prompted it? I don't understand what would take you from art to an interest in business development," I said. Silently, however, I questioned his audacity, thinking, "What gives you, an artist, the credentials to advise business people?"

"I think everyone and everything is in business in some way or other. The only question is how they go about it. Art and business are both about creation. Even when I was very young, I was in awe of the creative process. Where do ideas come from? What's the mysterious process from which images, poems and stories arise? In what way do our dreams take form?"

"So you teach people how to be creative? What do you have, some new techniques? I should probably warn you, I've already read all the books on creativity," I added.

"Really? All of them? Didn't find much in them, did you?"

I remained silent. It was true, and I didn't like acknowledging it. Besides, I certainly hadn't read all of them. What a waste of time that would have been.

"I don't teach techniques," Adam went on. "I help people *be* creators. There's a big difference."

"How long have you been doing this?"

"Oh, a couple of years. I began by teaching private classes in graphic design and painting. Some of my students were business people who were learning to paint as an avocation. Over time, however, an interesting thing happened. Many of my students would come up to me during a break and tell me how they'd applied some idea they'd learned in my class to their job."

"They applied art ideas at work?"

"Not exactly," he laughed. "When I was teaching the class, I always made it a point to articulate, as best I could, the principles behind the physical act of creating, so my students would become competent not only in drawing and painting, but would also be aware of the creative process itself. It was these principles of creativity that my students used at work — with outstanding results. They took the principles of creation they'd learned in class, incorporated the principles into the language and action of business and saw that it worked.

"I was fascinated. I saw the possibility for some real 'cross-over' learning. I wanted to see what would happen if I applied these creative principles to every other aspect of my life."

"What happened when I applied this plan for myself was extraordinary. To my surprise and delight I realized that there were no areas of my life where the principles couldn't be applied. I realized how much we overlook opportunities to cross-pollinate the different areas of our lives. I began to develop new ways to teach my discoveries, so other people could more easily put them into action. I knew I was onto something that could be transferred. All it took was communication.

"Soon," Adam continued, "I began to have requests to present lectures and programs at the university and kept getting good responses from people in a number of different fields.

"Then some of my students asked me to coach them personally on work projects. Their friends came to me. The next thing I knew, I was being asked to work with organizations!

"And Dave," Adam added in a mock conspiratorial tone, "all without my having the prerequisite MBA!"

He laughed. From the moment he answered the phone it had been obvious that he had no interest in playing the cool, professional consultant with me. He seemed genuinely fascinated by the unexpected turn of events that had created this new business for himself.

My guard had gone up a bit during Adam's spiel, though. My own background in business had been fairly traditional. I had earned my stripes providing the standard MBA practices. I knew how to do case studies, calculate the math, and chart projections. I'd been successful, and what I'd learned had been useful. I always had held business and the arts as two separate worlds, so I was a little unstrung by Adam's easy application of his philosophy of art to the business world with the same aplomb that he used to apply paint to canvas. Adam would be characterized in conservative management circles as a fringe guy.

"Dave?"

The sound of Adam's voice brought me back.

I could hardly believe the next comment out of my mouth. I guess I was trying to cover up for my lapse in attention. I found myself making an awkward attempt to impress Adam. I asked him, "What are the main consulting systems you use with clients?"

He hesitated. "I can't answer that, Dave" — almost as if that comment were a recommendation for his outstanding talents.

I had to grope. "Is it confidential? I hope you don't think I'm asking you to divulge any trade secrets!"

"No, not at all," he laughed. "It's just that I can't answer the question, because I don't know what I'm going to do ahead of time with any client. I don't mean it's shoot from the hip, though.

"Look, here is an analogy for you. There are ready-to-wear clothes and designer clothes. I do personally designed consulting, just the way I create individual works of art. And besides, how could I possibly know what my client's real needs are and what solution will work best until we've looked at the situation together in depth?"

Then he said what I considered to be a very strange statement.

"I trust that what needs to be done will unfold itself in my conversations with the client."

A pause, during which he caught my unspoken thought.

"And what I just said, Dave, is not New Age-speak," he laughed. "'Unfold' is a technical term here. Have you read the work of the physicist, David Bohm?"

"No," I replied.

"Brilliant stuff. Wonderful creative thinker."

He paused. He was obviously waiting for me to get to the point of my call. I decided to skip the judgmental stuff and cut to the chase.

"Adam, I've got a big problem, and I don't know what to do." Briefly I told him about the crisis I was facing in my career. More reluctantly I mentioned my problems at home.

"I understand," he replied softly.

It was the first time in years that anyone had said that to me and made me feel they were telling the truth; that it wasn't more social grease sympathy bullshit. Maybe Adam was one of those rare people who actually listened.

We'd had that kind of truthful relationship in high school, and I could feel it coming back to life now. It was a circling back, a connecting to an earlier time that seemed full of possibilities.

"Adam, can you hold a second, I want to turn on the speaker phone." The pressure of the receiver against my ear was becoming uncomfortable. Besides, I wanted my hands free to take notes as we spoke. As I flicked the switch, Adam's firm voice filled the room with a strange question.

21

"What gets you up in the morning?" he asked.

"What?" The question seemed disconnected from anything we had said previously.

"What gets you up in the morning? What mood are you in when you wake up? What do you observe to be your state of being at the start of the day?"

"I still don't understand what you are asking for or why," I replied, feeling both perplexed and annoyed.

"Answering that question honestly might provide you with some real insight into the way you are living."

"Well, why the hell in the morning?" I asked. "Wouldn't it make more sense to ask me how I am at work, in the middle of the day? That's when most of the problems arise."

I could sense my old need for control asserting itself. I was trying to guide the conversation where I thought it should go.

"After morning, it's too late," he chuckled, "you've got your armor on by then."

Adam paused, then continued. "Listen, Dave, I know that you're a guy who can hunker down and make things happen and yet be oblivious to the pain you're in as you carry on with a stiff upper lip. Remember, you and I go back a long way. I was standing on the side of the field during that district championship when you injured your knee *bad*, and you didn't let on, not even to the coach, and not even at the half, for fear that they'd pull you out, and then you kept playing through the pain until your knee finally collapsed. You're a fighter, so I know you can bleed without feeling it."

I was moved that he'd remembered that game, and the way he described it made me feel he'd been there with me in every detail of that horrifying moment, much more than I'd been there for myself. That alone would have made me want to hire him, because he'd understood one of the most important and devastating events in my life. That injury had taken me out of football and an almost certain college athletic scholarship. He wasn't only criticizing me, he was also acknowledging one of my strengths. My resistance to his question evaporated like dew in the morning sun.

"So, first thing in the morning is better?"

"Yes. Just at the point where you are first waking to consciousness. It's the most accurate time to gauge what I call 'your resident state of being' before you've put on your helmet and lowered your visor."

"I understand," I said. "What's the best way for me to get to the answer to your question?"

"Simply by recalling what it is like for you at the moment you awaken.

Take yourself back to a typical morning — your mind has it all stored there. Ask, and *ye shall receive*." Ever the wit, Adam had said the last few words with the emphasis and cadence of a Baptist preacher.

I was silent for a moment, and tried to do what he asked.

"I have a sense of the experience, but I am having trouble articulating it in words. I guess I'm very good at avoiding it and disguising it from myself."

"Let me give you a structure that may help," he offered. "I've observed that people wake up in one of three basic states. Most of us have experienced each one of these at some time in our lives, but the question is, which one is the primary ground of being for you most mornings?"

"Okay, I'm with you. What are they?"

"Let's do it experientially, as a guided inquiry. Allow yourself to be in touch with what you mentally observe as I go through these three states of being, and see if any bells go off. Keep your eyes closed and your mind open; then see what you get."

"Kind of like a visualization process?" I asked.

"Exactly. Are you game?"

"One moment," I said.

I got up and locked the door. I knew that Janet was still packing and I didn't want her to walk in and see me listening to a disembodied voice with my eyes shut. I leaned back in my chair and closed my eyes.

"Fire when ready!" I said.

Adam began. "How do you get up in the morning? Who are you when you awaken? Are you an *endurer*? Are you a *striver*? Are you a *creator*?"

"Which of the following three scenarios fits you most closely? Scenario number one: *Some people get up in the morning because they didn't die overnight. They are victims of life, merely enduring it.*"

The statement threw me for a moment. It was both outrageous and pertinent.

"If you fit in this group," Adam continued, "you experience life as something you're putting up with and suffering through; a journey that you don't recall requesting on a road littered with rusted memories and the faded tracks of unfulfilled dreams. You feel helpless, victimized by life's circumstances. You sometimes suspect there's an instruction manual on how to navigate the path of life, but you've never been given it.

"Each new day repeats the last — just another present time to endure, with hope for an occasional respite that will dull the pain and boredom of the life sentence you've apparently inherited. Your view of life's possibilities is one of apathy, hopelessness, resignation and despair. You do not know your real self. You are an endurer."

As Adam spoke, feelings suddenly crystallized that I'd glimpsed earlier but hadn't been able to articulate. Part of me resisted his description, wishing to deny its relevance. But my actual physical and mental activity told a different story. Hendersons's face loomed up, followed by the faces of scores of employees I'd had to fire. Worst of all were the images of Janet, Steve and Sarah. I'd been kidding myself — thinking I didn't feel anything about the disaster our relationships had become. I'd masked my feelings with the anesthesia of denial, just as I had done with my knee so many years before. I was shocked. Was this what life was like for me now, after all the years of striving and working?

This last question was like a cue line for Adam's next statement. "Here's scenario number two," he said. "*Some people get up in the morning because they have to, they are driven to. They are strivers.*

"If you are in this group," he went on, "you get up in the morning because you *have to*. You have to go to the bathroom, you have to pay the bills, you have to get the promotion, you have to get the kids to school, you have to show you are the best, you have to become rich, you have to gain approval, you have to maintain control, you have to avoid failing, you have to win — you have to make it. Awakening each morning in this state, you may experience only rare and fleeting moments of satisfaction and peace."

I experienced a tightening in my gut as Adam continued. I recognized striving. I knew it intimately.

"No matter how materially successful you are, no matter what you do, deep down you know that if you simply have a little more knowledge, work a little bit better, or act a little bit differently, eventually you will find the key to living a whole, satisfying, balanced life. Meanwhile the practice continues in preparation for the ideal life when it finally arrives.

"Until that magic 'someday' arrives, you know that your job is not your real job, it's a practice job, just a precursor to the ideal job with the ideal boss, the ideal employees, the perfect office, the ideal salary — which usually keeps changing as your real salary increases — plus, of course, the right stock options, the ideal balance of freedom, power, and authority.

"In your attempts to reach your ideals, you'll experience yourself more as a human *doing*, than a human *being*. You're prone to skepticism and its final slide into cynicism. You keep trying to find your true self and finally become undisturbed. You are a striver."

My feelings were all over the map, coming forward, tripping over themselves as Adam spoke. I was angry with him, and tried to deny that I was a striver. At the same time, I was justifying my life of striving, while grieving that I had come up empty. I raged at Henderson for attempting to cut me down at the height of my career, and lamented the years that I'd sacrificed.

I realized how often I'd opened my eyes in the morning already in that state, a tightness in my jaw and shoulders, as though I'd spent the night alert for action. I knew all about striving. I could have written Adam's copy for him.

"Then there is scenario number three," Adam continued. *"There are those who get up in the morning and greet the day with enthusiasm, awe, appreciation, creativity and reverence. They are the creators."*

"If you're a creator, life is not a static state to be endured, nor a force to be overcome and tamed. Life is a flow of fluid, vibrating energy, a limitless potential to be embraced, nurtured and shaped. You experience a rich interrelatedness with all of life. You are nourished by a deep well-spring of joy that is not determined by the circumstances of each moment. Like the eye of a hurricane, you are a quiet center in the midst of the events swirling around you. You're able to respond powerfully and innovatively. You have the freedom and ability to create moment to moment the meaning and purpose of your life. You are committed to the results of your actions, but have no attachment to them. You experience yourself as the author of your life. You are not waiting for life to turn out. Each instant is an opportunity for creativity. Each day is an opportunity to express and fulfill your intended destiny. You are a creator."

As Adam spoke, I recalled moments when I'd experienced that creative state — witnessing my daughter's birth, watching the flick of the sun's disc light up the world in an instant on the rim of the Haleakala crater on Maui at sunrise, creating a breakthrough project for my company — but those times had been so rare that they were only reference points from which to judge what had been missing from most of my life. Being enormously successful doesn't make you a creator. I'd met too many brilliant, financially successful colleagues who fit the striver profile to a 'T', their self-esteem solely a function of their accumulated possessions.

Adam had stopped speaking. Whether it was a few moments or longer I wasn't sure. He was patiently waiting for my response. I opened my eyes and looked at the telephone. I could feel my armor re-establishing itself.

Finally Adam spoke, his words even, his tone interested. "What did you observe?"

I decided that this wasn't the time to hold my cards so close to the chest. If I wanted Adam's help, I had better stick to the straight talk we'd established back in high school. Haltingly, I told him my reactions, not pulling any punches. "I can see that I'm a combination of all three: the endurer, the striver and the creator, and to be perfectly honest with you,

Adam, I'm not thrilled with the distribution of the percentages in my case."

"In what areas of your life does each appear?" he asked. "Some people may notice that they're enduring life in their family relationships, striving in their professional lives, and creating in their hobbies or avocations. How is it for you?"

Once again I noted with admiration the absence of judgment in his voice. With a flicker of regret I realized that I didn't have the ability to accept myself as fully as he did.

"Adam, to tell you the truth, I think that for most of my life I've been pretty well stuck between enduring and striving — kind of like a never-ending commute between hell and purgatory. It's been exhausting for my body, and even for my soul, if I have one left".

"You do. You just need to recover it."

His words plucked a chord of recognition deeper than the marrow of my bones. I felt a palpable shift in my body: the way my muscles sometimes let go of tension I didn't even know I had, after arriving home from a long, arduous journey.

"I've tasted what it's like to live as a creator. It was a long time ago, though." I laughed at the memory that surfaced. "I can definitely tell you, I haven't been waking up with that sense of joy and promise since elementary school, when I'd get up in the morning on Saturdays and Sundays before anyone else in the house, full of energy, excited about the coming day. And I can see that's because I knew the day was mine to do with as I wanted. I could barely get up during the weekdays, my Mom practically had to blow me out of bed with dynamite.

"Sometimes I endured school and sometimes I was striving, but I can't think of many times I was given the opportunity to create. That was relegated to the weekends.

"You know, the more I think about it, the more I realize that striving was the main thing they taught us in school. The emphasis was never on knowledge and thinking, though it was promoted as such. Knowledge was always in the service of something, *in order to* something. We learned in order to get good grades, go to college, get good jobs and die rich. I'm not knocking it, I just realize that it was rarely for the joy you described as part of the way of being as a creator."

Then I realized something else. "*Being* a creator is distinct from the act of creating, isn't it?"

"Yes. One's a process and the other's a state of being. Quite distinct. Strivers can create as a process, also, in a particular area of their lives, but they may be ineffective in more important ways. The world is full of folks who are

26

brilliant in one part of life, while dreadfully striving and enduring in the rest of their lives."

There was a pause in the conversation. "Now what?" I asked, not sure where to go next with the conversation.

"It's up to you. Being a creator is the natural state of a human being," said Adam. "Not knowing that we are supposed to be creators, that we are in our most basic essence creators, leaves us only two options: enduring or striving. Do you want to know yourself as a creator and live that way fully? I don't mean in some abstract way, but in a way that gives you some real power? If the idea of being a creator can't translate into action, if it can't alter reality, then it remains only a dream, and I'm not interested in dreams. Fulfilled visions, yes. Unfulfilled dreams, no."

"I'm very interested," I admitted. "Before this phone call I wouldn't have known what to call it, but it's certainly what I need."

"I told you I design my coaching and consulting work for each client," Adam replied. "The foundation for my design is what I call The Genesis Principle; the four step path of creation. It's the unfoldment of your natural wisdom, available when you are in the presence of your true, essential nature. It's based on the four worlds of creation described in the Kabbalah, the Judaic mystical tradition."

I was surprised to learn what was backing up his work but made no mention of my concern. Instead, I politely asked, "How did you happen to come up with this?"

"I didn't; it came up with me!" he replied with a chuckle. "I'm not being flip when I say that, Dave. I learned it by being open enough to allow wisdom to shape me, to form my voice, my expression, and my articulation."

I was very skeptical. In some ways Adam sounded more and more flaky. But I couldn't discount what he said because my guts kept telling me to listen. Besides, there had been those moments in high school when he'd been way ahead of me, and in this conversation he still seemed to be ahead, though I couldn't for the life of me figure out why or how. I'd had my own experiences of spontaneous creativity from time to time. I knew creativity had an irrational side. I could see that, perhaps too often, I'd discredited some ideas just because they didn't fit into my current level of understanding. But there was more to it than that. Clearly, Adam was looking at a picture that I could not see, so I couldn't judge its authenticity yet. This was going to be a risk, I knew, but then at the moment, my whole life was at risk.

"One other thing," Adam added, as if responding to my unspoken thought, "you'll have to be willing to question a lot that you've held sacred.

This will probably be tougher than the high school championship game was for you. It may even involve more pain."

I noticed a sudden tightness in my chest.

"I recommend we continue our talk in person," Adam said.

"You want to get together for a preliminary meeting?"

"I think it best to do the next step face to face."

"Okay," I said, "when is the soonest you're available?"

"Are you free this afternoon?"

My laugh had an edge of bitterness. "Right now, I have all the time in the world, I've got a week in organizational limbo to sort things out for myself. That's why I called you."

"Let's spend the afternoon together," suggested Adam," and see where that leads. At the end of that time, if you have a clear sense that I can be a resource for you, and if I agree that our working together looks like a fit for both of us, I can open up a number of days this week, and we can pick a place where we won't be disturbed."

"A few days in the woods, maybe?" I said, thinking of my cabin by the lake.

"Something like that."

"And accomplish what?"

"That's what we can clarify this afternoon. By the way, regarding my fees, I'm willing to work with you for a reduced rate, Dave; not only because you're an old friend, but because this may be a big learning opportunity for me, also."

"In what way?"

"Most of my business clients have been individuals, or small to medium sized firms. Working with you will give me a chance to apply my methods to a much bigger canvas. We both might learn something through the interaction."

"A consultant who doesn't pretend he knows all the answers. How refreshing."

"And it keeps me honest," he laughed. "Let's meet at one o'clock this afternoon."

"That will work fine. I'll drive my wife to the airport and head into town."

"Dave, plan on at least three to four hours together to talk things over."

"Where shall we meet?"

"The Museum of Art," said Adam.

The answer caught me off guard.

"Why?"

"The Museum is the perfect place to get started. It's where you will begin to see how your business concerns and the principles of creating are connected in a very real and practical way."

"What should I bring with me?" I asked.

"David, my friend, your first assignment is to figure that out for yourself. See you at one!"

"You're the coach," I said.

SIX

RELATIVE REALITIES

It is impossible for a man to begin to learn
what he has a conceit that he already knows.
— Epictetus

In my poetry class in college I once heard a story, probably apocryphal, about the American poet, Robert Frost. It seems that Frost had been teaching in a college somewhere and one day he gave out an exam with only one question on it. It read, "In the light of what you have learned about me in this class, do something you think would please me."

The only student who got an "A" was the one who immediately got up and handed in a blank sheet of paper — didn't even have his name on it.

Wrestling with Adam's riddle of what to bring to our meeting, the Robert Frost story came back to me. Almost thirty years after I'd heard this story, I finally got the point. It wasn't about some nice poetic ideal to strive for, it meant much more than that. It was a call for freshness, for receptivity, somewhat like the Zen practice of "beginner's mind." If I were to open up to what Adam had to offer, beyond the constricted boundaries of my own set opinions, I had to empty myself of the assumption that I knew anything for certain at all.

That was the antithesis of what I'd spent years learning how to do. As a successful executive I was supposed to project competence. "I don't know" is a profanity in certain corporate cultures. After all, to acknowledge that "you don't know" can be taken as indication that you might not have what it takes to get ahead. I was taught that the value was in having the answers, not in having the questions. All these years, my cup had been filled with answers, but now those answers were bankrupt. I had no room to pour anything new into my cup, so full was I with judgments and conclusions about what I already knew.

So Adam had thrown me a curve ball. I was to decide what to bring, and what I would bring was an empty cup — precisely nothing.

I arrived at 12:50 p.m. and walked gingerly up the broad steps to the white marble portico. I entered the central rotunda through the tall glass doors.

It had been at least ten years since I'd been in the museum. The rotunda had a look of comfortable formality about it that I remembered with fondness. The walls, floor, pillars, ceiling and circular fountain were all marble, with subtle variations of color for contrast and coordination. The floor had a mirror-like shine to it, its light gray tone setting it off from the creamy pillars, placed equidistant around the edge of the rotunda. The fountain supported a bronze figure of Mercury atop a slowly moving pool of water. Soothing and tranquil, the pool's trickling sound echoed off the high, hard walls that encircled the place. Reflections undulated across the water's surface as though sunbeams streaming from the dome's skylight had turned to liquefied light. The combined effect felt unexpectedly warm and welcoming.

I was experiencing some unaccountable anxiety over my face to face meeting with Adam, as though I were about to begin a job interview. But I was confident my apprehensions would dissipate quickly enough. Over the years, I had learned how to do the "executive unconfrontability" shtick pretty well. I knew all the obligatory expressions, the tone of voice, the body movements. The photos of executives in magazines like "Fortune" and "Forbes" showed exactly how to project the look. The CEO looks down at the camera's lens with a stern but knowing facial expression. Sometimes there's a hint of benevolence in the expression — but not so benevolent as to suggest a lack of toughness. The jaw is slightly clenched; the arms folded over the solar plexus. A touch of gray hair is useful if you're promoting your seniority, but only a touch. You don't want to come off looking old. A dark suit and power tie finish off the costume. In an informal photo, which means jacket off, wearing suspenders is preferable.

On my last visit to the Museum, walking through the galleries of European court paintings, I was struck by the familiarity of the poses and facial expressions in the portraits of Generals, Earls and even Popes that adorned the walls. They were Fortune magazine poses in robes, wigs and garters.

I interrupted my inner musings as I spied Adam across the rotunda. He had his back to me. He was inspecting a white marble bust in one of the alcoves. I was pleased that without seeing his face I could still recognize my old friend. He was about six feet tall, with a slender, wiry build. He would never pass for a body builder, no matter how much he exercised, but he wouldn't be mistaken for the Scarecrow in the Wizard of Oz, either.

He must have sensed my gaze, for he swung around as I approached, flashing a smile and extending his hand. His hair was shorter, whiter and sparser than I remembered, and his trim, white beard, which could have made him seem less accessible, was balanced by the openness of his expression.

31

I noticed that my executive assessment scanner was in high gear, sizing up Adam's apparel in a few nano-seconds: gray double breasted suit with subtle brown stripe... good material... Italian cut, definitely not Brooks Brothers... drapes well, fits him well... maybe Brioni or Zegna.... Tie is not the standard power tie, but it works... black shoes... look like Ballys...

Adam's long fingers reached forward and enveloped my outstretched hand. Simultaneously, he grasped the back of my right upper arm with a light but firm pressure. His grasp was both strong and intimate.

"You like the costume?" he smiled, reading my thoughts.

"What do you mean?" I feigned confusion.

"My consultant's costume. The suit. I wore it today for the luncheon meeting I had with an investment banker. It lulls conservative business people into a false sense of security, before I hit them with my radical artistic ideas," he said laughing.

"Well, 'artist' is not what I would have gotten from looking at you, if I didn't know your history."

"I'm loose about it. I never bought into that b. s. that 'clothes make the man,'" he said. "However, I'm smart enough to know that the world is often run like a restaurant with a dress code. If you want a seat at the table, you have to dress the part."

"You dress to give yourself access to do what you are up to, rather than for self-identification," I commented.

"Well said. It's like a Navy SEAL dressing for a mission behind the lines," he said in a dramatic stage whisper.

A couple of people turned quizzically in our direction. It was a forceful reminder that Adam was essentially a jester, a guy who seemed always to be joking about life. But inevitably he shifted your point of view in the process. Adam smiled at me and shifted gears.

"Are you ready?"

"That depends. What do you have in mind?"

"Let's look at the pictures."

"The pictures?" I asked dubiously, "Is that the best use of our time togeth..."

Adam's face and demeanor changed swiftly. Half crouching in place like a crab, looking around furtively, his mouth twisted to the right in a pursed-lip grimace, he leaned toward me in a conspiratorial manner that was a perfect imitation of the back alley con man trying to sell a hot TV. He put his lips to my ear, and in a gruff, hoarse voice whispered, "Trust me."

An instant later he abandoned the charade and looked at me, his eyes twinkling with mischief. "Not to worry! It will all be relevant."

I surrendered to his antics and his promise, my doubts placated for the moment.

He led me down the long west hallway of the museum. Blank-eyed statues posed along its length, deaf to our echoing footsteps. The painting galleries, designed as a series of interconnected rooms, branched off on both sides of the hallway. Each room was similar in its rectangular configuration and its dark wood floor. Most rooms had a simple wooden bench at the center, and in a corner, a narrow box containing an instrument that monitored the room's temperature and humidity.

We came to a gallery with the work of the Pre-Renaissance Italian painter, Giotto. Angels, the Madonna, the Baby Jesus, and various saints filled the frames. Adam pointed out Giotto's use of color, his use of symbolism; the flatness and linearity of his imagery.

During past visits to the museum I had never given these paintings more than a cursory glance. I'd always moved quickly past them on my way to more contemporary galleries, searching out images I was familiar with. I'd looked at art the way I'd read a memo or a spreadsheet at work with a quick, surface glance, catching the key highlights, picking out the relevant information, scooping up images on the run. Whatever delights Giotto's paintings provided, they had escaped my view. Access to that world demanded a change of tempo. I'd never had the time.

I glanced at my watch. I was not sure why Adam was taking me on this tour when we were supposed to be discussing my work situation. Time was marching on. Was this art tour a way of loosening me up? A way of getting us into relationship before we discussed my business issues? If so, it was taking far too long.

As we entered yet another gallery, my concern grew into frustration. I was about to protest this use of time, when he said, "Look, a whole room of Peter Paul Rubens! What do you think of his women?"

Momentarily distracted by his question, I looked around. From all sides cheerful and lascivious smiles, surprised looks, and coy glances beamed from the faces of Rubens's women, some clothed and some naked.

"A lot of naked ladies," I said with more than a hint of petulance in my reply.

"The correct word is nude," Adam grinned. "When they are hanging in the museum they are nude, no matter what they are doing. When they are at home in the shower or bedroom, they are 'naked'. Figure it out."

Clothed or not, all of Rubens's women had pink, ample bodies. I calculated that at least three of today's fashion models would have to be bound together with rope to equal one of Peter Paul's round-bodied ladies.

The men portrayed in the paintings certainly showed no lack of ardor.

Their lust for these generous examples of feminine pulchritude seemed fully contemporary. Weight, beauty and sensuality were quite comfortable with each other in that world.

"Ideals of beauty have certainly changed since Rubens's time," Adam stated, simply, uncritically.

I felt the pressure of Adam's hand on my elbow, telling me it was time to move on. I was still not sure what his point was, taking us from room to room like this. I was about to protest when he turned towards me, saying, "Just a few more galleries. Just keep looking. We'll discuss it all soon enough."

"How did you know I was concerned?"

"I'm not just observing the paintings, Dave. I'm also observing you and how you operate," he said matter-of-factly.

"What do you mean, you're observing me?" I said defensively. I felt insulted, even betrayed. The guard looked our way and I lowered my voice. "I didn't come down here to be evaluated."

Adam's expression didn't change. "You didn't ask me to, and I'm not. I said I was observing you, not evaluating you."

"That's a bogus distinction," I said with exasperation. Was he now going to mock me as well?

"As I said, I was simply observing you, not judging you."

"Sure, as if you could do one without the other!" I countered. Did he think I was stupid?

"By the way," he said nonchalantly, "haven't you been observing me? And haven't you been judging and evaluating what I am doing, how I look, and what my point is for what we're doing?"

I could not answer for a moment; I felt completely derailed from my aggrieved self-righteousness. He was dead accurate, of course.

"Dave, unlike you, I am simply appreciating your response to the paintings. I don't have a criterion that I am measuring your behavior against to see if I approve or not. Okay? You could be an ant crawling across the floor, or an angel thrusting your face through heaven, and I'd be doing the same thing. Just adding to my vocabulary of experience."

I finally began to hear what he had actually been saying, and felt a little chagrined on top of everything else I was experiencing. Whatever else I may have been doing in this life, I was clearly not just observing. No wonder I was so suspicious of Adam. I'd accused him of one of my own familiar traits. I relaxed and let my guard down a bit.

We walked into the next room, the French Impressionist collection that I had always loved! The room felt warm with the richness of color radiating from within ornate frames — all these attempts to capture transient light and hold it fast in canvas and oil.

Directly across from me hung four renderings of the same cathedral by Monet, each painted at a different time of day — the same subject matter, and yet each one unique in its colors, shapes, shadows and forms.

"These paintings should be required viewing for every elementary school teacher who ever handed out crayons," I said to Adam. "Do you know that one of my teachers actually subjected us to art drills!"

For a moment, I was back there again in my second grade class. In that cinder block classroom we were seated alphabetically at our desks, placed in five orderly rows on the overly waxed linoleum floor.

One day we were asked to draw a picture of the scene outside the window. Afterwards, our crayon drawings were pinned to the bulletin board. After looking at our drawings, She — (Mrs. Jamison, but we usually called her 'She,' as in: 'Put it away, SHE's coming!') — she must have felt some of us were dangerously veering toward unbridled self-expression, because she sat us down at our desks to do what she called an "art drill" in unison.

"And what color is the sky, boys and girls?"

"Blue!" the other students responded in a sing-song tone. I said nothing. I looked out the window and saw the changing light in the school yard. An enormous cumulus cloud obscuring the sun had rendered the sky a dark purplish-green. Pale yellow sunbeams burst through breaks in the cloud. At that moment, the heavenly palette was definitely not blue.

"Better not to argue," I remember thinking. "You'll never win this one."

My joy in looking at the Monet paintings now, so many years later, was the joy of a familiar recognition, too long denied — the spirit of an eight year old looking out at the sky. "Yes!" I exulted silently, "the colors are like that! Yes, the shadows do fall like that!"

Monet requires the observer's participation. Adam started to point this out to me, but I cut him short, telling him I could see that for myself, and besides, I was having my own epiphany, thank you. He backed away, smiling. For the moment, I dropped my nagging concern about time and surrendered to the four paintings on the opposite wall.

As I walked towards them, they began to dissolve. I realized that there was one critical step — about four feet from the canvas — that was the crossover point from form to formlessness. Within that one small step, all form broke down, giving way to colors, swirls and smudges. It was like seeing a loved one from across the room, moving passionately towards her, and then suddenly experiencing her dissolution into a kaleidoscope of textures, sounds, colors, warmth, moisture, touches, and thoughts whose boundaries are lost with the movement forward into her embrace.

I was entranced.. I stayed at the point of that defining step, moving back and forth in front of each painting, watching it take form and then dissolve. Creating it, dissolving it, with nothing more than a step. Then, in an instant, I experienced an even greater epiphany. Reality is not out there, or in here. It is taking place at the point of recognition.

There was something compelling in this realization, but I didn't know what. Images of Janet, my kids, and even Henderson flashed by and dissolved. I didn't know what to do with this. I couldn't make sense out of it, yet.

I finally stood back. Satiated. I turned around to find Adam standing near the wall, watching me, waiting patiently. He sensed that I was ready, and tilted his head toward the connecting gallery. "Check these out," he said.

The next room was awash in color. Vibrant brush strokes carved out faces, rooms, fields and sunflowers in colors more vivid than life.

Van Gogh. Even I knew the story — obsessed and sensitive, always strapped for cash — couldn't sell his paintings when he was alive, but a Japanese business shelled out over seventy million for one of his canvases. I tried to separate myself from that whole story for a moment and just look at the paintings in front of me. In the past I hadn't found that easy to do. Too often I'd gone straight to the name plate before looking at the painting itself, as though I needed guidance from some art historian spin doctor on the correct way to view the picture.

I confided my guilty little secret to Adam.

"Labels have the same dynamics as vultures," he said.

I waited for the punch line.

"Near each work of art in the museum a label hovers, still and lifeless, patiently awaiting our gaze. The label becomes animated the moment we ask it to speak for the painting. Then, in exchange, the painting becomes a corpse, embalmed in dead, conceptual explanations."

Adam looked at me with a slight smile, and suddenly asked, "And how does this fit with what happens in your organization?"

I was surprised by the turn about. I didn't have a quick answer, but I groped at one anyway.

"One thing comes to mind," I said. "The way we base our relationships on the labels we've created for each other, rather than on direct experience.

"Labels?"

"Yes, we label ourselves and each other with official job titles or job descriptions, or we do unofficial labeling through conclusions we make about others, based on our past perceptions of them, or even through what we think we know about them from rumor or gossip. I remember my first week of work at Allied Technologies. I was the new kid on the block and had no track record yet. I was attending a meeting with seven other managers and we were tossing ideas around. I actually had a great idea, but the response I got was lukewarm at best. Then, about twenty minutes later, another manager at the meeting — he was considered a real innovator and had a lot of authority at the table for his savvy — offered exactly the same idea, with only slightly different phrasing. His words were met with such enthusiasm that you might have thought he had stumbled on the holy grail. At that moment I realized how much of what we say is valued because of how we are labeled before we even open our mouths. The reception has practically nothing to do with the actual worth of our contributions. There is nothing objective about it.

"I think the labels give us an illusion of predictability," I added. "We hope they'll reduce the uncertainty of life."

"Maybe the most daring way to live, and the most frightening for most of us, is the possibility of an unscripted life," Adam said quietly. "Certainly a life lived and created moment by moment would be a threat to the status quo."

I could see how this conversation wasn't just about the world of art. It applied precisely to my life, to my organization. Hell, the very nature of the word "organization" pulls for order, design and structure, which for most of us also means static, fixed and stable. In the organizational models I'd inherited, the ideal life was the scripted life. So we're boxed in by a paradox. On one side we're calling for innovation, and at the same time we're cautioning against rocking the boat. It keeps looking like an either/ or situation: keep things static, or slash and burn and call it "downsizing" or "re-engineering".

I remembered the sign someone had given me the year before. I had it hung over my desk when things were beginning to get tough.

This life is a test.
It is only a test.
If this had been a real life,
you would have been given further instructions
on where to go and what to do.

Adam and I were both quiet for a while, much to the guard's relief, I suspected. In the last few minutes I'd been giving myself more permission than usual to actually appreciate what was in front of me without having to have a story attached.

Then Adam said in a stage whisper, "Another gallery, come this way."

He led me across the marble hall to the gallery on the other side. Inside, were paintings from the late nineteenth and early twentieth centuries.

"What do you notice about that one?" he said.

It was a picture of a woman crossing the street with a dog on a leash.

"Well, it's a way of capturing motion."

"What do you mean by that?"

"The way the leash is blurred and the way the dog's legs are blurred, to show they're walking fast."

"Good," said Adam. "And what does all this have to do with your problems with your organization?"

The question took me by surprise. "Beats me," I said.

"Here's something: none of the paintings in this room were done without a technological innovation occurring first."

"What do you mean?"

"Okay, let me make it more concrete. Do you think any of the paintings in this gallery could have been done one hundred years earlier than they actually were?"

"I don't know."

"What about the painting with the blurry leash. Did you see any paintings from an earlier period with any depiction whatsoever of a blur, or does the concept blur even appear?"

"Well, not that I know of, Adam, but I'm no expert."

"Don't worry that you're not an expert. Trust me, blur doesn't appear."

"Okay, I'll take your word for it."

"And do you know why it doesn't? I mean here we've got some really good artists, master artists in the Renaissance, right?"

"Absolutely."

"We've got some pretty good artists in the eighteenth and nineteenth centuries too, correct?"

"No argument there."

"So, how come none of these great artists ever thought to paint a blur?"

"Well, maybe because it wasn't important to them, or they had their attention elsewhere."

"Okay. I'll buy that to a certain extent. But there is something else I'd like you to consider. No artist painted a blur because up until the late nineteenth century none of them had ever seen one or seen a representation of one. It took a technological breakthrough for blurs to exist in people's imaginations."

"Wait a minute. I don't think I heard you right. It sounded like you said that blurs didn't exist until the nineteenth century."

"That is what I'm telling you, there was no blur. It did not exist in people's perception. What it took was a technological innovation before a blur

38

ever occurred. The first time any of these artists or anyone else ever saw a blur was in those old, slow film Daguerreotypes, in which, if you didn't sit there for five minutes, the image blurred. But the photograph wasn't capturing a reality, it was capturing the inability of a film plate to record the reflections of light off an object that was not completely static. And this became, to the public at large, a way of representing quick motion."

"Hmmm. Interesting."

"The impact of photography on all other art forms is usually played down, but it was tremendous. It forced artists to redefine the purpose of their work, because a photograph could register an event or capture a likeness."

"So they had to redefine what the role of the artist was."

"Yes, and that's pretty well understood. What isn't so well understood is that photography opened up new ways of seeing the world. There may not have been any Impressionists without the influence of the Daguerreotype. The French painters were bowled over when they saw how the Daguerreotypes were, in effect, painting directly with light. Suddenly they could see images captured on a flat surface with nothing more than light itself. This was a staggering revelation.

"Here's another one for you, Dave. Have you ever seen a painting of a horse galloping?"

"Mmm, I think so."

"Well, I'll make you a bet. If you have, you've never seen a picture of a horse galloping with all four feet off the ground in the correct positions unless it was painted after 1860."

"And why is that?"

"Until that time there was a running bet among racing aficionados on whether or not a horse lifted all four feet off the ground simultaneously — even the best horsemen were never sure. And then a photographer named Edward Muybridge set up a bank of cameras with trip wires, had a horse gallop in front of them, and proved for the first time that, indeed, a horse did lift all four hooves off the ground at the same time! Then a very interesting thing happened. Once people had seen Muybridge's sequential photographs, they were actually able to see the legs aloft as a horse galloped by! Muybridge's photos shaped people's perceptions from then on.

"Perception is not an objective phenomenon. How we see our world and our place in it is influenced in a very dynamic way, not only by our biology, but by cultural factors or technological innovations as well. New ways, new tools for perceiving the world alter our perceptions of the world itself."

"So reality is always in flux?"

"Could be," Adam grinned.

"Until recently, that's not something a corporate manager would want to hear," I said.

"Of course not. The original design of organizations always focused on order and stability, but the velocity of technological innovation makes it quite clear that the new question to answer is, 'How do we create a new order out of chaos, when everything about the world is changing faster than we can adapt?' As you know from your own experience, having more and more information does not equal clarity."

"I'm not so sure about that. Information can lead to clarity, but it has to be organized in relation to the whole picture."

"Good point," he said, raising one eyebrow.

"For me the question is real simple," I told him. "How the hell do I stay ahead of the curve? Or better yet, *anticipate* the curve."

"Or even better than that," Adam added, "be able to *create* the curve of the wave of change. Every one of the artists in this museum had to face that question. Each of them created a new way to see the world for the people of their time. Even if it was within an existing style, they took it further than it had ever been taken before. For our purposes, just as important as the artists represented in this museum are all the artists who aren't."

"The artists who aren't?" I said.

"Yes, most of the artists represented here had a school, and in that school were very talented pupils who basically replicated the vision of the artists who hang here," he replied. "But those students, with a few rare exceptions, are not hanging here. And they are not hanging here because, while they may have been competent in their execution of the master's view, they simply rode the wave that the artists on these walls created. So that is another question you have to face in organizations. Whether your company is going to be a competent follower of the marketplace doomed to play catch-up, or whether you are going to be on the cutting edge, defining what the market is."

"So, now we've got this major acceleration of change going on, and my company, as well as just about all of the people on the planet, are attempting to deal with it."

"Yes, and we've been building our systems for dealing with change out of a faulty model that denies that all of us have the power to create," said Adam. "Do you want to be a great executive and a great manager, or at the very least a satisfied and effective one?" he asked me.

"That's why I'm here with you."

"Then you're going to have to get beyond merely reacting to life or the situation in front of you. You have to know that you have the power to create your life ongoingly. You have the power to shift realities. So does your company. What has got to shift is your idea of who you are, of what your company is."

"A hot conversation topic in organizations right now is the idea of 'self-origination,'" I said. "Stop telling your employees what to do, stop micromanaging them. Instead share your overall intention and your guiding principles, and then allow them the freedom to organize themselves. That way, each of them will define what needs to be done in their particular area."

"That approach works," Adam said, "if the system is designed so it fits together as an integrated whole. Then it is effective, because the integrity of all the elements working together is far more powerful than direction from the top, where it's impossible to know what is actually needed in each part of the business.

"Unfortunately, in our current business culture, we continue to put a lot of attention on the content, the things to do, the information, but very little attention on the design of the field in which that information is organized."

"I lost you there, Adam. Can you try it again?"

"Simple. Let me give it back to you as a question. How can you effectively organize for innovation when your organizational structure calls for continuity, persistence, certainty, and familiarity, not to mention predictability? How can you pretend to be committed to allowing your people to be self-organized in a design that attempts to maintain control? How do you attempt to understand and operate from a total system which was designed to look at things only from the perspective of those at the top?

"No matter how much new content you put into a system like that, until you alter the underlying design or principle that determines how the organization functions, or what a human being is, it won't make any difference."

Adam looked at me for a long moment.

"Dave, If we work together..."

He stopped and chewed absentmindedly on his lower lip for a moment, his gaze focused inward. I guessed that he was choosing his words carefully, wanting to release only those words which would serve me the most. Finally he seemed satisfied. "If we work together — beyond helping you solve your immediate situation at work — our most important achievement will be a radical, fundamental shift in your experience of who you are and what you can accomplish. When you are aware of your self as the author of your life and begin acting from that truth, you are a creator. Then..." he said dramatically, swinging around in a circle, his arms making wide, sweeping gestures toward the paintings, "...life is a work of art!"

SEVEN

BEYOND STYLE

There is knowing about, and then, there is Knowing.
One is an expression of knowledge,
the other the expression of Wisdom.
— Dr. Hazel Parcells

We left the main galleries behind, walking slowly towards the quiet atrium at the end of the building. The atrium was deserted. Only the large palm trees flanking a rectangular pool of water kept us company. We sat quietly on a wooden bench facing the water.

"Dave, I was very lucky when I went to art school," said Adam, breaking our mutual silence. "I had a couple of great teachers. One of them taught art history in a unique, non-conceptual, hands-on manner. Instead of merely looking at great art, each week Professor Lendstrom would have us choose a specific painting of a particular school and ask us to paint something in that style, using a subject already very familiar to us, like our own room or the scene outside our window. That is when I learned that style is not some surface expression. To do this assignment we had to actually look with the same mindset as the original artist in order to organize and render reality in his or her way."

"So he had you learn to paint in different styles."

"Yes, but it was much more than that. The whole idea of style is a superficial take on what we are talking about because these painters didn't just develop a style. It is not like one day they looked at the world and thought, 'What would be a nice way to render all that complex reality out there in my unique style?'

"Style is a good word to use if you're talking about clothes. But for an artist, the objective reality itself is what's in question. What people refer to as an artist's 'style' is literally his way of relating to reality — his or her way of organizing it and perceiving it. The artist's expression is a function of the mind looking at the world and interacting with it. There is no such thing as objective reality apart from perception. In Professor Lendstrom's class I learned three lessons which have been priceless to me ever since.

"The first is that there is no one way of viewing or organizing reality.

"The second is that it is possible to step into someone else's reality and think from that place. So instead of reality being a game of comparison, or conquest — who's right and who's wrong — reality can begin to be shared inclusively. Then the question that emerges is not, 'Who is right?' but rather, 'What will work most effectively, given what I am committed to?'

"What was the third lesson?" I asked.

"The third is our power to synthesize, to listen to and integrate ideas that are new to us. That starts with our appreciation for them."

"It sounds like you found out you didn't have a lock on the truth."

"Well said. What I learned in my art classes served me to my advantage. Being able actually to shift perspective has allowed me to be more effective as a teacher and consultant."

"In what way?"

"Well, if you ask people whether they know that they don't have a lock on the truth, that there are other ways of viewing reality, most people will agree, won't they?"

"Yes, absolutely."

"Except, that's not the way people operate. I've noticed that in a crunch, most people want to prove they're right. Very few of us have the power to throw everyone's point of view into the mix, stand in the commitment that everyone has, and see which interpretation becomes the most effective. That is quite a different focus than 'who is right?'

"My other teacher in this area was my sister, Stacy. Thanks to her I learned that people actually see the world differently. Stacy would do these remarkable colored pencil portraits from photographs. Her pictures were sensitive and full of subtle gradations of hues and tints. She used purples, greens, and lavenders in the skin tones, and they looked fabulous. One day I asked her, 'How do you come up with these colors?'

"She looked at me quizzically and said, 'Adam, what are you talking about? The colors are already there. I'm just coloring in what I see!' At first I thought she was kidding. When I realized she was serious, I had to confront the possibility that my sister saw things I didn't.

"One day I took one of the photographs she'd used and studied it very carefully. Finally, with her drawing as a reference, I was able, very gradually, to make out colors that she saw very clearly.

"That is what a great artist can do, and that is also what a great entrepreneur or executive can do. They see the world in a particular light, which for them may look simple and obvious, but which others do not see, and they find a way to articulate that view so others are able to see it too."

"I think that's true," I replied. "Most of the breakdowns in business meetings occur because there are ten different people at the table, and therefore at least ten different realities, but nobody takes that into account. They all operate as if everybody else sees the world as they do, as if the way they see it ought to be obvious, and that if people don't agree, they are either stupid or just plain stubborn. Nobody's looking for alignment. Everybody's looking for agreement."

Adam nodded his head, and gave me a knowing smile of recognition. "In these galleries, you've got people who have raised the curtain on a whole new way of looking at the world. I can either look at each of these works as an entryway to a distinct view of reality and walk away enriched by that; or I can stand in front of the picture and see it only from my own point of view, assessing whether the artist's expression of the world conforms to the way I think things ought to be. Then I'll walk away agreeing or disagreeing, but not enriched or transformed."

"How do you begin that kind of change?"

"I'll tell you. But first, I want you to answer a question for me."

"Okay," I said laughing. "What else would I expect?"

"Here's the question," he said. "Which painting style in these galleries that we've gone through, captures the most accurate view of reality? Answer that question and you've got the first key to being an innovator, whether you're an artist, a physicist, or a business person."

I thought for a moment. Then I realized that Adam's question was another curve ball. Each of the paintings, each of the styles was a representation of someone's reality. I liked some more than others, probably as a function of how the artist's view corresponded with my own perspective of the world. As Adam said, it was never objective. None of the paintings, even from the same school, offered the same take on what was real. Each was valid as an expression, and each looked from a particular point of view. I noticed that even the most realistic painting was easily recognized as that of a particular artist. This, of course, made a lie of the whole notion of objectivity, since a truly objective view of reality would have no persona attached to it. I have never seen such a work of art, unless you count one of those mindless paintings they sometimes sell in shopping malls.

I looked at Adam. "The question you asked me is GIGO," I said.

"Ah, you mean 'garbage in, garbage out.'"

"Sure. The question itself is flawed. There's no single best expression... although... it may indeed be possible to experience 'the truth', I don't know. A lot of folks throughout history seem to have connected with something fundamental and authentic. The artists in this museum seem to have tapped into

44

something universal, though they probably weren't trying to."

Just then I was reminded of a poem.

"'*Something I don't know, that one may come on randomly,*'" I quoted to Adam. "Do you know the poems of the Spanish mystic, St. John of the Cross? I studied and fell in love with his poems in college — even learned to read them in Spanish. He composed poems in awe of what he called 'this knowledge by unknowing'. I think he was expressing something that I confess I've never experienced but wish I had. At best, I've sensed it subtly, in the way that you might catch a fleeting movement at the periphery of vision. Turn quickly to face it, though, and it vanishes."

"I know St. John's work," said Adam. "Whatever he experienced is not where the problem lies. St. John allowed it to use and shape him."

He stopped speaking, and sat quietly, seeming to want to give us both a few more moments of reflection.

When he again spoke, his tone was tinged with sadness. "I think what creates so much pain and mischief, deadening our hearts, is our haste to rush to judgment. In an attempt to make our world predictable and controllable, we turn our experiences into rigid beliefs. But this kind of certainty is lethal. It cuts us off from the flow of life and the multiplicity of viewpoints and experiences that arise. The inclusiveness of 'and' dies, and the exclusivity of 'either/or' takes its place."

"I can see a lot of that at the office," I said. "When it happens, the game shifts from inclusion and teamwork to a game of contention that polarizes us as winners and losers."

"Unfortunately," responded Adam, "we forget that no matter how sophisticated our beliefs may seem, they are merely one set of possible interpretations that we've fossilized in our vain effort to 'get it right'. Worshipping our beliefs, we break the second commandment: 'Thou shalt have no other gods before Me.' We live in fear of the unknown, and lack faith in the Mystery that's beyond all interpretation."

"St. John and St. Teresa got in trouble for saying that kind of thing, Adam." I laughed nervously. "You'd better watch who you say it to if you intend to work with large organizations. The idea of Spirit makes some people jumpy. They want practical stuff, not spiritual talk, or at least they think they do."

"Nothing is more practical than spirituality," he countered, "it's the word itself that has a bad rap. Too many bags of belief got dumped over it. If you don't like the term, don't use it. Use some term that physicists use, or make up one of your own. What could be more practical than tapping into the principles of creation, to live as a creator? It's either that or living as if you're

45

nothing more than a clod of complex protoplasm feverishly working your ass off in the service of the 'someday' god and waiting for some miracle to have it all turn out and make you happy.

"The philosopher, Bertrand Russell, said, 'Every great idea starts out as blasphemy.' Nothing is more blasphemous to entrenched beliefs than the possibility of a direct connection with the source of creativity. When you actually live from there, you are continually replacing your worn out beliefs. You don't need to believe in something if you know it directly! Most people believe in the seniority of the seeable over the unseeable. That leaves them living their lives ass backwards, making their beliefs sacred and static. They exclude all experiences and interpretations that don't conform to their view, and so the lie begins. All real understanding, compassion and empathy go out the window when righteousness walks in."

"I've been as guilty of that as anyone," I admitted. "All the wars that have been fought over that question you posed — over who has the truth, and who has the right to lay it on others — amount to a tragic cosmic joke. I can't imagine that any human point of view can encompass the whole of reality, the whole of all knowledge, the whole of 'the truth', much less articulate it. As I said, the answer to your question is 'GIGO' and knowing that it's GIGO provides the key to being a creator."

I stopped talking, suddenly aware that my arms and legs were trembling. I had no idea why I'd said all that, but I didn't even care to analyze it at the moment. I knew something important was happening, and I was willing to trust the process.

"Congratulations," Adam said quietly, "you passed the test. Let's get something to drink, and continue our conversation."

EIGHT
THE ORIGINATING ORGANIZATION

Do we decide questions at all?
We decide answers no doubt,
but surely the questions decide us.
— Lewis Carroll

The restaurant was relatively new, added during a recent renovation of the building's interior. For years only a small, simple food service had existed, tucked away in a far corner of the museum's basement, with all the ambiance and appeal of a high school cafeteria.

All that had changed. The Cafe, as it was now called, was a large airy room, with white-stained wooden floors. The walls were a bleached yellow, like stone buildings I'd seen in Tuscany. Floor to ceiling windows looked out on the landscaped sculpture garden, while tall glass doors allowed for passage from the cafe to the lawn and white gravel paths outside.

Adam and I chose a corner table near a window where we could have both privacy and a view of the garden. I ordered an expresso. Adam chose some strange tea concoction.

"I think it best if we address the larger issue of your company first," Adam suggested. "From there, we can talk about your own state of being. Obviously, who you are has a very large impact on whether or not you can make a difference in your company."

I listened to this suggestion with relief. I was more comfortable discussing my company than myself. Maybe we won't even have to get to me, an internal voice whispered. I told Adam, "That sounds good to me. The company is my biggest concern anyway."

Adam settled into his seat and took a long, slow sip of his tea, reflecting on how best to begin. "In most companies, the focus of attention is on the form the company takes — its identity as a culture — and the actions performed in its operation. Usually very little attention is paid to what determines those actions. That misunderstanding is the main problem. You can alter the company's policies, directives, orders, 'org' charts, and so on, but that only makes a superficial difference over time. These surface changes don't affect what is driving the behavior and actions in the company. In the long run, techniques don't alter behavior. But shift the way reality is perceived, and you have real change. Your practices become an expression of that shift."

He raised his cup again to his lips before continuing. "However, not every organization is at the level where they can make that kind of a shift. Your company sounds a long way off. In my work I've distinguished three kinds of organizations: the *reactive organization*, the *responsive organization* and the *originating organization*. When I walk through a new client's door I can pretty much tell within the first hour what kind of organization I'm dealing with. It's evident from the scale of view the company has, how large a perspective they have of themselves and their future. And do you know what really pegs them? The relationships among employees, the kinds of questions people ask when they're sorting out problems."

"What are some of the differences?"

"As I said, level of scale is a prime determinant. A reactive organization deals with what is happening at the level of scale called *events*. There is this event, then this event, and then this event to handle. People with an event scale of view talk about having long range plans, but it's all talk."

"That sounds like my company. There's a crisis to handle nearly every day. We don't have time to see the underlying problems, so they reoccur, again and again."

"That's because you're focusing on useless questions," said Adam, "like what went wrong and who did it. If you're asking *those* questions, you're in trouble."

"It's true. It's all about blame and shifting responsibility," I admitted. "It's about who's the victim, who's right and who's wrong. And that is the whole game, the 'blame/credit game'."

"So do people in your company feel pitted against one another?"

"Yes, I guess I'd have to say that. Everyone's trying to cover their ass. There's a lot of polarization."

"Aha," said Adam. "So, in addition to all the other problems, you also have your insiders and your outsiders in the company. Do you know what you get next?"

I didn't have a clue to what he was driving at.

"You get the pickle problem."

"The what?"

"P - C - L," he joked. "Say it out loud and it sounds like pickle — Pre-concluded Conditioned Listening. Pre-concluded means I've already made up my mind before it happens. Conditioned means mechanical and automatic.

"Hasn't this ever happened to you? You're in a meeting and everyone's doing pre-concluded conditioned listening, and you say something that is really extraordinary, but because you've already been categorized as one of the 'outer circle', your ideas don't count."

This had not only happened to me, I'd listened that way myself a thousand times. Getting beyond the cuteness of Adam's "pickle" analogy, I saw how true it was. To be pickled is to be unchanging, embalmed. I'd certainly had a pre-concluded conditioned response to Henderson. I'd made up my mind about him before I'd even met him: what he was like, what he would listen to. The idea that my conclusions about him might not be the whole reality had never even entered my head. And Henderson wasn't the only one I'd dismissed. My colleagues, my family, they didn't have a chance with me. I had stuck them all in the pickle barrel and sealed the top. There was no way they could ever make it with me, there was no way that I could see them freshly each day. I was in the barrel, too, drowning in preconceptions about myself. I didn't have a pre-concluded conditioned listening, I was that listening.

With wounded pride that I knew I was going to have to forget about if we were going to get anywhere, I told Adam what I'd realized.

"There is an old Sufi saying," he said. "'When a thief looks at a saint, all he sees are pockets.'"

What kind of thief was I?

If I could discover that and correct it, perhaps I could understand my situation in a new way. I decided not to dwell any further on negatives. That would be too easy in my present state of mind. I wanted to press on with the discussion, to get something I could use.

"What's the second kind of organization you mentioned?"

"A responsive organization," Adam replied. "They're a big improvement over the reactive kind. At least they have a larger view of the world and their place in it. In other words, they have a guiding vision and mature, positive relationships. In a responsive organization, when people ask 'what happened?' they actually mean 'what happened?' not 'what's wrong' and 'who's to blame?'

Adam took another sip from his cup before continuing. "They can step back from the problem and view it objectively. Blame is not the issue. In a responsive organization we can look together to see what needs to be done. Fear doesn't take over to gum up the works."

I nodded in agreement. Fear. I realized that was an important issue. A person in a reactive organization is not going to want to take creative risks because it's too threatening to stick your neck out that far.

This was making a lot of sense to me. "If I'm authentically responding to what's in front of me, I have to be able to observe the situation without it being unconsciously colored by my ideals, expectations and past estimations. I have to see and listen to what is present 'as it is', not as I believe or think it should be."

"If you really create your company as a responsive organization," he replied, "it allows you to move to the third kind of organization, the originating organization. But first your company has to be at least a responsive one, because it is not possible to become originative unless you are being responsive, being count-on-able for what you are up to."

"What exactly do you mean by 'originative'?"

"In the dictionary it says: *To originate is to bring into being, especially to create something original; to invent, or thinking or acting in an independent, individual, fresh way.* As you can see, I like the definition so well, I've memorized it."

"...creating someting new...thinking or acting in an independent, fresh way," I repeated. "Then an originating organization has the capacity to continually bring forth new ideas and projects. It's not a one time or sometime thing, but originating on a sustainable, consistent, ongoing basis."

"Yes. And you have to understand," he said, "the originating organization is aware of itself as able to bring forth new realities both within itself and within its markets. There's a place for incremental improvement in what a responsive organization is doing," said Adam. "They will take a tradition and improve on it. But this is something else. Origination may grow out of a tradition but then it takes that tradition to a completely new level, which the organization hadn't been focused on at all before. Having your past, but not stuck in it, that is the key."

"And you can help our company do this?"

"With the right commitment, yeah," he nodded. "I can."

"And the right vision?" I asked.

"Sort of, but the key is not getting stuck in your particular vision. You need room to grow, to keep asking certain questions, and to shift and refine your vision and your mission as you go along. Of course if you have a reactive organization the vision is irrelevant anyway. You may post it in the halls, but no one takes it seriously or believes in it, because everyone except top management knows that it's just an exercise in futility. A responsive organization might benefit some from a vision, but not much. Only origination makes an organizational vision viable, and then it's an open-ended flexible vision that eventually becomes woven into the spirit of the organization to the point where it's transparent."

"What are the questions that can lead to all this?"

"I mean questions like, 'What might we build? What might we create?' but also, when problems come up, 'What's the possibility that we have in this breakdown?' That is another dimension. An originating organization asks the questions that nobody else is asking, like how you might do something in a completely different way, in a completely different field that wasn't seen to be possible before.

"And the people in the company have to be very participatory, not holding their cards close to the chest, allowing a flow of information, trying things out non-judgmentally—which doesn't mean not rigorously. You have to be rigorous, but you also must have the ability to delay your judgment and avoid premature evaluation of ideas — even making room for the crazy half-baked idea, the idea that may seem silly when you first hear about it; yet if acted upon, may be capable of altering reality. Change on the grand scale!"

I remembered Adam's promotion piece and my reaction when I'd read the part about "creating change." I'd been suspicious of that idea, dismissing it as just so much hype. This is what he meant by creating change. He meant origination.

"You know in your promotion brochure where you talk about creating change?" I asked. "I was pretty skeptical when I read that, but I think I'm beginning to understand what you mean."

"I love it when someone gets what I'm talking about!" he replied with a grin.

"You know," I continued, "over the years I've seen a few companies shift their identities, so I know it can be done. But usually it's been in response to unavoidable market demands, rather than as a function of a free creativity that itself steers the marketplace."

He mulled that over, gazing contemplatively at the garden outside. "The problem is," he said, finally, "that without that originative spirit, the new identity becomes the new Truth to be believed. However effective it might be, the company will eventually slide downward, unless a new breakthrough comes along to make it possible for them to redefine their identity again."

"But what if an organization didn't just initiate a change when things began to slide?" I asked, an 'aha!' forming even as I spoke. "What if a company kept re-inventing itself, not merely as a response to a demand, and not in any kind of arbitrary way, but because its very nature was to bring forth new expressions of itself that transformed the marketplace in which it was a player? Then it would have fulfilled itself in every aspect as an originating organization."

"By George, I think he's got it!" Adam teased. "The nature of its *being* is originative. To get to that state, it is necessary to create a critical mass of people in the company who are willing to *be* originative on a daily basis, not only within their company, but in the way that their company relates to the larger world. It would require a transformation in the very nature of what people consider themselves to be — creators."

NINE

THE FOUR WORLDS

Look, it cannot be seen — it is beyond form.
Listen, it cannot be heard — it is beyond sound.
Grasp, it cannot be held — it is intangible.
These three are indefinable;
Therefore they are joined in one.
— Lao Tzu

"Given the way Henderson is and what he cares about, an originating company is probably the farthest thing from his mind," I said resignedly.

"You just fell into the PCL barrel," Adam replied with an accusatory chuckle. "Notice how easy it was to get sucked back into it? It's the automatic human condition, this pull to take reality, which is malleable, and view it as a fixed, static thing. Your company's not a static thing, it's dynamic energy in motion, and so are its people."

I became defensive. This was not my best move. "I know how I'd like to respond to the changes I see happening at work," I said lamely, "but other people keep getting in my way."

Adam just laughed at me. "At your age and with your position you ought to be more in charge than that."

His mockery was oddly refreshing. Everyone else I knew took my position too seriously. For a moment I let my guard down.

"Sometimes," I said, "I think there's no position more powerless than one which appears to be formidable, like it's bolstered by a huge arsenal of power and prestige."

"What do you mean?"

"Simply that I have to answer to so many different people, situations and abstract forces that I can't get a grip on *my* agenda. I serve too many masters, that's the problem. It's never a question of just trying to please myself. I'm always obligated to a whole slew of folks, many of whom I don't even know."

"Has it always been like that for you? This feeling of powerlessness?"

"Not constantly, but I've had attacks of it off and on as far back as I can remember. I've felt continually thwarted, lately, and that sure brings it on." I stopped. This was beginning to sound like a therapy session. I didn't want to get so personal. I refused to go on, preferring the awkward silence to continuing with the whining.

Sensing my reticence, Adam switched direction.

"If we look at your feeling of powerlessness from the point of view that the universe at every level is composed of energy, then you're experiencing a blockage in its flow," he said.

I silently mouthed an expletive. "With all due respect," I said, "I'm sick and tired of getting yet another cute but useless metaphor laid on me. I have big problems. Your energy metaphor makes me want to puke, to be quite honest. I just can't translate it into anything useful."

"That's the trick, isn't it?" said Adam. "Otherwise it's just another pile of interesting but useless information."   .

His response to my outburst was not at all what I'd expected. It hadn't fazed him in the slightest.

"Maybe the first step is for you to realize that I'm not speaking metaphorically," he continued.

He paused to let that register. "Look, Dave, my intention is not to drown you in platitudes. What I'm telling you is not my opinion, it's my experience. It also lines up with views of the universe that have been around for a long, long time. I'm speaking about a force that can alter your reality and release the energy that you need to accomplish whatever you've decided is really essential.

"Of course if you like being stuck where you are, that same force will give you the momentary illusion that things are staying in place. But they're really not, you know."

Adam's next statement reverberated in my head as an ominous warning.

"Either you are going to create change or change is going to create you, but there will be change. Who are you going to be in the face of it?"

"Go on."

A slight smile flitted across his face. "Look, listen and understand," he intoned with the sing-song cadence of a tent-show evangelist. Then his expression shifted to intense concentration. "There is a difference between *creating* and *making*. The latter has to do with taking something that exists and turning it into something else: ore into steel, a tree into a piece of furniture, a blueprint into a building. To function we need to be able to do that effectively. Making is integral to the creative process. But creating itself is not merely the ability to reshape what already exists. Creating is the power to bring forth something from nothing, whether it be an idea, a view of the world, or a new technology.

"Here is a principle you can find in both ancient religious texts and in Quantum Physics," Adam continued. "Everything is an expression of energy, and all energy is expressed on a continuum, from nothing to something. It starts with what might be called 'undifferentiated nothingness': no form."

Adam leaned forward, his body mirroring the intensity in his voice. *"Now the earth was unformed and void, and darkness was upon the face of the deep..."*

He paused before continuing, letting the quote sink in. "That's the second line of *Bereshith*, the 'Book of Creation,' popularly known by its Greek name, *Genesis*. There's nothing except unformed potentiality before the beginning. It's nothing and everything simultaneously. From this infinite potentiality, an energy emanates. *'...And the spirit of God hovered...'* unfolding itself into invisible fields and patterns of intention. *'And God said, 'Let there be light.'* These organizing fields shape the diverse expressions of matter that subsequently arise from it. *'And there was light.'* From the flux and flow, the infinite manifests itself in finite structures which evolve and eventually dissolve back to nothing, from which to create newly again."

My curiosity heightened, I started to wonder, Was there a connection between human creativity and the creation of everything? Was modern science really pointing to the same things as the Bible?

"These organizing fields," I asked him, "are they similar to the 'strange attractors' in chaos theory?" The relevance of chaos and complexity theories to my work had so far eluded me.

"Possibly."

Suspecting that his answer was intentionally ambiguous, I was somewhat frustrated. But I had to admit to myself that I was curious about this stuff. At the same time, if I was going to listen to it, it had to be relevant and verifiable. I wouldn't put up with a lot of b. s.

"I just want to make sure that this discussion is relevant. I've got books at home with this kind of information in it, and some people think they are a great cure for insomnia. I'm drowning, buddy. I don't have time for philosophical ruminations."

"Complaint noted," he chuckled. "Let me try again. I admit that much of what I am saying may not seem pertinent at first, but the flow I just described will give you the fundamental dynamics of creating; be it for an individual, a team, or an organization. The subject is both practical and apropos. It isn't just a theory or a metaphor, but an essential piece of knowledge for living life as a creator."

"All right, go ahead," I said.

"In late 1997," he continued, "a team of astronomers recorded a tremendous blast of energy, twelve billion light years from earth. The energy blast lasted only a few seconds, yet it was equal to the energy of all the billion trillion stars in the universe. Do you understand what I just said? In the time it takes me to look at you and then glance away, an energy was released from the depth of space that equaled the energy of the entire universe. And then it was gone. Back to nothing. And they have no certainty about what could have produce that amount of energy or where it came from. What they *have* learned over the years is that the whole universe, from the cosmic scale all the way down to the cells in your brain that are firing measurable bursts right now as you sit here, is energy in form. Energy lights the sun, allows a small woman to lift a car off a child and an athlete to run faster than ever before. It powers every creative thought you have ever had and is what you are providing to your body with every breath you take.

"I'm asking you to do a thought experiment. I'm asking you to imagine that the world, the whole universe in fact, is made up of interrelated fields of energy. Now in doing that, I'm not asking you to imagine some abstract, sterile concept. Instead, imagine that all the many forms and expressions of the universe are made of vibrating energy — whether it's the flow and power of a river or the frenetic action on the floor of the futures exchange. So I'm including everything, every form, as an expression of energy."

"Even business?"

"Of course. Leave anything out and the hypothesis falls apart. In fact, "it's all or nothing."

"Okay, go ahead. I'm game."

"Good. Now this is a completely different way of looking at the universe than the way you and I learned in school. We were taught that the primary stuff is matter. Of course many Oriental traditions have been saying that it's all energy for eons. In England over one hundred and fifty years ago Michael Faraday attempted to tell his fellow scientists that the field of energy comes first and the forms follow, not the other way around! It's all energy in motion, and we just believe it's solid! Guess what? They've measured it — even the things that look solid — and they're mostly made up of nothing! Meanwhile, most of the rest of us have bought into the view that we grew up with, so we can't see the consequences."

"That's certainly true of me," I said. "I can't see the consequences of what you're saying."

Adam looked at me hard. His right eyebrow went up and he pursed his lips.

"Okay, let's make it practical. A field of energy has a certain direction or flow and organizes the flow of the contents within it into certain patterns. A simple example, the one Faraday pointed to, is the way iron filings line up within a magnetic field. It doesn't matter how you try to put them down, they will rearrange themselves in a pattern consistent with the direction of the field.

"Now remember that you can't see a magnetic field. You can't register it with any of your physical senses because it exists only as energy. It's invisible, but its effects are not."

"You mean like radio waves?" I said. "They're all around us, but we can't perceive them until they're translated into sound vibrations through the use of a radio."

"Good analogy. But you started in the middle. A radio broadcast begins with the announcer's voice, which is translated into radio waves, then back to sound waves in a radio receiver, and then to the listener's ear. There, the same kind of shift occurs when our internal decoder translates sound into words, which are then given meaning which we understand internally, and all within a millisecond. That process happens spontaneously."

Then Adam delivered the punch line.

"How could this be possible unless energy itself was the basis of it all, no matter what form that energy might take, moment to moment?"

"That certainly makes sense."

"The hypothesis I'm offering you," he continued, "is that it all starts with the formless and moves toward form. Once the process is in place, it moves continually back and forth between those two poles: the formless and form, energy and matter."

He paused for a moment and looked quizzically at me, assessing whether I was following his line of thought. "Can you give me an illustration of a pattern which determines the flow and shape that matter subsequently takes?"

"How about DNA?"

"Very good. Give me another illustration."

"The movement of waves in the ocean?" I offered.

"Yes, as long as you understand that the wave itself is not the water we are perceiving but the current of energy that is giving the water its shape and direction," Adam cautioned.

"I think I understand. A wave in the ocean is not the water that we call the wave. The wave is literally a wave of energy which the water takes the shape of and rides on. It's invisible. So if you're a surfer, you are actually surfing waves of energy, not water."

"Well said!"

Then I had another thought, this time about thoughts.

"How about this?" I suggested. "A thought can't be seen, but the action that follows from it can be."

"Precisely, now you're getting it! Pure energy expresses itself in fields that fill the entire universe. That's the creative force you must seek to cultivate if you want to become truly creative. You could call the outward forms that you create manifestations of the underlying field. They resonate with it."

"These effects, the created things, can be recorded by our senses, but not what generated them, is that what you're saying?" I asked.

"Yes. In fact Faraday's point was that the realm of the unseeable is senior to the realm of the seeable and controls it," he said. "Try to line up the iron filings another way in a magnetic field and it won't work. The field will re-organize the filings every time.

"Now what if you began relating to your organization not as a thing, not as a static structure of buildings, not as the number of breathing bodies talking or moving around, not as its traditions and history, not as its policies, rules and procedures, and not as its statistics, products or bottom line?"

"That's hard to imagine. If you take all that away, it looks like there's nothing left."

"Exactly. That's all the stuff you and I can register with our senses, and therefore they're all junior to the organizing field from which they arise. Now what if you held all of those forms and permutations as visible and measurable outcomes, and instead related to your organization as a dynamic field of energy? What if you could design the field of energy that shapes your company, its ideas, actions and behaviors, the same way the magnetic field shapes the direction and design of the iron filings?

Suddenly I saw new possibilities in what he was saying. "Maybe the relevant question for me is, 'What in an organization is analogous to the way a magnetic field shapes and controls the forms and patterns within it?' If I knew that, it might be a key for shaping the company."

Adam grinned. "You're right on the money. A creator has a relationship with energy that allows it to be shaped into new and innovative forms of expression. You're asking the right question, all right. When you know that, you know the DNA of Being. Have patience, we'll get to it."

Have patience! Same old Adam. Questions for me to wrestle with when what I'm longing for are answers. I decided not to press the point yet. Besides, something else was troubling me.

"I see a possible hole in the argument," I said. "I can understand it when we talk about iron filings and waves. But an individual, a family or an organization is not just made up of physical components. There are the emotional and mental realms to consider."

"Excellent, excellent!" Adam replied. "What you are saying is key. Energy is energy, and it manifests at every possible level of form from the gross to the subtle. Our thoughts are expressions of energy. Hell, we can measure how much energy it takes to think with MRI and EEG machines. And we can measure our emotions, which are certainly forms of energy."

"Okay, so you've included the emotional and mental realms. What about the spiritual? Is that within the context you're talking about?"

I was surprised and annoyed by my own question. It seemed to have leapt unbidden from my mouth, as if asked by someone other than me. I was perplexed. Remembering my prayer of the night before made me even more so. What was going on with me? Spirit was not something I normally thought about. If I couldn't see it, touch it, smell it or hear it, I didn't consider it had much reality or value in my life.

What I'd learned about spirit from my religious education and from my undergraduate philosophy classes had left me deeply dissatisfied and skeptical. The one remaining thread, tenuous as it was, that connected me to the possibility of spirit was the poetry of St. John of the Cross. When I first read St. John's words, a potent recognition had registered in my heart, though I couldn't say why or how. The pale echo of that epiphany resided there still, albeit unexplored and maybe even exiled. Perhaps it was this once glimpsed hope that leapt over the wall of my present skepticism and uttered the question about spirit.

Adam stopped and poured some fresh tea into his cup. I wondered if my question had him stumped.

"I don't want to give a facile response to your question," he said. "I'm asking that you listen to what I'm about to say, but not from whether you believe it or not, or from whether you agree with it or not.

I was perplexed. "Well, what the hell do you want me to do?"

"Just try it out, each thing that I say. Look from there, without judgment, and see what arises."

"I'll try," I said, still not sure what he wanted.

"You're going to try to try it out?" he noted ironically. "Don't try. Trying is an illusion. There is no try. How much value do you attribute to 'trying' when you ask someone in your office to give you a report you requested a week before, and they come up empty handed or with a half-assed attempt and say they tried?"

"Zero. It annoys the hell out of me too. I get your point. Please go on."

"The question you asked about spirit leads to another, bigger question. If the whole universe is energy, what's ultimately determining its design and shape?"

"I sure haven't spent much time with those kinds of questions," I replied.

"I've paid a lot more attention to the stuff you can see and measure. But I'm also familiar with some of the ideas regarding complex adaptive systems; how a system re-organizes itself, and the hypothesis called 'sensitive dependence on initial conditions' that's been popularized and misunderstood as the 'butterfly effect'. You know, the idea that the smallest vibration of energy may affect the behavior of the whole."

"And maybe that hypothesis seems far fetched only in a world view that we are all separate objects, not connected," Adam suggested, not missing a beat. "Inside a theory of interrelatedness it might make sense."

"Can you give me a real example of that theory?"

"How about your body? It works as a totally integrated system."

"Okay, I'm with you."

"What if an organization worked with the same kind of deep understanding of the interrelatedness and systemic nature of itself and its marketplace, and consciously had the power to change the organizing field that shaped its systems?"

"I wouldn't be dealing with the main problem that I've got at work right now, that's for sure," I answered.

"And you would be able to lead your company to the full expression of its field of *being*."

"And what's *being* an expression of?"

"The possibility, intention and power to *bring forth being*."

"And beyond that?" I asked sarcastically.

"The Crown of it all. Pure Awareness. The Awareness, I AM — your true unchanging nature."

Before I could protest the fairy tale direction the conversation was taking, he added quietly, "Even some of the top physicists hypothesize that."

"Anything you're suggesting that exists beyond that?"

"Maybe what you were asking about. Spirit. The Prime Cause. The Ain Sof. The Void. The Source. The Infinite Silence. B. T. B. B. Pick your name, none of them can capture it."

"B. T. B. B.?" I asked.

"Before The Big Bang," Adam said mischievously. "I made that up for the science types." Then his expression grew serious. "Are you familiar with the phrase about not 'throwing pearls before swine'?"

"Yes. So, what's your point?" I could tell that I was getting ready to defend myself.

"This conversation illustrates the point perfectly," Adam said. "You expressed an interest in learning the principles of creating."

"That's still the case," I said.

"Well, Dave, I just ran three principles of creating by you, and you brushed them aside with a pinch of sarcasm. I told you not to believe or disbelieve. Instead, I asked you to try on what I say. You didn't do that. You asked me about spirit, yet when I answered you, your pre-concluded bias made the truth worthless to you."

I was at a loss at first as to how to respond. "Would you be kind enough to run that by me again — whatever you said I missed?"

"I didn't say that you missed it, I said that you disregarded it. That's different." It was a 'zinger,' but not because Adam was rubbing it in.

"Okay, what did I disregard?"

"Are you ready this time?"

I nodded.

"Dave, a few minutes ago, whether you were aware of it or not, you dismissed the possibility that Spirit is the source of creation and all creativity. In fact it was so easy for you to do this that I wonder if you have any clear conception of what you so blithely tossed out of the picture. Spirit is the source of all form. But it cannot ever be grasped or understood fully through any form, since it is beyond all forms.

"You can't capture it with language, though sometimes poetry comes close. Listen.

That in whom reside all beings and who
resides in all beings, who is the giver of
grace to all, the Supreme Soul of the
universe, the limitless being — I Am That.

"That was from the ancient Amritbindu Upanishad of India.

"Ultimately," he sighed, "all words fail at the threshold of the Presence itself."

"Well, then how can you connect with it, if not through some representation of it?" I asked. I was asking it of myself as much as I was of Adam.

"You can only know it by being aware of your true nature. Then you know it directly as the field from which you come," he said.

"What do you mean by my true nature?"

"Again, words and symbols are not it. They can only point to it. The description or symbol will never give you the experience itself. Your true nature is your Original Self, your essence. It exists at the threshold where Unity brings forth the possibility of Diversity. It's the emanation that originates life, and from which multitudinous expressions spring forth.

I could hear the words Adam was saying, but I could not grasp them. I felt like a rodeo performer trying to grab a prized greased sow as it runs out of the chute, feeling its slippery form within my grasp; then suddenly finding myself face down in the mud with empty arms.

"That is what makes this so hard to hear in the beginning," he said with empathy. "You are used to listening for subject-verb-object. But here is a subject whose verb acts on its own Self. It's self reflexive. It's subject-verb-subject. And that is hard for the mind to understand at first, and impossible for it to grasp as a concept." He shook his head with a smile. "How can a mere concept — which by its very nature is finite — ever expect to hold the infinite in its embrace?

"You have the ability to experience yourself not as a thing, but as the unchanging, timeless field of awareness from which your thoughts, your emotions, your moods, your actions and your world arise. You are the awareness that creates and inhabits your identity. You are the I AM that is breathing each breath in and out of your nostrils."

"Stop!" I called out, slamming my palms down on the table top, sending my spoon flying in an arc toward the floor. Adam responded immediately, and fell silent.

"What does all this bullshit have to do with helping me out of my business predicament?" I was yelling, and I didn't care who heard me.

"I've just about reached my quota of conversations about being," I hissed hoarsely. "I challenge you to come up with worthwhile suggestions about what I can do!" I pointedly looked at my watch, again. I could feel the tension in my face. "You've got two minutes to convince me that I shouldn't walk," I barked curtly.

"O.K. Two minutes," said Adam, checking his watch. He looked at me calmly and said, "If you could recall a time when you experienced the state of awareness I've been trying to describe for you, would that give you permission to continue with this seemingly bullshit tangent for a while longer, just on the off chance that you will be able to see how ridiculously practical and relevant this conversation turns out to be?"

"Yes, yes," I replied gruffly. "You've now got about a minute and a half to make your point, if there is one. But I don't see how you can. I have no recollection of such an experience."

"You don't think so, huh? Well let me ask you this. Have you ever been so completely absorbed in what you were doing that you've lost all sense of your identity? You may be working on a project and suddenly ideas are just coming to you easily, seamlessly and you have no sense of where you are, or of time passing, or of being Dave Carey — not even a sense of having a body. You're just purely aware and absorbed in what you're doing and everything is flowing effortlessly like magic. Has that ever happened to you?"

My mind flashed immediately to a time when I'd been up late working on a new sales promotion plan for a product we were considering for production. As I worked, the plan suddenly sprang alive in my imagination, as if it were actually happening, actually out there being implemented. I filled page after page with ideas, drawings, bits of ad copy, memos to various people — a helter-skelter of stuff that had its place in the three dimensional technicolor dream going on in my mind. As I worked in my home office I sat across from a window which was pitch black with the darkness of night. The next time I looked up, it was full daylight.

Was that what this was all about? Achieving that state? Of course I'd experienced that kind of awareness several times. I'd wished it could happen more often. Those memorable (but too infrequent) times that I'd achieved that state had been exhilarating. I probably owed my career to those occasions. And the strange thing was, after it had happened it did feel like magic, like receiving a gift, as if all my good ideas were out there just waiting for me.

"Dave? Answer me. Has that ever happened to you?"

I knew it was petty of me, but I didn't want to let him see the interest he'd aroused in me. In as perfunctory a manner as I could muster, I told Adam that I had remembered some times that were similar to what he was talking about, after all, and that I felt okay about continuing our conversation.

"Are you saying that you can help me achieve that state of awareness more often?"

"I'm saying that you are that awareness. Dave Carey the identity, however, is not so real."

This seemed like a strange thing to say. Still, I tried to make the connection. I reflected that while working on that project I had lost all sense of myself as a person. I was simply the process of what I was doing.

I remembered a Biblical phrase which went something like, "Who so would find himself must lose himself."

It made sense. I had lost myself in the project and thereby found myself as pure energy. I was the creative activity I had been performing. There had been no room in my mind for thinking about other things like a headache or a few bills I had not paid or an annoyance with a neighbor.

By projecting out from that experience I could sense that one might be that way much if not all of the time, feeling totally creative in all, or nearly all, the aspects of one's life. It would be a wonderful way to be, I thought, because it would be a sort of collaboration with the universe, the flow of energy coming through me from somewhere else as I concentrated on doing only that which totally absorbed me.

Could such a way of life really be possible?

Adam fell silent, and in that silence, as though called forth by his voice, a fragment of St. John's poem floated to the surface of my memory:

> *Without a foothold you must seek*
> *Him out — no face, nor form, alone —*
> *tasting there something I don't know*
> *that one may come on randomly.*

A missing piece in a puzzle that had eluded me for years fell into place. "Then this state may also be the domain of St. John's 'knowledge by unknowing,'" I offered.

"Yes," said Adam, " and it may be the answer to the zen koan, 'What was your original face before you were born?' You can't see it, because you're looking from it, but you are aware of it as your essential nature, as that which is living your life."

Adam let out a sigh.

"But it's 'pearls before swine,' again!" he growled, shaking his head. "Understand," he continued, "that 'swine' means those whose noses are so deeply rooted in the material world that they are oblivious to any existence beyond tangible matter. People are asleep to their own nature."

While I couldn't pretend to understand Adam's words fully, I could at least follow him this time, and I was aware that I had heard echoes of this before, though it had never gotten beyond mere concept.

"I AM THAT I AM." The phrase came suddenly to consciousness. "I'm recalling the story of Exodus," I told Adam. "Moses wants to know what to say to his people and God says to tell them, 'I AM THAT I AM has sent me unto you.' Is that related to what you're talking about?" I asked Adam.

"Look for yourself," said Adam. "It is that from which all else emanates!"

As Adam spoke, I noticed a curious expression in his face. He seemed to be responding to something within himself, something deeply felt, which he was reigning in for my benefit.

"Say, are you all right?" I asked, somewhat concerned about him.

He looked at me with bright eyes.

"I'm fine, Dave." he said evenly. "What I am talking about is not conceptual b. s. to me. It's very much alive for me, particularly when I speak about it."

He paused for a long moment, looking at me.

"Is this conversation, scaring you off?" he asked finally.

"A little, I admit. The only way I can grasp it is to go back to our earlier conversation about fields. It sounds like what you are talking about is the field of all fields. The field that originates fields."

"Brilliant!" he said, jumping to his feet. "That really captures it! Good!" He seemed both delighted and relieved. "For the moment, without any need to believe any of it, let's just say that Spirit is the field of all fields."

He pulled out a folded sheet of paper from the inside breast pocket of his suit coat and spread it out on the table in front of me. It was a simple drawing of four circles, one inside another.

"This diagram represents the whole four-step principle of creation as

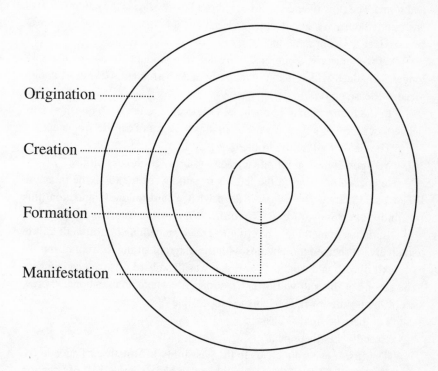

described in the beginning of the Bible. I had an insight about this universal creative principle years ago, when I first studied the teachings of the Jewish mystical tradition of Kabbalah. I knew that if the path described in *Genesis* truly reflected creation, then that path would be consistent at every dimension of existence, from the creation of the whole universe to the creation of the most infinitesimal particle. Then, of course, its validity would apply at the human level too.

So I tried it out. As an artist, I could see immediately that this path (which I've taken to calling The Genesis Principle) was not merely some esoteric theory about the creation of the universe, for it authentically mirrored the process I'd experienced each time I'd successfully manifested an idea or intention into reality. Its four worlds or dimensions of creating are the processes that one moves through in bringing something into being."

Here he pointed to each of the circles, beginning with the outer one, as he named them. *"Origination, Creation, Formation and Manifestation.*

"The outer one, Origination, is the context for the other three. It's also called Emanation in some texts. The process ends with Manifestation in physical form. The flow of energy through those four worlds is the natural flow of creation, whether it's manifesting as a galaxy, a human being, or an innovative product for a corporation."

"Of the three you mentioned, why does the product always seem to take longer?" I added with a blend of sarcasm and wistfulness. "Sorry," I apologized. "Please go on."

"In the first principle of creation, Origination, there is no division, only oneness or unity. It's the Crown, the first expression of Spirit."

"The field of all fields?" I interjected.

"Yes, containing an infinite capacity to bring forth possibilities."

He cocked his head to the left, as if waiting for me to chime in again. When I said nothing, he asked, "Then what would follow Origination, this possibility of creation, of bringing forth? What would naturally be next?"

"Initiating something? Starting to create something?" I offered, a little tentatively. It seemed too obvious with the diagram sitting in front of me.

"All right.," said Adam. "Now, that wasn't so hard was it?" he laughed. "The second of the four worlds is Creation. It's where an intentional expression of the formless whole begins to be possible."

"Let there be light?" I asked.

"Exactly. Let there be..."

"The first move from chaos to the possibility of structure," I added.

"Well said! Then, if the possibility and intention at the level of Creation is unimpeded, it will naturally evolve to more form and structure — ideas, blueprints, strategies, and finally actions. That's the world of Formation.

"From there," Adam said, "the design takes on more and more form until it appears completely realized in physical reality."

"And that is what the fourth world, Manifestation, is all about," I jumped in, "achieving the results."

I looked again at the diagram in front of me.

"If I knew how to generate that flow on a regular basis, it could really make a difference for my company. But the truth is, our successes have been hit and miss, with all kinds of blocks, surprises and economic uncertainties damming up the pipeline. For instance, I've had a lot of projects get stuck in the third circle, the formative stage, and die there, good ideas wasted, not to mention time and energy. How do you master the Genesis Principle so it's not just another metaphor?"

"That's the right question," Adam said. Across the very top of the diagram he wrote with his pen:

OCFM=YHVH

I studied the letters for a minute. "I can guess that 'OCFM' stands for the first letters of the four worlds," I said, "but what do the letters after the equal sign mean?"

"What we have here," Adam replied with a mixture of excitement and awe, "is the essential equation of creating. Just as E=mc2 is a fundamental equation in physics, in the realm of creation itself, YHVH is the ancient equation for The Genesis Principle. It's the formula for ongoing creation, universally and personally. And it's thousands of years old. YHVH is the English alphabet's equivalent of the Tetragrammaton, the four sacred Hebrew letters that make up the name of what we call 'God' in our culture."

"How do they look in Hebrew?"

"Like this," said Adam, drawing them on the diagram.

$$יהוה$$

"It's read from right to left."

"How do you pronounce the name made of the four letters?"

"Nobody knows for sure. The letters are all consonants. The Hebrew letters are pronounced Yod, Heh, Vav, Heh, but the vowel symbols that normally would be placed under these letters were never written down, and only the priests were allowed to utter the name on special occasions in biblical times. Which is kind of a nice touch, if you think about it — the relationship of the invisible with the visible. In fact, some Kabbalah traditions had meditations based on repeating those four letters with different vowel sounds to create shifts in meaning.

"Now translation is always a dicey proposition at best, and when these four letters of the sacred name were translated into English, they were often expressed as 'Jehovah'. But that is certainly not the correct pronunciation, plus it makes it sound like the Creative Spirit had a proper name. You know, 'Jehovah' being a name like 'Frank' or 'Sam.' It doesn't communicate the fact that those four letters are a sacred expression of the Infinite I's process of creation. And it completely hides the fact that the Tetragrammaton is the whole process of creating — the four worlds in a mystical equation that describes the way in which the world of form continuously comes into being — and then, reversing the process, returns to nothing."

"If it's not a proper name, but the process of creation, what do the letters mean when they're put together?" I asked.

He laughed. "It depends on which rabbi, scholar or philosopher you've read! The Tetragrammaton comes from the Hebrew root *Hayah*, 'to be.' Some say it means, 'I AM THAT I AM,' a self-referential and eternal declaration of the unity of the Divine Nature. If you follow Rashi, it's rendered as 'I will be what I will be'. Another states it means, 'I Am Present.' Yet another says it represents a causality from the future to the present, a yearning to create that reaches from the future and moves us toward fulfilling the possibilities that we are. And some say it gives expression to the fact that 'I WAS, I AM and I SHALL BE.'"

He paused to make sure I was following him. After a few moments he seemed satisfied, and leaning forward, added quietly. "In my experience, 'I AM THAT I AM' includes all of the possible interpretations. I AM, in that case, is not a statement about the present — that's in time. As itself, I AM is timeless, the infinite field from which time itself unfolds, from which past, present and future appear."

The air around us felt electrically charged, almost palpably energized. When Adam spoke again, it was almost in a whisper. "The Genesis Principle — the four worlds of creation — and the four sacred letters that make up the name of God are the same. The Tetragrammaton is the formula for creation."

I looked at the four letters again. There was a simple but elegant logic to them. The second and fourth letters were the same. The fourth world — Manifestation — represented in English by the letter "H," was a repetition of the second world — Creation. At the level of Creation there is an energy form, an electrical potential, an idea. Through the process of Formation the idea takes on more and more structure until it is finally manifested in the outer world. The fourth world is the second world fulfilled in physical form. It is a tree grown from the seed of intention.

Wasn't that what I was looking for — creating? Being able to create an idea, go into action and make it real? If only I had the freedom to do that in my own life! Why was creating so difficult and sporadic for me?

I recalled Adam's words of a moment before... "and then, reversing the process, returns to nothing," he had said. The Genesis Principle, like Jacob's ladder, was a two way street, the sacred formula of the Tetragrammaton flowed in both directions — from nothing to something and back again to nothing.

No wonder I had little freedom to create. I was stuck in the illusion of permanence. Adam was right. I did live as though reality were static. I was like a man clutching a bouquet of faded flowers, attached to their memory and meaning, afraid that there would be no others as beautiful to replace them. I had done that often. So had my company. There had been no room for origination.

In a flight of fancy, I imagined the flow of the universe, constantly forming and dissolving back into energy, to be resurrected into new form in the next instant. Creating and dissolving. Energy formed into billions of stars, released as light and heat and gravitational fields that formed into planets, then chemical structures, taking forms of earth, water, and air; then microorganisms, plant and animal life, and then sentient human beings — the energy of creation in form, aware of itself as an expression of the creative power.

Origination, Creation. Formation, Manifestation.

"You want to know what can provide you with mastery in creating?" Adam said. "Living in harmony with The Genesis Principle."

TEN

THE TREE OF LIFE

An epiphany enables you to sense creation
not as something completed, but as constantly
becoming, evolving, ascending. This transports
you from a place where there is nothing new
to a place where there is nothing old, where everything
renews itself, where heaven and earth rejoice as at the moment of creation.
— Rabbi Abraham Isaac Kook

Adam took out another sheet of paper, and with his pen, quickly divided the sheet into four horizontal sections. Hovering over the paper for a moment, his hand began to move in circles, lowering slowly toward the paper. I was fascinated by the motion, which didn't seem to originate in Adam's fingers or wrist but in his right shoulder. It was amazing to watch him. His arm seemed both still and in motion at the same time. His face showed a detached but focused attention on the arm, pen and paper before him, as though he was not connected to them, but was simply an interested and attentive witness to the process. Slowly and calmly his hand and pen descended. With no hesitation, no jolt, no bump or drag, the pen touched the paper with the smoothness of a master pilot landing a 747.

Within moments, ten circles lay in a geometric design upon the paper, one in the section he'd designated Origination, two across from each other in Creation, six in the section marked Formation, ending with one again under Manifestation. He then wrote words in each of the circles, and completed the process by drawing a series of connecting lines from the top circle to the bottom one.

"This is the design of the *Sefiroth* — The Tree of Life of the Kabbalah," said Adam. "Kabbalah is a Hebrew word that means, 'to receive' — and this is important. Most people think that creating is a function of doing something. The Kabbalah, by its very name, sets the record straight. What if creating is not a function of doing, but of receiving? Allowing something to occur, being open to receive from the infinite — that is where the real creative power lies.

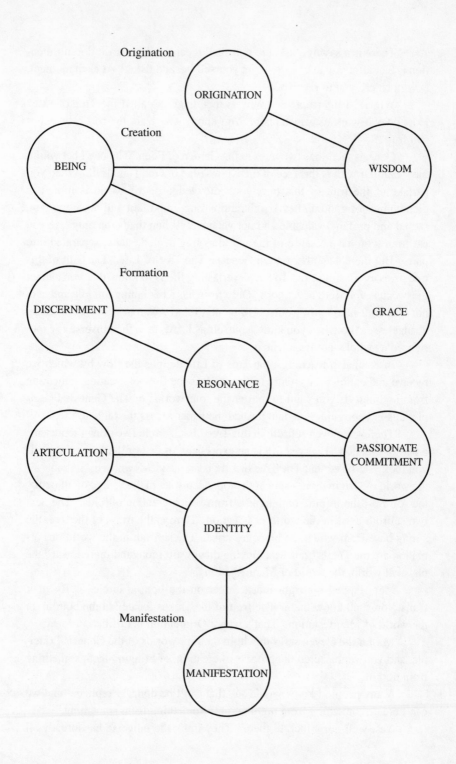

"There is a saying, 'ask and you shall receive.' The part it doesn't mention is that after you ask, shut up, let yourself be, and listen! At each moment, how open are you to receive?"

"Whoa!" I interrupted. "Why is this diagram called the Tree of Life? How does it work as a metaphor? You know, where are the roots, branches and fruit?"

"Genesis mentions two trees in the Garden of Eden. The one I bet you're most familiar with is the Tree of the Knowledge of Good and Evil. When you partake of the fruit of this tree, your knowledge of the world is rooted in dichotomies of good and evil, right and wrong, important and not important, sacred and profane, valuable and not valuable. When that's the only tree you eat from, you have a sense of the world as fragmented, static, separated into parts. But there's another tree in Genesis: The Tree of Life. The fruit of this tree gives everlasting life. To have everlasting life is to know that you cannot die because you were never born. Only form has a beginning, middle and end, not Spirit. It is to know yourself to be that I AM Awareness that is timeless, changeless. And when you know yourself as I AM, then the universe is experienced as whole, not fragmented.

"In Kabbalah teachings, the Tree of Life defines the flow by which we receive and express the energy of Spirit. It is the flow of creating something from nothing. If you want to master the four worlds of The Genesis Principle, this is your guide." Adam pushed the paper across the table to me.

"There are eleven sefiroth in this Tree. Each circle I've drawn represents a part of creation. Every sefira is an expression of one of the four worlds. If you look you'll see that The Tree of Life is an upside down tree. Its roots — the world of Origination — are at the top, deeply set in the source of all being, the Ain Sof; the infinite nothingness from which creation unfolds. The next two sefiroth exist in the world of Creation. Here is the trunk of the tree, the strong base from which the branches arise. The sefiroth in the world of Formation are the Tree's branches, moving downward more and more toward the physical world, the world of Manifestation."

Adam tapped his right index finger on the bottom circle. "'By their fruits, you shall know them.' The fruit of the Tree is located at the bottom, in the world of Manifestation. That's where Origination is fulfilled in form.

"Master the eleven sefiroth within the four worlds of the Genesis Principle, and you've mastered the process of creating, of bringing forth something from nothing."

"Many people I know would say that can't be done," I replied, "that we can't create something from nothing, only something from something."

"Yes, well good luck to them. They think the universe has already all been created, that it is a static thing and God is now out to lunch, and the best that human beings can do is to 'make' things from things. I prefer to operate as if the Creative Spirit created us in its image. Now that certainly can't refer to arms, legs, and kidneys unless you hold God to be a guy on a throne on a cloud somewhere. My experience is that to be created in the image of the Creator is to be a creator. The Genesis Principle, if it is valid, must function at every level and dimension of the universe. It is the universe in process at the levels of a galaxy, a world, a society, an organization, a relationship and an individual. Physics too is saying just that more and more."

I studied the diagram for a moment.

"What does that pattern of lines from top to bottom mean?" I asked.

"That's the *Lightning Flash of Creation*. It expresses the direction of the journey from formlessness to form, from the intention for an idea, through to its physical expression. On a practical level, this is a diagram of the steps people go through to create something, whether they are aware of it or not. Each is a step in the creative process. If one of those elements is missing, there's a barrier to the natural creative flow.

"Do these develop one after the other, from the top down?"

"Only in a linear dimensional view," he said. "But to understand correctly you have to think multi-dimensionally. The Tree of Life is like a hologram in that each circle or sefira holds within it all the others."

I looked again at the diagram and held the sheet up to Adam. "There are only ten circles on this diagram. I thought you said that there are eleven sefiroth."

Adam's eyes twinkled. "Ah, you noticed! The eleventh is hidden, for now. It may be the key to insuring the integrity of the other ten. It makes them unassailable, and allows for true mastery. But we're not ready for that one yet. If we choose to work together, we'll address it," he said, and dropped my question.

"Are you going to explain the words in these circles?" I asked.

"All in good time. Addressing the words doesn't do much good. They have no power as concepts. We'll experience each sefira directly. But we can talk about the first few."

I studied the drawing again as Adam spoke.

"The first circle is *Origination*, the same name as the first world. The Hebrew word for it is *Keter*. It means Crown, the light of creation itself. It is the only sefira in the first world of the Genesis Principle. In the world of Origination there is only unity. So there can't be a difference between the world of Origination and its sefira. They are one and the same."

"But what does it mean? How can I get a handle on it" I asked.

"You know already. You said it earlier. It's what God told Moses to say to his people."

"Ah! I AM THAT I AM has sent me!"

"Yes, the I AM Awareness, the power of creation — the emanation and its expression — are indivisible. In some mystical writings they make no distinction between I AM and the Ain Sof — the Infinite Undifferentiated Ground of Being, the Cause of all Causes, from which all unfolds, except to say that I AM Awareness is Ain Sof's window to express the Infinite in the finite."

"What is this principle at the practical level? At the level of my individual self?"

"Living each day being aware that you are a creator and that you are one with the Infinite creative power."

"And how do I do that?" I asked with barely concealed chagrin.

"First, you start with the possibility that I AM is who you always are, that you have the power to create, and that you've been lying about it to yourself. I AM Awareness is the opening for all the rest of creation. Second, become aware of the form you have identified yourself to be and dismantle that fictional attachment. Here's a hint about the fictional you — it's who or what you really believe yourself to be."

I looked again at the diagram. At the level of Creation there were two parallel circles which created an equilateral triangle when looked at in relation to Origination.

"How do you say the Hebrew name for the second sefira?" I asked.

"*Chokmah*," he replied, saying the letters "ch" with a deep, gutteral sound that doesn't exist in English. The closest I could come to pronouncing it was a soft "h" sound. It wasn't even close. "*Wisdom* is the English for this sefira," he continued. "It's an ancient and perfect name for this sefira. Wisdom yields a deep and direct understanding of the Creative Spirit and the ability to shape the flow of creation from Awareness. Unfortunately when people hear the word 'wisdom', they usually think it refers to an accumulation of inherited knowledge, which it certainly does not. All the big deal about the 'Wisdom of King Solomon' is not merely acknowledging that he knew a lot of stuff. What's celebrated was his ability to see to the core of something, to its very essence, and from there to create a new future beyond what others could see."

Adam looked at me expectantly. "Any responses?" he asked.

I thought for a few moments.

"I remember you said that the world of creation was about intention. If I look at where it is placed in the Tree of Life, Wisdom is I AM's initial intention to create."

Adam nodded approvingly. It was satisfying to find myself keeping up with him.

"The intention to bring something into being," he muttered under his breath.

He pointed to the third circle, directly across from Wisdom. "Here is where the design of the intention gets determined. Your intention begins with the words I AM THAT I AM. Whatever finishes the statement, fulfills the intention of 'I AM.' I AM... whatever... fill in the blank. This full intention is the third sefira of the Tree of Life, the *Field of Being*. Its Hebrew name is *Binah*."

"What does that mean?" I asked, checking out the diagram.

"The usual English translation is 'understanding,' but that word doesn't even come close to capturing the depth of it. So, I prefer to call it *Being*. The problem with 'understanding' is that it usually means 'knowing about' something. And if you think the Tree of Life is some kind of esoteric intellectual exercise, that will probably satisfy you. But that's not what Binah means. It is not related to 'knowing about' something, it is related to direct knowing. And direct knowing — which is *true* understanding — is not a function of knowledge, it is a function of Being."

I didn't grasp the difference yet, but I knew it was important, so I asked him to explain it.

"Let me give you what Sri Aurobindo said on the matter: *'You cannot relate to anything if you don't know it, and you can't know anything until you can become it.'* Target. Aim. Bull's eye. Don't you think?"

Suddenly I understood the basic problem in my relationship with Janet. With all my shallow attempts to understand her I had never even tried to become her. Not physically, of course, but at the level of being, experiencing her world from her reality, not from mine. I never even thought to try. Everything I had learned told me this was not possible.

"Ah, I see a light has gone on over there!" said Adam, looking at me with amusement. "Shall I continue?"

I merely nodded. I was feeling a little shaken by this insight into my marriage.

"Wisdom and Being; that is the dynamic of the second world of the Genesis Principle," he continued. "When Wisdom unites with Being, a field is created that organizes energy and determines how it will appear. What unfolds from that union is the *Organizing Life Principle*. It's who you say you are in the world. It fundamentally determines the meaning and purpose of your life. It shapes the way reality appears to you, what you are aware of and what you are not. What follows the words 'I AM THAT I AM' shapes your whole being. Whether you create 'I AM THAT I AM... the Light', or you create 'I AM THAT I AM... not good enough', you will begin to manifest yourself in word and deed to be a perfect expression and reflection of that field. The created field of Being is a womb where the seed of intention is planted to take a form that expresses that intention."

"So the second and third sefiroth are like two halves of a complete statement?" I asked. "I AM... Being... whatever I say."

"Yes, the created field of Being gives form to everything that arises within it."

An image came to mind of an enormous, glowing television screen with an infinite selection of channels, each channel broadcasting a particular view of reality, a distinct state of being. However this is no ordinary television set. The flickering story on every channel is the same — it is my life. Yet the episodes vary with each channel's view of my reality, and I am the one selecting the channels. If I say to myself, "I am a person with a hard life," my story as serious drama flickers on the screen.

If I stick with a particular state of being, the channel selector remains stuck on that station, showing only that version of my life over and over again, with no other options — like a timeless re-run, until my television screen finally burns out.

I shook myself out of this reverie.

"Is this 'I Am'ing' the same as affirmations?" I asked.

"Absolutely not! Intention at the level we're talking about is not a function of the mind or the identity, it is a creation of the Spirit. It's a pure creation."

"So it's no good just to repeat 'I am a creator' twenty times a day every day?"

"No good at all. Your being has to be 'I am a creator.' You know, *'The Word made flesh.'*"

That last phrase set off a nagging search inside me. The Word made flesh. It connected with something I had seen before. Suddenly I remembered da Vinci's painting of the Annunciation. The light of the creator, the angelic messenger of intention, and the pure, receptive field of being, the Virgin's womb, it was all there in the painting, the first steps in the Creator's Word Becoming Flesh.

I was stunned. I had never before realized the deep archetypal nature of those images and symbols. The first three principles of the Tree of Life were captured in Leonardo's masterpiece, waiting to be recognized.

"I just thought of a remarkable connection," I said to Adam. "Do you know Leonardo daVinci's painting of the Annunciation?" By his smile of recognition I realized that my insight, so startling to me, was not so unique.

"It's all there, isn't it?" he responded. "The creative power creating a field of being for its expression to grow, to take form and manifest in the world."

"These are fundamental principles of creation," I murmured, partly to myself and partly to Adam. I shook my head with amazement. What was most staggering was how often I had failed to see past the story line, to grasp the underlying meaning of these great archetypes. Pearls before swine, indeed.

I paused for a long time, contemplating the rarity of conversations like this in my life. I could always count on Adam to get my mental juices flowing. I was feeling happy and expansive. Then all of a sudden practicality, which had been in hiding, inserted itself.

"I am beginning to see some potential in this," I admitted to Adam, "but I don't have any idea about how to use it at work. I'm not going to ask people to do a lot of esoteric things or have conversations like this during office hours, you know."

"You don't have to. First of all, the most important thing is to be a creator, coming from I AM. People will notice. Remember, when you shift the field, the contents of the field shift as well. Secondly, the people in your organization are determining the form of their reality all the time, whether they are aware of it or not. They have already created the field of their own reality, or more to the point, they've inherited one without questioning it, calling it 'the way things are.' But no reality is a static thing, a creator can create new realities for other people too.

"Does the organizing life principle apply to a company too?" I asked.

Adam nodded emphatically. "You bet! It's not just individuals that have life principles; these fields also exist at the level of relationships, companies and cultures. And all these levels interact. Remember, Dave, the Tree of Life applies at every level of existence. It's not practical to try to change the personal field of each person in your company, but if you could influence what the company's life principle is, that would be effective leverage."

I recalled numerous times I'd seen new management theories fail. Maybe, just maybe, all the theories and practices were like the iron filings in Faraday's experiment. You could throw new filings in all day, in new arrangements, and it wouldn't make any difference. They would inevitably line up with the prevailing pattern of force. In a company, this could apply at every level. Every division, every department and every individual employee was being shaped or constrained by the invisible field in which they all functioned together. When we talked about this invisible force, which was rare, we called it 'our culture.' We didn't use this force, it used us. It controlled and constrained us. And we almost never addressed it directly. Instead, we kept working hard, trying to correct its effects. We were like ants trying to re-order the iron filings in the magnetic field without altering the field itself, moving the filings into new configurations only to have them return to their original design the moment we turned our heads away.

Adam was suggesting a radical departure. What if this Genesis Principle of his could really be incorporated and acted on in a practical way?

I had a sense of what it might be like, but I couldn't yet see a clear pathway for achieving it. I knew, of course, that without going forward all of this information would be of no consequence to me. I was sick of theories with no grounding in action. I had to determine whether Adam had that critical piece, and even if he did, whether he'd be able to transfer it successfully. I hoped that he could. But I needed to know more before our meeting that afternoon was over. My future — maybe my whole life — was on the line.

ELEVEN

THE DNA OF BEING

This world has no existence on its own.
It is through the qualities of our perception
that we perceive reality.
— *Rabbi Nachman of Breslov*

I gazed out the window at the sculpture garden. The light had changed since we first sat down at our table. Darker, richer colors had replaced the washed-out hues of the earlier light, coloring the mute metal and marble sculptures with glazes of greens, pinks and golds. Slowly lengthening shadows marked the grass with silhouettes, weightless ghosts of their silent progenitors. I appreciated these works with a newly found insight. The sculptures did not exist by themselves in an artistic vacuum. They were part of a dynamic, fluid, vibrant reality, their fluctuating shapes and colors subject to many interweaving factors: their placement in the garden, the ever-changing light, and the cultural meaning assigned to them by the observer. All of these variables were influenced by the personal organizing field that shaped the observer's perceptions, beliefs, thoughts and actions, the organizing life principle, as Adam had called it.

"Is the life principle the most important factor for creating change?" I asked.

"The first step is to know yourself as I AM Awareness. Then, yes, you're right on target," he said. "At its most fundamental level the life of an individual or of an organization is shaped and determined by the life principle because it literally creates the context that gives us life, that shapes our essential way of being. It creates the core design or field of meaning from which a person, organization or country structures its beliefs, values, and priorities — its whole reality."

"You just used the term 'field of meaning.' So the field of Being, gives meaning?" I asked.

"Let's make this practical, Dave. The field of Being is the context for whatever arises within it. All meaning is context-bound; the same situation, behavior or word can have different meanings depending on the context in which it appears. Change the context and you change the world within it. That's what makes the life principle such a high point of leverage for causing change. Let's take something simple, like the word, 'driver.' It can be invested with quite different meanings depending on the field or context in which it arises. For instance, think of the meaning of 'driver' in the context of the Indianapolis 500.

"Now I'm going to say the exact same word, and all I'm going to do is change the context in which I want you to listen to it, and tell me what you get. Ready? The word is 'driver.' The context is golf."

"I see what you mean. Now it's a club that you swing to hit a ball down the fairway."

"And its not just the definition that alters. You see a whole different background picture in your mind, almost as if you had shifted into a different world. For example if I shift from 'driver' to 'club', a tiny piece of the picture changes, but when I shift from 'driver of a car' to 'driver on the fairway' the entire scene changes, and along with it everything about your reaction to what's going on."

I could see Adam's point. In the context of the Indianapolis 500, there was a whole world of race cars, speed, teams, crowds, and noise. Then, with nothing more than a change of context, it is replaced in a flash by a world of tee shots, bunkers, and the slow pace of a weekend foursome.

"Now what we're going to see here is that the life principle creates a context for everything that happens in your life. But as long as it remains invisible to you, it becomes a prison. You are locked into it. It's as if you were forced to spend your entire life on a golf course and could never get behind the wheel of a car."

"That seems absurd," I said.

"It's literally true," said Adam. "A life principle limits the ways you can adapt. Let's say you had the organizing life principle, 'I don't need anyone.' Now this belief could give you a lot of personal strength and self-reliance. It could allow you to be very daring and entrepreneurial. But that same self-reliance could make trouble for you in a context where you really do need other people's assistance. For instance, if, with that same entrepreneurial spirit, you created a successful business for yourself — you would be hampered and eventually diminished if you believed you could do everything yourself. The business couldn't grow. You wouldn't be able to delegate responsibility. You'd be stuck in a smaller sphere, locked into a single context — one where you had to do everything yourself.

"The way you interpret your world — the people, actions and situations in it — is all context determined," continued Adam. But when the context is unconsciously locked in by a life principle that says, for example, 'I am what I do,' or 'Intimate relationships are threatening,' then it is no longer perceived as a context, it is perceived as reality."

"So all meaning and interpretation is context or field dependent, including the meaning of life itself?" I asked. "Change the context and everything else changes? If that's true, wouldn't this organizing life principle be the secret weapon for causing change?"

"The organizing life principle could be said to be the *DNA of Being*," Adam replied. "Like DNA, it determines who and what you can and cannot be, both in yourself and in your relationship with the world. The statement 'I AM...,' even if unconscious, shapes the scope, limits, boundaries and parameters of the actions you can take and what you can manifest in your life."

"I never even knew I had a life principle," I said.

"You do, and so does everyone else. But very few people are aware of it and as a result they have little ability to shape their field of Being. It's like water to a fish; you aren't aware of it because you are so fully immersed in it. Human beings just assume they are the way they are, and that they either lucked out in life or they didn't. As a result, they learn to cope with their circumstances and make up stories about why they are the way that they are. Some people have a life principle that gives them a lot of freedom and opportunity to create. Others have a life principle that is constraining and debilitating — which is especially sad because they don't recognize they have a choice in the matter."

"Wait a minute, wait a minute!" I protested. "I don't get it. You say that most people don't even know they have a life principle, yet it is running their lives?"

Adam nodded.

"Well where did their life principle come from then, if they don't even know it exists?"

"Correction. They may know it exists. They just don't recognize it as a life principle. They simply call it 'the way I am' and spend their lives trying to live from it, avoid it, defeat it, or be defeated by it. Whatever action they take will be a function of the life principle itself. It's self-reinforcing. It's only when you recognize yourself as the creator of your life principle that you have any choice about it."

I was beginning to feel alarmed by this conversation, and was noticing a number of uncomfortable sensations in my body. This was becoming less and less a merely interesting intellectual exercise. I tried to maintain my cool as I repeated my question. "If we don't remember creating it, where did it come from?"

"A lot of it we inherit from our family and environment. We buy in, at an early age, to the identities others impose on us. We don't usually think to question them. Sometimes an event happens which we'll interpret in a way that unconsciously defines the limits of our being: our raison d'etre if you will."

"You mean a traumatic event?" I asked.

"Not necessarily traumatic," he said. "It could be something you don't even pay much attention to."

"Could you give me another example of a life principle?"

Predictably, he turned my request into a question.

"Let's look at it on the individual level of your organization," he said. "Do you have someone in your company that you consider an outstanding entrepreneurial thinker?"

"Sure, Fred Marx."

"What do you notice about the way Fred operates?"

"Well, if we have a meeting, Fred is invariably able take what has been said and put that information together in ways that other people do not."

"So some people come out of the meeting with disjointed pieces of information."

"Correct."

"Yet Fred is able to synthesize that information in a way that other people don't. Other people walk out and feel that it was a good meeting. Fred walks out and he's got a great idea. Fine. I say that what allows Fred to be effective is not just that he listens, because everybody else in the room is listening too. Rather, it is the way he organizes and processes the information he is hearing."

"True. That's clear enough."

"So, we might say that Fred listens in a field of new possibilities, actually listens for new possibilities, while other people may only be listening for accuracy or what fits their existing understanding."

"I'll buy that."

"So Fred is *being* an entrepreneur. He is able to see opportunities that other people don't see."

"Yes, I guess so. Are you saying that that is a function of Fred's life principle?"

"That's exactly what I'm saying. I don't know what his exact principle is, but obviously it allows him to hear opportunities that others cannot."

"How do you know this is not just a result of the strategies that he follows?"

"Has he ever tried to train others to think like he does and failed at it?" Adam asked.

"As a matter of fact, he has. Numerous times. Some of his protégés succeed better than others, but only a couple have come close to functioning like Fred. And Fred is a generous guy, he wouldn't be holding back what he knows. He tells them everything he does."

"But what he hasn't transferred is who he is being as a result of his life principle. They are definitely not going to get it if they merely try to imitate Fred. That will just make them inauthentic. It's also not as simple as learning rules, steps, or strategies. If it were, you'd be able to turn out clones of Fred without any problems. There are, of course, some jobs that you can do that with because they are 'doing' jobs — just following instructions exactly, no original thinking necessary. But you can't do that with Fred's job. The transfer of a way of being is needed there.

"The effect of the life principle is enormous," he continued. "It can override the influence of all the training and information we feed to someone, no matter how outstanding that training, no matter how much money or how many hours have been invested. We've both met people who have life principles that cause them to sabotage themselves. Have you had any employees who consistently shot themselves in the foot, just as they were on the verge of success?"

"Sure," I said. "We call it the 'snatching defeat from the jaws of victory' pattern. It's heartbreaking to see, because you know that these folks are really able, really could make a contribution; but they have a time bomb that goes off and causes them to fail at the critical moment. They don't stay around."

"And they have no power to alter this pattern of behavior," said Adam, "because they misidentify it and think it's bad luck or fate or something their mother did to them when they were three years old. It becomes an unconscious negation of their own power."

"What might be the life principle of someone who acts in that way?" I asked.

"It's hard to say," said Adam, "because a life principle can be expressed in different ways: as something to fulfill or as something to resist. People may construct quite different scenarios for their lives and ways of behaving. But hypothetically a person such as you're speaking about might have a life principle of 'life is hard', or 'it will never turn out', or 'I can't win', or maybe, 'I'm not good enough.' Their self-sabotage is a natural expression of their Being.

"But you have to watch it, Dave, because sometimes the life principle manifests itself in ways you wouldn't expect. I've coached clients who were extremely successful, but had the 'I'm not good enough,' life principle. In their cases, however, it didn't come out as self-sabotage, but as the worst kind of striving. They'd accumulated all the symbols of success, but could never rest; they continuously strove to prove themselves, over and over again."

Adam waited until that had sunk in.

I noticed that slight choking feeling in my throat again.

"Isn't what you're calling a life principle just another name for a belief?" I challenged.

"No, not at all. Beliefs are quite junior to a life principle. A life principle is a field phenomenon, not a content phenomenon. The life principle is the 'you' that maintains all your beliefs and judgments. You could say that the life principle is the meta-belief that allows for all the other beliefs you hold. It is essential to your existence and as close to you as your next breath.

"A number of years ago I was in London," Adam continued. "A friend of mine invited me to lunch with a famous author of children's books and his actress wife, both of whom she knew quite well. In the course of what had been a very pleasant meal together, we talked about the life principle and its impact on creativity. The man confessed that he thought his life principle was 'I'm not good enough.'

"However when I mentioned the possibility of freeing himself from it so his writing could flourish as an expression of creation rather than striving, he wouldn't hear of it. He acknowledged that he completely identified his current life principle with who he was, and he was certain it could never be changed.

"In addition, he had decided that his success as a writer depended on being 'not good enough.' His logic went something like this: if I were to be freed of my life principle, 'I'm not good enough,' I would no longer be 'good enough' to write. That's because my writing gets its strength from attempting to disprove that 'I'm not good enough.' If that were no longer present, my writing would no longer be 'good enough,' and I will have proved, by finally escaping from 'I'm not good enough,' that in fact, 'I'm not good enough.'"

"Whew!" was all I could say at first. My mind was whirling. I was appreciating in a new way something my philosophy professor had said in college about how the logic within a system could always argue for itself, no matter how illogical it appeared on the outside.

"And that's how the majority of people live their lives," said Adam. "They live inside a life principle that they've unconsciously created for themselves, quite by default. If you live with the awareness of yourself as the author of your life principle, it occurs as a field of expression for you, rather than something you're stuck in."

"But you're saying that in most cases people simply never arrive at that awareness, isn't that true?"

"Yes. Most of us have forgotten our original Self. We've forgotten we have the power to create who we are in each moment. Instead, we've created our life principles unconsciously. That is why I call it a *default* life principle. We haven't created anything else to replace it."

"Is there a way out of a negative life principle? The writer you mentioned, for example; your assurance that he could change it seemed only to increase its power."

"That's right," said Adam. He rested his elbows on the table and leaned forward to underline the importance of what he was about to say. "I have an operating principle I use in my work: *resistance causes persistence*. Now what does that mean? It means, when we resist something, we make it stronger.

"Let me explain it this way: The universe is in a constant state of change. Each moment of now dissolves into the next. If you can experience the truth of this flux and embrace what is, you have the freedom to create, to re-interpret, to shape and to act at each moment. It's all right to appreciate, understand and be informed by the past and present, but not to be chained to them. Better to be part of the flow, part of the constant reforming of the universe. Otherwise, you're trying to stop the flow. Part of you becomes stuck at a moment in time, succumbing to an illusion. You become attached to this illusion, either trying to avoid it or trying to hold on to it, rather than letting it flow through its complete cycle of creation. Then you find yourself bewailing the way things are and whining about the way things 'should be' or 'shouldn't be.' That simply strengthens its hold on you. Ignoring something or someone is a form of resistance. Trying to change something is a form of resistance. Seeing yourself as a victim of it and rolling over and succumbing to it is a form of resistance. And that's so at every dimension. The more you resist it, the more it persists."

Adam stopped for a moment. I knew that he could see my confusion.

"I know that makes no sense to an endurer or striver," he said, "but that is because you are asleep and don't know your Self."

I was trying to decide whether I should be insulted by this last remark, but obviously I'd called him in the first place because something was missing. I decided to shut up for the moment and let him continue.

"In that walking sleep that you call awake," he went on," you believe that you are your identity, your body, your story or your personal history. You're not seeing yourself as a constant flow and expression of energy. You're identifying with a static and stillborn illusion of that energy. The moment you

85

identify with any of the levels, you are stuck with them. Then you don't *have* thoughts, you *are* your thoughts. You don't *have* feelings, you *are* your feelings. You don't *have* circumstances, you *are* your circumstances. Most of all, at the very foundation of it all, you are no longer the creator of your organizing life principle. You experience actually being that life principle. Since you do not recall authoring it, you are living it by default.

"The joke is: there is a strong likelihood that you inherited your life principle from someone else, or you put your life principle together unconsciously in reaction to a moment of trauma and fear, as a way of making sense of reality. Of course then you live, if you can call it that, believing that the world as organized and perceived from that point of view is the truth: static and unchangeable.

"Then you're stuck," I said.

"You bet! Oh, things may get better circumstantially. You may get richer, smarter, more attractive, more powerful or more famous. You may even have more fun — better toys to play with — and I'm not knocking having these symbols of success, by the way. Not having the symbols and being righteous about that is the same game in reverse; it's called martyrdom. But whatever the circumstances, within yourself all the same dynamics persist, even though the cast of characters and circumstances may change."

I scowled and shook my head. "I don't know if I agree with that. I'm certainly better off now than when I was younger. I'm more comfortable..."

"Dave, wake up! Your circumstances are more comfortable, not you! How is your stress level these days? Your sense of peace, freedom and well being? With all of your past successes, can you honestly say to me that you are experiencing more joy and satisfaction, a greater sense of fulfillment, vitality, intimacy and love than you were ten years ago or twenty years ago?"

I shook my head. "But it's the circumstances...."

"The circumstances keep changing," he said emphatically. "Have you ever been with someone who spent years trying to achieve something, absolutely certain that when they achieved it they would finally be happy and satisfied?"

"Yes," I said, not letting on that the person who came to mind was sitting in my seat.

"And then when they finally do achieve their goal, what happens? Are they happy? You bet! Maybe even for as long as twenty minutes."

This was way too accurate for me. I shifted nervously in my chair.

Adam looked at me with just a tinge of pity. "You know, you don't have to stay in this insane relationship with yourself."

"Don't you think 'insane' is a bit strong?" I heard myself protest.

"Too strong? What would you call it? Look at yourself. You fear change and you're obsessed with change. You're upset when things don't change! And you're upset when things do change, even in the way you said that you wanted them to, because now you're upset that they might change back, or stop changing, or change too fast, or change too slowly! Every state of change causes anxiety for you!"

Adam twisted his face into an expression of incredulity and exasperation, rolling his eyes toward the ceiling, making a gesture with his right hand as though he were flicking salt over his shoulder. "Is this crazy or what?" he said loudly enough for a few people in the cafe to cast looks in our direction.

"It's crazy all right," I muttered. "But what's the way out, if resisting it, fearing it, succumbing to it, and trying to overcome it don't work?" I asked. "If they are all part of the problem, what can anyone possibly do?"

"To find the way out, you must shift your relationship with everything. But to do that, you must know yourself directly, not as a finite identity, but as the field of awareness in which life is occurring. Then you can embrace change because you know yourself to be the creator and interpreter of your life.

"But we do come into the world with certain 'givens', of course, that are not amenable to negotiation after we get here," I interjected, after giving myself a moment for my head to clear. "Our physical DNA gives us our body type and certain inherited physical attributes. Then there are the factors like who our parents are, and what environment we are raised in."

"I'm not dismissing those 'givens' at all," he said. "They do exist. But who are you being in the face of them? In what way do you organize your reality to include both the 'givens' and those factors that you have the power to create for yourself?"

Adam looked at me intensely, and grasped my forearms with a strong grip. He seemed to want me to hear him in my bones. "I say that you can create your life's purpose and your own intentional destiny, not just live some destiny prescribed to you by others! You can create your personal sense of yourself and your place in the world. You can experience life as an opportunity to create. It's all fluid and flexible."

Adam released his grip on my arms and sat back in his chair. He turned and looked out the window. He put his legs straight out in front of him and leaning back, assumed a posture that would have seemed almost languid were it not belied by the energy in his voice.

"One of the most freeing things I've discovered about life," he said, turning his face to me, "is that what happens to you is not what ultimately determines who you are. Both good and bad things happen to people. The real test is who you are in the face of your experiences. I've met people in the worst possible situations, in bodies that couldn't move, or with chronic pain, or terminal illnesses, who nevertheless managed to be powerful, loving human beings, living generously and joyously. And I've met others who had everything, all the things people assume will make them happy, and they're still bitching and whining their way to the grave."

Adam looked out again at the garden. "That's what makes the life principle so powerful, you know. It's not what happens to you that determines who you are in life, but what you decide your experiences mean."

"What do you mean by that last comment?" I could tell that my voice had an edge to it.

"Later," said Adam. He saw my distress and dropped what he was saying for the moment. "Let's look at an organization. It also has an organizing life principle. Everything, from the company's vision to its day to day policies and procedures, is affected by it. As with an individual, the life principle frames the design, the shape, the possibilities, the boundaries and the limits of what the organization can and cannot be, what it can and cannot do, and what it can and cannot accomplish.

"The life principle is analogous to a river bed. While all of the attention is on the river — its sound, its speed, its velocity, its color, its temperature, its shallows, and its depths — the river bed itself, which is the prime determinant in forming the characteristics of the river, goes unseen and unnoticed. As the riverbed molds the shape and direction of the water within it, a life principle dictates and ultimately molds the ideas, decisions, choices and actions in the life of the organization.

"Intentionally creating a life principle for your organization establishes the riverbed, the fundamental ground of the company's life. And from this ground spring the architecture, strategies, priorities and actions relevant to the company's current and future commitments. Then an organization can be designed by its people from the whole rather than from its parts, with elements that have strength, flexibility, effectiveness and integrity.

"I'm particularly interested in what you're saying here, given the situation at Allied Technologies," I added. "I realize that I've never sat down with my boss, Diane, and asked, 'who are we'? Of course up until now it never even occurred to me to create an organizing principle. I just assumed we all knew what our company was about," I said.

"That can be a dangerous assumption," said Adam, "as the life principle may not necessarily be what people think it is."

"What do you mean?"

"Let's say that you have a traditional products company that says its vision is to transform itself into a successfully innovative company. Now remember, that vision is going to exist in the field of meaning, flow, and forces shaped and given by the life principle."

"Okay, I'm with you on this," I said.

"Now what if this company has been around for years, and what if the unexamined, unconscious life principle of this company is, 'Be Careful'? As the fundamental principle that has organized and shaped the company's life, all of the policies, procedures, strategies, and support for risk-taking will have developed over time to fully express this 'Be Careful' life principle. Now someone sells upper management on this new vision to be an innovative company. What happens?"

"Ouch! I've been there!" I said with a grimace. "There will be effort, struggle, grand gestures and superficial changes, but no substantive change. The place will be back to business as usual within a year, under the pretense of innovation. Have I got it about right?"

"Unfortunately, you've got it perfectly," replied Adam. "To put it into practical terms, before asking the question 'What's our vision?' it's important to ask, who is the 'we' that is asking? You won't believe some of the life principles I've uncovered in the companies I've dealt with."

"Like what?" I asked.

"How about, 'Winning is everything,' 'We are mavericks,' 'Trust no one,' and 'We know best.' On the more creative side, I've seen a couple where the principles were something like, 'We are innovation and inclusion,' 'Our people are the difference,' and 'We are service, integrity and effectiveness.'"

"You know," I added, moving my spoon around absentmindedly in my empty cup, "I can see that the life principle our company started from may no longer be appropriate, or might even have been fulfilled, and we don't even know that. We need to restate who and what we are. In addition, it can't be done in a vacuum, given the recent takeover by Henderson's group. We have to deal with who and what he says we are as a subsidiary of his larger company. There is no way that we can speak with him effectively unless we fully understand where he is looking from and know what reality we have to address."

"You're starting to see the impact of this," said Adam.

"One of the insights I'm getting," I said, "is the power of the life principle to both reveal and conceal possibilities, like new opportunities or new directions. My life principle allows me to see opportunities that agree with it, but as for the possibilities that don't fit within my organizing principle, well, that's a different story. I'll either not see a new possibility, ignore it, or invalidate it. And doing so will seem to be the most logical and intelligent choice I could make."

"And it will be," he added, "viewed from within the field of the life principle itself."

"Is it accurate to say that the only way to make a sustainable difference in outcomes over time is to alter the life principle itself?"

"The field is essential, but it's not the total story" he answered. "It's the beginning of the process, but you can't stop there, because the field is the potential for the forms that arise, not the forms themselves. You have to understand that the field has to take into account or include all the content that expresses the field. In other words, it has to take into account the worlds of Formation and Manifestation. So the company's structures and policies have to make sense in the context of the field.

"It's like DNA. DNA is a complete blueprint for a human being in potential, but it has to go through a gestation period to be realized in form. Once the form exists, of course, you'll find that the DNA inherently shaped it all."

"So you have to include the integrity of the whole design, not just the top end?"

"That's right. It's just like everything else in the universe. If people in organizations actually knew that, they would have a deep understanding of systemic thinking. And systemic thinking is far more than merely a step beyond linear thinking, or a summation of all the different linear processes. Ultimately, a linear approach will result in a collapse of the whole system. True systemic thinking is multidimensional, interrelating different levels of reality at the same time."

"How many levels are we talking about?" I asked.

"If we're speaking about the dynamics of the creative principle, there are the four worlds. Within the four worlds are the eleven sefiroth you and I have begun looking at together, the Tree of Life."

He responded immediately to the thought that he must have seen pass across my face.

"It may sound complex, but it's not complicated. "Once you're clear about the Genesis Principle, the rest of it unfolds naturally.

"When I'm working with a group of executives, I use the Genesis Principle to show them new possibilities for what leadership can be. I believe that's how originative leadership develops, as mastery of the whole multidimensional creative process, bringing forth intentional results on an ongoing basis."

While I liked Adam's idea of originative leadership, it was only a concept on my wish list. Maybe he could show me the key. I hoped so. After all these years I still hadn't found the secret of effective leadership. The more Adam spoke, the more I suspected that I'd been looking in all the wrong places.

TWELVE

A MATTER OF IDENTITY

To be, or not to be: that is the question.....
— William Shakespeare, Hamlet, Act III, Scene 1

I glanced at my wristwatch. It was 4:45, almost closing time, and certainly late enough to be wrapping up for the day. But I had a nagging confusion about the life principle and how it intersected with the question of identity. I moved the Tree of Life diagram closer to Adam. He looked at me expectantly.

"Maybe I shouldn't jump ahead like this, but I see that the ninth circle on the Tree of Life is *Identity*. Yet, you say that the life principle is a function of Being, the second circle. What's the difference between them?" I asked.

"The life principle generated by the field of Being comes first," he responded. "Identity — which includes your personality, your memories, your learned behaviors, and your emotional and physical characteristics — is the vehicle for expressing the life principle — the vehicle through which Being takes action in the world. I dentity is also called Foundation, because it provides the physical structure through which all the sefiroth above it are expressed. The expressions of Identity are like pilings driven deep into the ground of physical reality, anchoring the worlds of Origination, Creation, Formation to Manifestation."

"I think I see the difference," I confided. "Could you say then, that the life principle produces a person's identity?"

"You could say that, as long as you recall what you yourself pointed out earlier — that there are certain 'givens' that must be included in the mix. Our identities are shaped by three sets of factors: the genetic traits we are born with, the environment we are born into, and the organizing life principle that makes sense of it all. The life principle is the expressed intention of Being. All of your experiences are sorted through the sieve of that intention, and that's how you decide what you are, what works, and what doesn't work to fulfill the intention of your Being. And notice, I said what you are — not who you are."

"Should we not have any identity at all then?" I asked, though the question really didn't make any sense to me.

"That's not possible. That's like a driver without a car. But you don't have to be so attached to what you think you are. Then you can respond more flexibly in the face of changing circumstances. But don't worry, the matter of identity takes care of itself when a new, empowering life principle is created. That's why I focus on the Self and the life principle in my work with clients."

"What's the process of discovering those?" I asked.

"First, know who you really are. Second, unveil your current life principle and the circumstances in which you created it. Third, unburden yourself of all the ideals, myths and beliefs that have kept you asleep all your life. Fourth, create a new life principle. Fifth, learn and master the principles, practices and tools for creating on an ongoing basis."

"And how the hell do I do all that?" I asked.

"If we work together, you'll learn," Adam said. He took one last sip and finished his tea. It must have been cold by this time, though it didn't seem to bother him.

As fearful as I was about getting my hopes up, I believed that Adam might really have something to offer me, and my company too.

"Adam, you said before that organizations have life principles too, can you tell me more about that?"

"Yes, their life principles organize their identities as well," he said.

"What do you mean?"

"Let's take a really big organization with a long track record, so you can't miss the import of this. In the nineteenth century, what was the organization or industry with the most power and clout?"

"Well, let's see, it was probably steel or mining or railroads."

"Good, so let's use railroads. The owners of the railroads were among the most influential people of their time. They had an enormous impact on the way this country was settled. Now compare that with the financial viability and power of railroads today."

"Quite different."

"Good. Why? What happened?"

"Well, you had the invention of the airplane."

"True, but in itself that didn't do it."

"I don't think I'm following you."

"The decline of the railroads was not so much caused by new technology as by the fact that the railroads didn't take advantage of the new technology. They couldn't adopt it, because they didn't understand how it could contribute to their growth.

"Now remember, they have an organizing life principle, 'We are railroads.' So, when two bicycle merchants from the Midwest flew a burlap and wooden bi-plane on the dunes of Kitty Hawk, the railroad companies looked the other way — 'not railroads, not what we do.'

"But suppose their life principle had been, 'We are transportation,' knowing that the form of that principle — their identity — might evolve?"

"Ah, then they could have invested in this new technology because they could have seen it as another expression of their business," I replied, excited now. "Being 'We are railroads' limited them to a narrow, past-based technology that had already matured. God, if they had been focused on being, 'We are transportation,' maybe you and I would be flying on Southern Pacific Airlines."

"Exactly," said Adam. "See, it didn't matter how smart they were, and these were very, very smart people. The edge in business is not just a function of smarts, it is a function of how you organize the information and energy around you.

"Being the life principle 'We are railroads' gave them freedom and purpose in the beginning. But as they matured, in the arrogance and certainty brought on by their success, they never again questioned who they were. That's how they missed the possibility of developing new transportation technologies.

"Dave, a friend of mine was in a meeting where he heard the CEO of the most successful software company in the world publicly state his company's organizing principle. You know what he said?'

I shook my head.

"He said, 'Who we are is communication' — not hardware, not software, not even the Internet. The form of communication was not fixed. And if you look at the phenomenal success of his company and their ability to innovate, outflank, swallow, include, buy and use their competition, you can see how their strategies, tactics and actions are in harmony with their life principle, which is very big and inclusive, and yet is still focused.

"If you are in the communications business, there is an awful lot you can see that your competitors, who define themselves more restrictively, cannot. Whether we're talking about you as an individual or about a whole company," said Adam, "things go up and down. They change. Change isn't the issue. The issue is, Who are you going to be when things do change? Who and what are you going to bring forth? That is where the power and freedom are, not in attempting to avoid change, or attempting to reach some mythical homeostasis."

He folded his napkin neatly on the table. "The subconscious comes up with whatever is appropriate at the moment," he said matter-of-factly. He stood, waving his hand for me to come with him. I heard the familiar crack of my knees as I pulled myself up from my chair.

We left the cafe, climbing the curved marble stairway to the main floor of the rotunda. Adam took the steps two at a time in that effortless, long-legged stride that I recalled from high school. But he did it slowly, so as not to outdistance my one-step-at-a-time effort. I grasped the shiny brass railing as we ascended, but it was more to enjoy the feel of its curved, cool surface in my hand than any need for support.

It was closing time.

We left the Museum together and walked halfway down the long, broad flight of steps in front. We stopped there, our shadows stretched and rippling on the landing, and watched the familiar crush of homebound traffic crawl by on the street below.

Adam turned and looked at me for a long moment before speaking.

"Dave, I know that we can work together," he said. "But our success hinges on how hungry you are for a transformation in your life. I know that you want things to change at Allied Technologies, but it's really going to start with you changing you. How committed are you to altering your fundamental way of being?"

He was silent. He wanted me to actually ask that question of myself. After a few moments, he spoke again.

"Without that, nothing else matters. I have no interest in superficial changes; that's just cosmetic surgery. You'll need to be committed to a major shift in your ground of being, or both of us will be wasting our time. I know I can help you. It's really up to you. We've had the philosophical conversation. Now you have to make it real for yourself. From there you can discover for yourself what steps are needed to make a positive difference in your organization."

He turned his face toward the traffic, but he wasn't really watching it. His gaze seemed focused on some inner scenario, as though he were watching the trailer for a new buddy picture called "Dave & Adam" on an internal screen.

"As I mentioned before," he continued, "I hope to get something out of it too. In our case, the student is also the teacher and the teacher is also the student. We both play each role. If teaching and learning happen between a student on one end of a log and Socrates on the other, then we can both sit on a log someplace where we can be undisturbed for a few days and see what we create. Plus, it will be fun. What do you say?"

"Which of us would play Socrates?" I probed, expecting him to cast himself as he always had.

"I don't know. Which of us would you say is trying to learn something?"

"You mean, which is the student?"

"No. Which is Socrates? That's the joke, get it? Socrates never gave up the role of student."

Adam looked at me again. "I can have this week clear if you say the word."

I hesitated, mulling over his offer.

"It's also fine with me if you choose not to engage my services," he said, smiling. "I won't feel rejected, and it won't devalue our friendship. We should do this only if it's a fit for you, because if we do work together..."

He paused for a moment to make sure that he had my full attention. "If we do work together, I intend to be ruthlessly honest with you. That's the way I paint, and that's the way I teach. It's your call."

I'm pretty sharp at observing what's going on with people, aware of their eye movements, facial expressions, body language, changes in tone of voice and the like, and I have seen some very clever people use some very slick techniques that they've learned in the field over the years, or in some seminar on "listening and eye contact techniques for effective selling" or "how to make a great impression." It amuses me to see them in action, as they adjust their nonverbal cues so they can more successfully manipulate the situation.

My experience of Adam was different. There was no fawning or calculation in his manner, nothing of the salesman closing a deal. Yet he was not poker-faced or detached either. His face was open and completely lacked self-consciousness.

He was quite a guy, Adam — occasionally over the top in his antics, but I had a lot of respect for him. He seemed to have complete control over his life and could do whatever he wanted.

He never mentioned his reasons, but I guessed that he wasn't doing this consulting work for the money. He didn't need to. So why did he do it? It was hard to tell.

"Adam, let's do it," I said, feeling relieved to have resolved the matter. "I can hear a possibility in what you've been saying that I've been hoping for for a very long time. I am hungry for it, and if it's possible for me to get it, I don't want to live without it any longer. You already know I'm no quitter. I'll do whatever it takes, though I don't promise I'll enjoy all of it."

I extended my hand. Adam's eyes shone with obvious pleasure. "Good," he replied, gripping my hand in both of his to seal our agreement. "Dave, you've just expressed the sefira that opens the door: *Passionate Commitment*. It's the seventh circle of the Genesis Principle. Without it there is no chance for success. With it, there's the opportunity for miracles. Where shall we get together?"

"I have a place about two and a half hour's drive northwest of here," I told him. "It's just a simple cabin by a lake, but we could stay there if you could stand it. It's got plenty of logs."

"Are there fish in the lake?" asked Adam.

"Last time I was there they were waiting for me."

"Sounds perfect."

We made arrangements, deciding we'd bring very little with us. The cabin was already outfitted with the basic equipment. We just needed a few items of camping gear and some food to last our stay. We planned the visit for the following day. Adam insisted that we each drive separately, so parting would be simple if things weren't working out.

As we descended to the street he said, "I'm going to bring my sketch book, not for me, but for you."

"I can't draw a straight line," I called after him.

"Neither can Mother Nature, so you're in good company."

THIRTEEN

THE META ROOM

No limits are set to the ascent of humanity,
and to each and every one the highest stands open.
Here it is only your personal choice that decides.
— Hasidic saying

Fifty years ago my father bought the cabin by the lake as both an investment and vacation retreat. Like so many of his investments, it had not paid off. The area suffered a collapse in property values when the local economy faltered ten years after he'd bought it. The cabin had paid off, though, as a family vacation retreat. We'd used it a lot in the early years. Wooded hills full of birch and pine surrounded the lake. If you'd never been near the Rockies you might call them mountains, but they were closer to hills. The trails and roads that circled the lake were encroached now with underbrush. Over the years most of the cabins had been abandoned. But a few houses, in various stages of disrepair, continued to be used on occasional weekends, the last remnants of the original camp community that had thrived here during the summers after World War II.

I ambled down to the shore behind the cabin. Originally each lakefront property had a wooden boat dock. Now only skeletal remnants rose from the weeds that clogged the shore. Our own dock had been built at my father's direction as an extended pier into the lake, allowing him to fish from the end of it, and to moor our now long-gone canoe and the rowboat with the notoriously unreliable inboard motor.

I walked back to unload the gear from my car, recalling that the lake had been well stocked with fish the last time I'd been at the cabin. With a little luck, Adam and I might find our dinners there.

I unlocked the cabin, opened the shutters, did a cursory dusting of the place, and unrolled my sleeping bag onto one of the two wooden bunks. Just then, I heard the sound of Adam's vehicle crunching and pinging along the gravel road. I walked out onto the front porch to watch him pull up. He was driving a Land Rover. Even disguised under the newly-laid blanket of dust, the dark green vehicle looked so new I thought that he must have bought it only weeks before, and realized I hadn't warned him about the dirt road.

"But, hell," I thought to myself, "that's what those four wheelers are designed for!"

Adam stepped out and stood for a moment looking around at the scenery, breathing deeply, apparently taking in all the sensations. Then he walked back and forth, kicking a rock here and there as if to test the tires of nature. He rubbed a leaf on a nearby sapling between his thumb and forefinger and looked up toward the hills.

He was wearing a pair of khaki shorts, a denim shirt and a tan poplin jacket. On his head he wore one of those waterproof Australian outback sun-hats.

He hadn't even said hello to me yet. He was like that. He could stand around maybe three or four minutes without a word, though he did glance my way a couple of times, nodding and smiling the first time. But his very act of not speaking made me feel as if I were with him again in all the old ways, when sometimes we would walk together for as much as a half hour without speaking, me paying attention to the way he was paying attention to everything around us.

"I like this place," he said, as if it were a professional opinion.

As we finished unpacking our gear and supplies, we talked about old memories: our classmates, the teachers we'd loved, as well as the ones we'd tormented, Roy's Place, where we used to hang out together in the evenings — even how we'd irritated our classmates by demanding more homework, first as a joke, and then because we'd genuinely talked ourselves into a greater thirst for knowledge.

"Mrs. Motovich. She was a great English teacher," he remembered, smiling. "As for most of the other teachers, they seemed only concerned that you knew the right answer. They didn't care if you did any thinking. Did you ever notice that half of what we were taught isn't true anymore? I probably wouldn't have had such a problem with the information if it had been presented to us as what it actually was: the currently accepted and agreed upon 'likely story.' But no, it was the 'truth,' which I always questioned. Fortunately, that discrepancy created a tension in my life that's benefited my painting ever since."

"You weren't painting at all when I knew you."

"I didn't take up painting much until I was in college."

"And now you're a celebrated artist."

"I'll be celebrated in another five years. Right now I'm just very expensive."

"Maybe I should buy one of your pictures."

"Be careful, no shoulds. Besides, you might hate them," he laughed.

"I always wondered, what allowed you to slip through the public indoctrination system unscathed?" I asked. "You know you were always questioning things. I learned how to do that from you, though I can see now that what I got from you then was only the tip of the iceberg."

"I had to think," he replied. "I couldn't buy what society was telling me. From the time I was very young, I was aware that my perception of the world, and what other people said and believed about it, were quite different. I think many children are aware of this when they're small. At first, they may even try to point out this discrepancy to the adults around them, only to find themselves being squashed and needled to 'get with the program.'"

"The program?"

"Yes, like that art drill you told me you experienced in second grade. When you are young, the choice looks simple. Either you trust your own experience, and risk the ridicule and constant pressure to conform, or you give up on your own capacity to think and allow yourself to be co-opted by the agreed upon myths. I found that I could hold onto my own experience of reality if I just kept my mouth shut and pretended to go along with the cultural hypnosis."

"How did you manage to avoid succumbing to this... what did you call it?... cultural hypnosis?"

"I realized I had to rely on my own thinking so I could make some sense of the world, and to do it in a way that I could survive and not be considered crazy. This in a world where it looked to me as if people were often calling sane insane and vice versa. You helped me do that sometimes. And joking around, too, was a method, of course. Being the Fool is an age-old method.

"But what really gave me the strength to trust my own experience were the books I read. They were my first real teachers."

"The books?"

"Yes. When I was a teenager, I discovered a certain bookstore in the old section of downtown. It was close to the building where my father worked, and I discovered it one day — a Saturday — when I'd accompanied him to his office for what I thought would be a few minutes. But he got sucked into some crisis or other, and I ended up waiting around with nothing to do. So after a few hours he told me to take the bus home or hang out downtown until he was done.

I began to walk, exploring some streets I had never been down before. Soon I found myself on Ninth Street where I discovered two bookstores nestled near each other in adjacent buildings, each occupying the lower sections of dilapidated brownstones. These were not at all like the bookstores I was used to in the suburbs.

"One of them had a wooden sign out front that said, 'George's, Old and Used Books.' The other one didn't even have a sign. Of course, that was the one I was most curious about. Its windows were coated with years of grime. I remember pressing my face against the glass to take a look inside. Any patch of glass that wasn't entirely opaque yielded a filmy view of an interior so dim that the one electric light bulb barely illuminated the teetering stacks of books inside.

"I opened the door slowly and stepped in for a look. The air inside felt heavy and dense. Dust hovered, wrapping itself around me, inserting itself into every crevice of my clothes, hair and eyes. Its taste was unmistakable, an instant coating of antiquity upon my tongue, tickling my throat with the cast-off dust motes and mold accumulated from generations of brittle, deteriorating pages.

"Walls of books surrounded me like natural insulation. The few sounds from elsewhere in the shop were muffled, as if heard through cotton batting. There was only the dull thunk and shuffle of my rubber soles upon the wooden floor, the softer than soft sound of a page being turned and muted pencil scratches from the clerk behind the counter.

"The interior of the bookshop seemed to be a series of three narrow, high-ceilinged rooms broken up by free-standing book cases, all filled to capacity and laid out like an intricate labyrinth. Adding to the confusion were the numerous stacks of books that could find no place of rest on the shelves, rising from the floor in vertical columns, placed wherever there was a modicum of floor space to accommodate them. In some places, the visible floor was no more than twelve inches wide. To avoid hitting a booby-trapped stack and setting off an avalanche of books, I had to make my way cautiously, twisting and turning my body and carefully placing my feet."

"Is that where you found the books?" I asked.

"Ah! I'm coming to that," he replied.

We had moved out onto the front porch of the cabin and were now sitting with our feet dangling over the edge. We watched the miserly shadows of noontime begin to lengthen. Adam sat quietly for awhile, as though listening to something I could not hear.

"The fourth room," he finally said.

I looked at him quizzically.

"That's where I found the books. In the fourth room.

"I've always tended to trust my intuition to lead me to what I need, even if I'm not always consciously aware of it. That was the way I browsed through the bookshop. I didn't pay attention to the category signs above the shelves, I just walked through, receptive to whatever pulls and eddies I could detect in some unseen flow, allowing myself to be drawn in a particular direction by a feeling that said, 'go that way.' I guess you could call it 'the Tao of Browsing.' Anyway, I allowed myself to be drawn in a particular direction. At some point, this sense would get stronger, and I would find myself reaching for some book within arms' length that seemed to have 'read me, Adam' written all over it."

"So, you guessed which books would be relevant?"

"No, no, I just knew it."

Adam paused for a moment, absentmindedly stroking his beard.

"The problem with attempting to describe this," he continued," is that words can't capture what I am pointing to.

"What I'm talking about is a kind of knowing that's beyond words. Some people call it instinct, some call it intuition, some call it a gut sense or a hunch. Ultimately, though, all words fail to describe it, and you are left with either being someone who has had that experience and knows it, or someone who hasn't — or more likely, you've denied the experience when you've had it. In dealing with my students and clients, however, I've found that people can learn to access that ability for themselves on a regular basis."

I had experienced first hand what Adam was struggling to describe, but I was no better at verbalizing it. Some of my most important and successful work had come about from following that gut instinct he was referring to. Unfortunately, I often didn't trust my instincts, only to end up regretting that later. It was particularly heartening to find out that Adam felt this ability could be strengthened.

"What about a fourth room and books?" I urged.

"Ah, yes. As I said, I'd been following my method, moving through the crowded, narrow aisles, until I found myself drawn to the third room all the way in the back of the store, happily lost, divining my way through the shelves. Nothing particularly caught my interest, and I was about to make my way back toward the front of the shop when some sense told me not to leave there yet. Then I saw a narrow corridor to my right. It ended abruptly at a short stairway. There was another room at the top of the stairs. An internal magnet was pulling me forward, up the stairs and into the fourth room.

"It was much smaller than the others, with a low ceiling. The illumination came from a single bare light bulb and a small circular window. I remember that the window had been covered with cheap colored plastic, in a poor imitation of stained glass.

"The faded, cardboard sign above one of the bookshelves said, Meta, but the rest of the word had been torn off. It was probably better that way, as I reached for a volume having no preconception of what kind of book it was. I opened it at random and read the first thing I noticed."

"I remember exactly what it said: *'Facts based upon reason and the evidence of the senses, which oppose the idea seeking expression, rob you of the belief in the reality of the invisible state...faith is the evidence of things not seen.'*

"I looked at the facing page. A line at its center caught my eye: *'Make results and accomplishments the crucial test of your power to create.'*

"I was excited. The book was telling me to have faith in the reality of the invisible state, of the idea not yet given form, even if there is not yet any physical evidence for it. But the line across from it meant to me that it didn't refer to 'blind faith.' It actually was a call for accountability, for acting on a vision, to make the 'spirit become flesh.'

"I read more. These were not ideas I was being taught in school or at home. I picked up other nearby books, reading a paragraph in one, a page or two in another. The books fascinated me. They spoke about the powers of the mind. They spoke of intention, vision, direct knowing and non-attachment. They warned of the suffering caused by living a whole lifetime locked in an illusion of oneself as merely a biological and psychological entity, acting out a script written by someone else.

"When I looked at my watch, three hours had passed. It was late in the afternoon. I had just about decided to leave when I reached for one last book. Its pages were yellowed and dog-eared, with barely decipherable pencil notes scrawled in the margins. The text was a dialogue between a teacher, designated as 'M' and his students, 'Q'. I looked down at the underlined words. I remember them still.

"*M: Stay open and quiet, that is all. What you seek is so near you... you know that you are. Don't burden yourself with names, just be. Any name or shape you give yourself obscures your real nature.*"

"For a brief instant, I had a sensation like an electric current passing up my spine. The words had resonated with something inside me that awakened and cried out, 'Yes!' It was unsettling, since this was different from understanding logically what I was reading. In fact, I was grasping for meaning, as the words seemed to defy rationality. I was sure I didn't know what they meant. Yet some part of me recognized and responded to them."

Adam leaned back and rested on his elbows, seeming to gaze at an image of long ago.

"That may have been my first conscious awareness of *Grace* — the fourth sefira — the effortless and abundant knowing that flows to one as a gift of creative Spirit. When you receive what you need as a flow of Grace, it leaves you with an awed sense of the infinite abundance of creation."

"The open hand of Grace," I whispered to myself.

"Did you bring your chart of the Tree of Life?" Adam asked me.

I nodded.

"Take it out and look at it."

I fetched it from my backpack and brought it back out to the porch to examine with Adam. I studied it, noticing that the flow of the lines of creation went from Wisdom to Being to Grace. After the world of Creation, the first step in the world of Formation is Grace. Adam pointed out that the Hebrew word for that sefira was *Chesed*, which was often translated into English as love, mercy and loving-kindness. He said the word Grace included all of these meanings and captured the sense of unconditional love, openness and abundant flow that arises once a field of Being has been created. Grace is the realm of intuition, of 'Aha!' of the inner voice or image arising to give specificity to the infinite.

"Over time I realized that my experiences of intuitive knowing were expressions of Grace in action," he said. "They were always preceded by a strong desire or intention."

"Ask and you shall receive?"

"Yes. By the way, do you know what the word *desire* means? *De-Sire.* It means 'of the Father.' Interesting, don't you think?"

He paused for a moment, then picked up where he had left off in his story of the metaroom.

"It was late, and my parents were expecting me home for dinner," he continued. "I looked around at the hundreds of volumes and knew that this place had been waiting for me. Here was a treasure of knowledge that both provoked powerful questions and confirmed ideas I had kept to myself. Up until then I had believed no one else was thinking such thoughts. Now I knew I wasn't alone. I bought the first book I'd picked up and took the bus home at twilight."

"I assume that the torn sign in the fourth room had originally said Metaphysics?"

"I'm sure it did," said Adam, "and that's what was so auspiciously wonderful about it being torn, because the part that remained described the contents of the room so much better."

"How so?"

"Well, what do you think of when you hear the word metaphysics?"

"I think it refers to an esoteric or occult body of knowledge that's not much related to the real world, and it's not concerned with the laws of the physical universe."

"That's probably the most common and popular interpretation out there. Do you know who coined the word metaphysics?"

"No, but I'm sure you'll enlighten me!" I laughed.

"Aristotle. It's the title of one of his books, probably named that way because he was either very straightforward, or he was feeling too tired to come up with a more original and sexy title. He had already written a book on physics, and this book was the sequel, or the next volume. Since the Greek word 'meta' means beyond or after, he called it Metaphysics. But the word metaphysics was never meant to indicate that it was unrelated to physics or its laws. In fact, it was meant to illuminate the underpinnings and principles behind the perceived reality."

"Then quantum physicists may be our century's metaphysicists," I suggested, "which may be more accurate than saying metaphysician. And they use their own esoteric language, the language of science: mathematics. They create models of what is beyond our common, direct perception. They've gone beyond the Newtonian mechanistic model, dealing with things that most of us assume are no more accessible than the most ancient mystic teachings."

"They are attempting to come up with new models for themselves. Their theories are, more and more, converging with ancient spiritual teachings. The language, metaphors, and packaging are different.

"I think the sign over the bookcase was more accurate in its torn state. The owner of the shop was not especially meticulous about what he shelved in that fourth room. It seemed to be the place where books on metaphysics, intuition, creativity, bio-feedback, spirituality, mystical religious practices, yoga, meditation, Buddhism, Taoism, and whatever I haven't mentioned of that ilk, ended up. Even the more esoteric books of philosophy were placed there. So I took my cue from the sign and christened the room my metaroom, and it really was that for me, a place where I could go beyond what I was learning in school and from my peers."

"Did you go to this metaroom often? I seem to remember you taking a lot of mysterious trips on the weekends."

"During that first year I went to the bookshop at least one Saturday a month, spending hours poring over the books in the fourth room."

"Weren't you afraid of becoming as indoctrinated by those beliefs and ideas as you were by the ones you were questioning at home?"

"Becoming a reverse True Believer, but a True Believer nevertheless? Good question. An appropriate concern. I think a few things saved me from that danger.

"First of all, a lot of these ideas worked. I would take a new idea and try it out in my life to see what happened. I knew if I couldn't re-create it for myself, it would remain merely informational, which I've never considered of much value — except for taking tests.

"Second, I explored the different traditions. The metaroom gave me access to more than one point of view of the world at the same time. As I read the books, studied them and compared them, going back and forth among the different traditions, I began to discern certain fundamental principles underlying their surface differences.

"Actually, I marveled at the consistency at the heart of these various traditions. Eventually I was free to discover my own voice for what I was experiencing.

"You know the fable of the six blind men, all trying to describe an elephant based on the part of it that they were touching and feeling? Each of them was absolutely certain their point of view represented the whole truth of the elephant."

"Yes, I know it well," I answered. "I've been in meetings that felt like that, except it was more like fifteen blind men around a table, not six, and all of them were certain they were the only one who could see."

"Well, I was very blessed," Adam said. "I felt like someone who had the good fortune to have interviewed all of the blind men, and by doing so, had developed a real sense of what the elephant was actually like. Because I could connect the views, I could sense the whole. Each view could illuminate part of the whole, and like a hologram, each view was a view of the whole from its point of view. None of them were invalid, they were just incomplete because they were points of view. I realized that no one had a lock on the truth. I knew that no system could ever capture the source of systems, they could only look from it. The more I read, the more the words drew me in. It was all new, and yet, it was somehow familiar, as though I had known it before."

"Did all of your present work develop simply from reading those books?"

"No, but that was the foundation for it. You must remember I also experimented with what I read, so I was active in my relationship with the ideas. I was constantly testing them."

"Did you have any live teachers?"

"For sure. As I said, the books were the foundation. They gave me a basis for what came later. There's an old saying, 'when the student is ready, the teacher appears.' I've found this to be true. I've mentioned the teachers I had in art school. There were other teachers, also. All of them seem to have come into my life at just the right moment. I've been fortunate in that way."

I was thinking of the way I had connected with Adam myself. "Did the teachers find you or did you find them?"

"All I can say is that we connected. Once I traveled to a valley in the west of India, to see some large statues of the Hindu god, Ganesh. It was only after I'd met one of my most remarkable spiritual teachers there that I realized why I'd gone to that particular place. This teacher had a small ashram near-by. From my experience of being with her I got a direct knowing of my Self as I AM Awareness. In India, they call this the knowing that I AM THAT. It's a knowing beyond certainty.

"I finally understood to the depths of my soul where all of those books from all those different traditions had come from. I experienced ananda, or bliss, which changed the way I've lived ever since."

I looked at him. I had no idea what he was talking about. I don't mean that I was dismissing what he said, it was just that I had no reference point for it. It was like telling a person who had never seasoned their food about the taste and smell of an herb. You could talk all day and it wouldn't make it any clearer until they had experienced it for themselves. Even so, I asked Adam to say more about his experience. He would only say that he had experienced a profound shift in his fundamental ground of being.

"You must be able to say more about it than that," I persisted, hoping for one small hint to hold onto.

"A moment before this shift," he finally offered, " I had experienced myself as an 'I' awareness located somewhere within my physical body. A moment later, I experienced myself as an infinite field of awareness in which what I had called 'I' and everyone and everything else were ONE. This was accompanied by an indescribable bliss beyond words or finite comprehension, a sense of inner peace and knowing that has never left me."

Absorbed in some quiet inner reflections, he said nothing for awhile. When he finally spoke, it was in a voice hardly above a whisper.

"A great yogi of India, Bhagavan Nityananda, spoke of it this way:

To see the One is subtle;
To see the One is to see the same Self in all.
This is 'same-sightedness,' equal vision.
Seeing the One in all by looking inward.
Seeing that this world and the next world are One.
The union of the individual Self and The Absolute."

Then he was quiet again. I felt like a deaf man trying to hear the crash-ing of waves upon the beach.

After awhile, Adam looked over at me and said softly, "Dave, don't sweat it. It's the direct experience that matters, not the words. Have patience and have heart." He offered this last encouragement so gently, I choked up.

I at once changed the direction of the conversation to one less immediately threatening. "Have you had any teachers in this country?" I asked.

"Many," he replied, taking my offered bait. "The world is full of wonderful beings ready to instruct you, if you are open to their message. Some teachers appear when it is time to learn a particular practice: mind/body control, meditation, guided imagery, or the knowledge of how to translate creative ideas into effective action. Sometimes their purpose is to awaken you to the Infinite, to listen to and trust your inner knowing. Sometimes the teachers you meet appear for a particular purpose: to clarify a question you have been wrestling with, or to give you the key to a mystery you are attempting to unravel, and that is their main contribution to you at that moment.

"A few years ago, I was drawn to some of the key principles found in the Kabbalah. Thirty years before, I'd had my first introduction to this tradition in the metaroom. I was fascinated by the ideas, but couldn't see their relevance to my life. This time, my experiences with other disciplines and my ability to see beyond the surface of things yielded a new understanding. I could see within the teachings of Kabbalah an accurate expression of the way the creative Spirit works in the universe. Now remember, the word Kabbalah means 'to receive', and that is of paramount importance. You can read and appreciate knowledge, that is one level of receiving. But knowing ultimately is not an intellectual process, it is a shift in being. Ultimately you have to trust your own experience and to listen to the Infinite I speaking within you.

"As I studied the diagram of the Tree of Life, I found that many of the English translations for the sefiroth seemed insufficient. The words didn't resonate with what I intuitively knew was a potent template for creating. It was a somewhat frustrating situation, because I didn't speak fluent Hebrew. Yet I knew that for the Tree of Life to be of full value not only for me, but for my clients, it had to be as powerfully accessible as possible in English. But, taking the word Kabbalah to heart, I remained open to receive.

"Around this time I happened to be staying at the home of a friend. On the second afternoon of my visit, I was sitting in the living room with his wife, and I told her about my frustrations with the Tree of Life translations. I was expecting no more than a perfunctory response, when she started to give me possible English translations for the Hebrew words. It turned out that she spoke Hebrew fluently, and would have studied to be a Rabbi had she not chosen marriage and a family instead."

"So she helped you out?"

"That doesn't begin to say it. We spent two whole days together going back to the root of every one of the eleven Hebrew words, trying to capture their essence in English. It was as if she had been waiting for me. After I returned home, I put all of the roots to the words, and the words themselves on my wall, along with a whole collection of possible expressions for the same principles in English. I used those yellow squares of 'post-its' so I could move them around. I looked at them for a month, just contemplating all these possible English meanings, noticing which ones resonated for me and which seemed most consistent with regard to the others, knowing that all of the words had to work together if I were to capture the whole essence of the Tree of Life. The translations I now use were developed organically in that way."

"What do the experts and scholars say about your translations?" I asked.

He looked at me with genuine surprise. It was the first time I remember ever catching him off guard. "I've never asked, and to tell you the truth, Dave, it never even occurred to me to ask before you mentioned it."

He stopped for a moment.

"You know," he continued, "it might be interesting to find out, but it's not a major priority of mine. I know that there are many variations on what the words can mean, particularly if you go back to the roots. The Hebrew language itself is designed to get to the roots of things. Each Hebrew word has three root letters. The tense of the word or the gender or person is indicated by adding letters to the root in a predictable way. Its predictable patterns make it one of the simplest languages in the world to learn because it is completely consistent with itself, while also being expressive and poetic. So, at the heart of each word there's a root word with a meaning that is always consistent, the way your pulse is. The melody of meanings changes around it, but the pulse remains the same. Thus you're always adding onto a root without departing from it. This helps to anchor eternal meanings as the words acquire dimensionality for people through personal experience over time. The priority for me was whether they resonated with the inner voice I've learned to trust, whether they fit my experience, and whether they provided greater access to living from the LIGHT of the Creator."

"What kind of teacher are you hoping you'll be for me?" I asked.

"The answer to that question is never clear until afterwards," Adam said, "sometimes not until quite a bit afterwards."

Adam walked over to the ice chest he'd left by the front door, and with a dramatic flourish he produced two cold bottles of Guinness stout and passed one to me.

"Does this call for a toast?" I asked.

"Of course! Of course! "L'chaim!" he said, raising his bottle. "To life! That's why we've come here — for vital and vibrant new life!

FOURTEEN

INTUITIVE KNOWING

Trust your Inner Authority

— Jack Schwarz

"This inner knowing you speak of, how do you do it?" I asked.

"Dave, there are many methods..."

"No, I mean how do *you* do it?"

"Oh, you mean my personal method? Hmmm... the truth is it's more intention than technique. For something like walking through a bookshop, it is nothing more than what I've already told you: I have faith in my intuitive sense and let myself be guided. For coming up with creative ideas I do follow a particular procedure.

"What I'm going to tell you will sound ridiculously simple, but it works for me and I trust it.

"First, I find myself a place where I won't be disturbed. I close my eyes, relax, and hold the question, problem or idea before my mind until I'm absolutely clear about what I'm asking. Then I vividly imagine the end result having already been achieved, putting no attention or concern on the method or process of getting there. Then when I feel as if 'it is done' I release that intention and go back into action, trusting I'll receive whatever information, insight or assistance I need. I don't anticipate how it will arrive, and I stay open to it as I go about whatever I think makes sense at the conscious level. It's worked pretty well for me over the years. The more I trust it, the more it opens up."

"That reminds me of a quote from Einstein," I offered. "He asked, 'Why do some of my best ideas come while I'm shaving?'"

"I think it answers itself. Shaving, showering, walking or meditating are all conducive to reverie, which is a mental state that allows ideas that have been percolating to settle out gently without having to be forced through the constricting channels of the linear, analytical mind.

"Understand, I'm not discounting rational, rigorous, thought. Rationality is a critical part of your arsenal when you're trying to make things happen. Logic works hand in hand with intuition. But logic and intuition are distinctly different and give you different outcomes. Logic allows for continuity, stability, tradition — the past brought forward and improved on with order and consistency. But if you want to create new territory, logic alone can't fill the bill. To reach the promised land of invention, you must let go. You must launch yourself from the very edge of your known world into chaos, allowing unseen currents to carry you aloft until you land, quite unexpectedly, on the shore of a new reality."

"There have been lots of times when an idea or solution suddenly just came to me," I said, "but I've always thought it was a fluke."

"Dave, there's a difference between merely logical processing, and what I call the intentional process (which includes both logical and intuitive thought.) The logical process may lead you to a certain point or conclusion, but it will always be an extrapolation of what went before. Even if it is an extraordinary improvement, it will still be subject to the old paradigms.

"The intentional process, on the other hand, allows you to leap beyond current knowledge and open your mind to new perspectives on a problem. These leaps literally re-organize the current reality. By the way, when first shown the light of day in the land of the status quo, these intuitive leaps are usually attacked as nonsensical, and are predictably referred to as 'so and so's folly.'"

"I understand," I said. "If I look at my most successful achievements — and I'm not talking about ideas that were merely improvements on what was already known, but the real leaps — I can see how it was the rational that led me up to the doorway of the solution, and as such, was vitally important for that purpose. But that was never what got me across the threshold to new ideas. That always required a leap of faith that allowed me to see possibilities beyond what I'd been able to conceive of as feasible up to that time."

"And I'll bet you didn't learn a lot about that method of thinking in business school."

"True, but I think its use among creative people in any field, including business, must be more widespread than most people imagine, because most of those who do it don't talk about it."

"The joke is that it has been talked about and written up for years," said Adam. "The list of creative men and women who have used this intentional process would make a book in itself. A lot of them got their insights through dreams or reveries, or perhaps merely by their ability to know what question to ask and how to frame it, until the answer unfolded itself as they worked.

"There are lots of scientists, lots of artists and musicians who call on this intuitive capacity pretty consistently. As I've pointed out to you already, in the Kabbalah this phenomenon is called 'the lightning flash of creation.' Some authors even anthropomorphized it and gave it a name!"

"What do you mean?" I asked.

"Robert Louis Stevenson called the source of his inspiration the 'Little People'! He nicknamed them his 'Brownies,' and said they did the work while he was sleeping, and then he just wrote it down."

"I can't see that explanation really going over big in a corporate board-room."

"How about 'Make friends with your Daemon' month?" Adam offered.

"Your 'Daemon?'"

"Rudyard Kipling used that particular name. He wrote that the way he called up his 'Daemon' was to 'drift, wait and obey!'"

"I can just see me telling that to Henderson," I remarked ruefully.

"I think lack of context for the communication might have something to do with the problem," Adam said dryly, "though I must admit it can be tough to get this idea across to people who have spent their lives as 'human doings' rather than human beings. They don't have much patience with the idea of being with something instead of immediately reacting."

"Kipling's 'drift, wait and obey' sounds a bit like your method," I said.

"It does, though I developed mine independently before I ever knew this about Kipling."

"Are there many examples of business people functioning that way?"

"Of course, though it's often hushed up. There's an illusion in some businesses that most things are determined by the 'Dragnet' method."

"What's that?"

"You know, 'just the facts, ma'am.' But in most companies what are called the 'facts' are, in reality, just a jumbled collage of statistics, interpreta-tions, assumptions, past and present fears, and reactive responses. The truth is that even the most mundane human communications are laced with intu-ition. Without it no communication could take place because you wouldn't have any sense of whom you were talking to.

"So the question isn't whether you operate intuitively, but how well developed your intuition is. In business, most creative people do cultivate their intuitive side to a high degree. It's one of the things that gives them an edge over their competitors; giving themselves permission to use both rigor-ous, logical thinking and free-wheeling intuition. All in the service of what I call an 'intentional vision.' It just hasn't been okay to speak about it so open-ly, because you might be seen as flaky, even though there's tons of evidence now that most of the great breakthroughs in the past fifty years in science and technology have been in the realm of the unseeable," Adam continued.

"Good Lord, Dave! Alexander Graham Bell, without whom that old giant AT&T wouldn't even exist, called the creative power, 'a conquering force within.' He said something that any creative, effective, no-nonsense business person should be able to connect with. He said that creativity was only available when you were in a state of mind where you knew exactly what you wanted...."

"That's why it's important to be clear about the end result, isn't it?" I said.

"Yes, and that's only the first part of Bell's statement. The second part is that knowing what you want must be paired with determination not to quit until you get it."

"Why don't more people practice utilizing both aspects of their minds? It would seem to me, that when we don't, we're like golfers who use only our right arms to swing our clubs," I said.

"Indoctrination, my dear Watson!" said Adam, laughing. "If you keep the new kids hypnotized with the lie that everything is a function of analysis and logic, the innovators keep quiet and walk off with the prizes," he added melodramatically. "Then they explain their success as a function of logical extrapolation, which keeps their competition from getting suspicious and horning in on a good thing. How's that for a creative conspiracy theory!"

He dropped the glibness, and looked at me soberly.

"But if your purpose is to lead an organization towards greater effectiveness, rather than to merely establish a corner on the creativity market, you may want to create a corporate culture in which you combine the power of intention with rigorous, logical thought. This will open up new avenues for innovation beyond what's predictable."

"Is that part of the work we'll be doing, together?" I asked.

"I think we're going to discover what's necessary as we go along."

"Maybe the correct term to describe you is a mystical pragmatist," I said with a smile.

"I prefer practical mystic," he replied.

"You certainly would never be called cynical," I added.

I was surprised by the vehemence of Adam's response.

"God no! Cynicism is a walking death. It kills all possibility, all spirit, all innovation and all creativity."

"Is skeptical a better word for your position?" I asked.

"It's better, but not quite it. I don't like it because it has a slightly negative connotation. I think 'curious' is the best word...open and curious, but not naive and gullible."

"How do you know the difference?"

"Well, sometimes you don't find out until afterwards. If you end up getting conned, you say that you were naive and gullible, but if you benefited, then you say you were open and curious." He tried to say this with a straight face, but as he finished his last words, Adam could no longer contain himself and broke out into laughter.

I didn't react very much to this frivolity, but that didn't constrain Adam's enthusiasm one bit. When he composed himself again, he looked at me with what I felt was a mixture of pity and admonishment.

"Dave, maybe the most brutal sentence that could be imposed on a human being is to be condemned to go through life with no sense of humor. If you can't tune into the cosmic joke from time to time...Whew!"

We were both quiet for a few minutes. I was thinking about this. Was I really that humorless? The last few years had been pretty grim, I realized.

I felt a click, like a rusted latch opening, and a feeling somewhere between sadness and despair climbed up from my gut and into my throat. I gritted my teeth tightly to keep it down and swallowed hard. I couldn't even remember when I'd last been in touch with the joy of living. Maybe it had just gradually faded out, like a color photo hung in the sunlight too long. One day you look and there are only flattened, faded shadows, mere hints of its vibrant, original state.

Adam finally turned back toward me, speaking passionately.

"Look," he said, "a creative life is a risky life. If you want a life without risks, where everything is predictable, then you're basically saying you don't want to play in the game of life as a creator. Because creativity and risk go together.

"But if you refuse the opportunity to be creative, what you're left with by default is either being a resentful, angry, destructive pain in the ass, or a dedicated preserver of the status quo, relating to change the way a child takes castor oil."

Then he abruptly changed the subject.

"Creating is what's primary.

"At one time it was difficult for me to think with colors and brush strokes. I had to integrate my desire to make sense of the world on the one hand, with my passion for self expression. It didn't come easily for me. But I suppose if it had I wouldn't have driven myself so hard to make visual sense out of my life."

He jumped off the porch and lay down on the ground, looking up at the sky, his head cupped in his hands. I could tell he wanted to relax the conversation a little.

"Art is a peculiar kind of struggle for me," he said. "It didn't come easily. Not at all. Sometimes I wondered if it was worth it."

"Why did you do it, then?"

"If it doesn't challenge you to the limits of your capacity, if it isn't like Jacob wrestling with the angel, it seems to me it's not worth doing — as a life's work, anyway." He rolled over to face me, leaning on his elbow while his other hand plucked some grass by the roots. "I worry about the people who sleepwalk through life with jobs they hate and a home life that's borderline torture. To me life is such an incredible gift, it's to be consumed with every ounce of commitment you've got."

He sat up and smiled at me, wagging his finger in mock reprimand. "It's far too important to take seriously, though, so don't let's get maudlin about this!"

Then he lay back down and was silent for a long time.

"It's like looking into the deep blue core of the sky," he finally said. "Something takes shape in you without your realizing it. You have a mission, maybe. You don't know that, and then suddenly you discover it, almost by accident.

"There was a turning point in my life, when I became an artist. For some people that point occurs when they think they're going to die. Like they're in a foxhole being shot at, or something. For me it came as a kind of joke I couldn't stop laughing at. I guess I was on the prowl anyway in a sort of serious but whimsical way. As you know, I've always loved music, and I had some thought once of being a concert pianist. I soon realized, though, that I didn't have the talent.

"One time I was in a store that had the latest in sound equipment, and they had this machine there for translating sound into light.

"I took one look at that sucker and thought it was the silliest thing I'd ever seen. The colors and shapes I saw when I listened to music went so far beyond what that little mechanical contraption was producing that I suddenly realized I wanted to capture the effect music had on me when I listened to it."

"But if you gave up the idea of being a professional musician, and I personally always thought you had a real talent for it, what made you think you had the necessary talent as an artist, when you weren't even used to thinking about art?"

"That's a good question," said Adam, and remained silent again for a while. "Sometimes you just know things. I've never thought about this before," he said. "Let's see. I'd always doodled compulsively, but barely noticed that I did it, and certainly never tried to structure it."

But he didn't take it any further.

"You didn't know, of course, that I nearly died during the summer after my second year in college."

"No, I didn't."

"I had pneumonia. It shouldn't have been difficult to cure, but it was.

"I remember lying in bed, at one point almost wanting to die and get it over with. But much of the time, when I was so sick I could barely focus my mind, I'd have these fantasies about what it would be like to be well again. Then I remembered some of my readings in the metaroom on intentional visioning. I'd visualize myself well, running and playing outside. I'd create the experiences in my mind as fully and vividly as possible, using all of my senses. I'd see myself doing something joyful and active, feel it in my body, smell it, taste it, hear it, and create the emotions and mental attitudes of well being, and know that this was my natural state."

"And all the time your body was lying in a hospital bed?"

"Yes," he said. "See, the mind can't tell the difference between a vividly imagined experience and a real one. It will respond to both, not just psychologically, but biologically. What we imagine, positively or negatively, has a powerful effect at emotional and physical levels. Visualization can actually weaken or strengthen the immune system.

"Anyway, as I practiced this intentional visioning, I began to create more and more vivid images in my mind with spectacular colors, textures and shapes. I fell in love all over again with the beauty of the universe around me and within me. I felt a deep appreciation for the gift and miracle of life."

I was more and more put off by Adam's reminiscences, feeling envious and agitated. When I thought about my own life, I felt nothing but emptiness. It had been a very long time since my life had seemed like a gift.

"When I started to get my strength back," he continued, "I knew I wanted to spend the rest of my life painting images on canvas."

Adam was silent again for maybe two or three minutes. Unlike me, he felt no need to fill the lull with unnecessary sound and chatter.

"What's particularly interesting," he resumed, "is that what I paint now has little or nothing to do with trying to copy nature. It doesn't come close to the real thing, or what I visualized when I was sick. But I'm always attempting to capture its essence in human terms, in a way that speaks first to the eye and then to the heart, hoping for a response from the viewer that says, 'Yes! I get your world! I know what you are saying!'"

He paused, then continued almost in a whisper.

"That's both the challenge and the joy."

He lay on his back and closed his eyes, apparently talking to himself now. "Each of us has something we want to express, some contribution we want to give the world. If you were spiritual, you might say it's why we came here. But whatever it is, it's sort of a defining element of being. Our lives are either involved in expressing it or being frustrated and thwarted because we're not."

The sensation I had felt earlier was back, crawling up my insides again. Feeding on years of thwarted intentions, it had just heard its name called.

FIFTEEN

SHAPE SHIFTING

As long as I am this or that, I am not all things
— Meister Eckhart.

I felt almost sick with anxiety. The sensation in my gut came in rippling, concentric waves. In my heart, I knew this turmoil was somehow both my terror and my salvation. I struggled to my feet, trying to shake off the feeling, praying it would beat a hasty retreat. I walked in a circle in front of the cabin, feigning nonchalance for Adam's sake, but not very convincingly.

Adam lay on the ground, looking casually in my direction. "Dave," he said softly, "allow yourself to experience your feelings. Don't try to avoid them."

I stood still, embarrassed, not knowing what to do.

Suddenly, in one continuous motion, Adam rose to his feet. Now, nose to nose with me, he gazed at me intently, rubbing the whiskers on his chin reflectively. "Your problem is you don't know your Self," he said. "Would it be safe to say that you identify with your feelings? Are you aware that you're presently allowing your fear to shape who you are?"

I grudgingly nodded. I was impressed by Adam's incisiveness and annoyed at my own transparency.

"If we're going to accomplish anything, you're going to have know who are you. You don't know yourself, so you're all muddled, flip-flopping with every change in the passing scene.

"I don't understand what you're saying at all. I know who I am. I'm Dave Carey."

"Bullshit!" Adam shouted, "Dave Carey is your name. Your name doesn't shape who you're being! But who you are being shapes what you are doing. A couple of minutes ago you shifted to being your emotional state."

"I don't get what you're driving at," I protested.

Adam grabbed me by the shoulders. I tried to pull away, but his grip was strong and held me fast. I was always the more muscular, but something was making him stronger now.

"Dave, listen! Right now, finish the phrase, 'I am...' with whatever comes to mind at this moment. Quick! Finish the statement! I am..."

"...afraid!" I blurted out.

"There. In fact, you're completely at the mercy of that fear right now. You could have chosen lots of other ways to feel, but you identified with fear and closed down all other possibilities of being!

"Remember the principle, 'resistance causes persistence'? Instead of experiencing your turmoil, and allowing its energy to flow and dissolve back to nothing, you're identifying with it and trying to avoid it! There is a world of difference between observing your experience and becoming it."

Adam's hands now gripped me by my upper arms. For an instant I thought he was going to shake me; then realized he was holding me so I would calm down and not miss what he was saying.

"Dave, wake up! If you have any interest in living as a creator, if you really want to be an effective leader, you've got to know who you *really* are."

Adam released the pressure of his grip, but did not remove his hands. Now that he could see he had my attention, his tone of voice became gentler, but no less intent.

"The majority of human beings never consciously create who they are," he continued, "they never know themselves as the aware expression of Spirit, I AM THAT I AM, itself. They never know they have the power to create their experience of reality moment to moment. Instead, they adopt other people's beliefs about themselves, or just identify themselves with the mood, body sensation, or feeling of the moment.

"They're stuck in the world of Manifestation, victims of ever-changing circumstances, like pieces of cork bounced to and fro by every wave that passes by.

"And these waves, my friend, are nothing more than the different shapes and forms that the ocean of life takes on for an instant! There are all kinds of waves waiting to pick you up and carry you away: the waves of your history, your job, your family, your accomplishments and your symbols of success. You can either ride them like a master or identify with them and be churned up and tossed around.

"Remember what I say: *Anything you identify with will eventually dominate you.*"

"But I have to identify with some things it seems," I said with exasperation, "or I'll end up merely floating from one wave to another, with no center or direction."

Adam let go of my arms, took half a step back and spoke, almost in a whisper.

118

"I know it looks that way to you. But it is possible to be a particular role without being attached to it. The key is knowing your fundamental I AM Awareness. As the director and actor in the story of your life, you may have many roles to play; and with each role there are actions for you to *do* and things for you to *have*. All your parts then become an expression of your creativity — be it husband, father or COO. Each is like a costume you wear for a particular occasion. It is only when you forget that you are creating the role that you become stuck. Then it's like putting on a mask and forgetting that who you really are is faceless.

"The only real quest is the one Yeats spoke of so simply and eloquently. *'I'm looking for the face I had before the world was made.'*"

Adam put his hand on my shoulder, gently now, an old friend sharing an important truth.

"Dave, to live as a creator is to be unassailable, able to withstand both the outer forces of the world and the inner hurricanes of thoughts and emotions. So what's the solution, Dave? How do you become unassailable?"

He stopped speaking. I felt as if the entire universe was poised in suspension, awaiting my answer. I had too much respect for him, however, to rush into a perfunctory response. I knew he expected me to take his question to heart.

I turned away from him, and walked slowly behind the cabin to the shore of the lake where I sat down to think for a while. I scooped up a handful of pebbles, revisiting an old habit I'd learned as a child during all those summers at the lake, skimming one small stone and then another across the surface of the water while my mind wrestled with Adam's question. I didn't have the answer. Doubts and questions rushed through my mind in quick succession.

I'd accrued a lot of power and money over the years, more than most people ever do, but where had all that gotten me to? My job hadn't made me unassailable. My relationships were the biggest source of pain in my life. So after all, who am I, I wondered. If I'm not my job, my name, my history, my beliefs, WHO or WHAT am I? It's always seemed that I am at least my body, but Adam was saying that my body, like everything else, is just an identification too.

Everything I identified myself with had a form, a shape of some kind. Whether it was physical, emotional or mental, it was some *thing*. That's what Adam had been saying. I could see that when I identified myself as being some thing, I gave up being a creator and turned my life over to something other than my Self. I was then the effect of what I had identified myself to be. I might still be able to manipulate my world, reshape it, or move things around, but I could only react to what already existed.

Yet as mired as I was in these various forms that seemed to be me, I did sense that I was not really any of the shapes I took. I was changing my shape all the time. Moment to moment my emotional shape changed with my feelings and moods, my mental shape altered with each thought that arose, even my physical body completely replaced every atom in its structure every seven years. What I called 'me' was in flux all the time. Adam had said that even the field of energy called my life principle could be altered.

I suddenly realized, in one swift and trenchant insight, that if my shape can change, I cannot *be* any shape. I finally understood what Adam was saying. I can only be the empty field that allows shapes to appear; the power that shapes. I was *all* shapes in potential. I was no shape at all. Just as the actor is not any of the roles he plays.

In attempting to answer 'who am I,' I had gotten to what may be the most powerful place —the place called 'I don't know.' Only in the silence of that response can my original state ever be known. My mind stopped its searching. A feeling of calmness suffused my whole body. I was approaching the entrance to the first world of creation. At this place, no words can plant their roots, for the true nature exists always beyond the describable.

What was left? Nothing. No-thing. I was not a cork floating on the ocean of life, nor was I any of the forms and expressions that I had identified myself to be. *That* is what Adam kept saying to me. I am the infinite ocean itself. All those waves are but my expression. I am the first world of creation — Origination, the pure awareness of being before any form is brought into being; before any waves exist.

How could I keep this pure awareness as my resident state of being, rather than something I accidentally experienced from time to time? That's what Adam was asking. 'How do you become unassailable?' Somehow, I would have to know directly that what I call reality is an extension and expression of Spirit, that Spirit is All.

I looked out at the lake. There, in front of me, was an upside-down tree, a reflection on the water. Its solid counterpart, on the opposite shore, was a large, gnarled oak. But it was the flickering reflection that captured my fancy. It was as real and recognizable as its land-bound equivalent, but had no corporeal form. The water itself showed no trace of its presence. Yet it glowed brighter than the real tree; its form interrupted by luminous, silvery ripples.

I gazed awhile at the shimmering tree, an ephemeral offspring of the light which had fathered it, a confluence of energy and matter meeting, given form by my awareness. I looked around at my world. Maybe all of these things, my list of identities included, were like the tree in the lake, changing and flowing with the light, the tide and the wind.

Only I AM was the invisible, unchanging reality. The invisible giving birth to the visible.

The Sefiroth was an invitation to "return to my roots," my real roots in the infinite, in Origination. Then I am home, and free to create. The other three worlds of creation become my playing field, and the flow from Creation through Formation and Manifestation is uninterrupted. The world of Creation — the trunk of my Tree — is the field in which my intention to bring forth first presents itself. How did Adam say it? Spirit becoming flesh.

A deep sense of sadness washed over me. I had spent most of my life grasping for the fruit of the tree — what I called 'reality.' I had spent very little time watering the roots from which that reality had sprung.

I took the diagram from my pocket and carefully studied the six sefiroth in the world of Formation.

Passionate Commitment was very clearly the lifeblood of Formation, the wellspring of imagination and emotional expression and perseverance. *In the beginning there was the Word, and the Word was with God, and the Word was God.*

Passionate Commitment was, at its essence, a function of one's word.

Passionate Commitment was the threshold I still had to cross. Was I more passionately committed to success — looking good and staying in control — than I was to being true to my Self?

I suddenly had the sense that I'd been thinking with every part of my body — my toes, my earlobes, my gut, my elbows, even my eyelids throbbed. I began to notice that different parts of me were hot or nauseous or tingling.

I felt divided. Part of me felt liberated, while another part questioned the insights I'd discovered. My skepticism was fighting for its life.

I looked around for Adam. He was stretched out comfortably on a sunny patch of grass, looking as if he would be quite happy to lie there forever. But I guessed he had been watching me.

"You're having some trouble with this, aren't you?" he said quietly.

"I'm doing the best I can."

"I know you are. I don't question that." His tone was reassuring.

"We'll just have to shift your perception pretty soon so this isn't so tough on both of us," he said with a chuckle. He held his right hand up, his palm facing me, as if directing traffic. "Wait. Have patience, Dave. The awareness you seek is not distant from you. In fact it's closer than your breath. It's who you are. In Deuteronomy, Moses says to the people of Israel: *'IT is not hidden from you and IT is not distant. IT is not in heaven... nor is IT beyond the sea... rather IT is very near to you, in your mouth, and in your heart, that you may live IT.'*"

At these words, I choked up. I didn't know why. It made no sense. Yet, there I was on the verge of tears with no ready explanation for it. This time, I didn't resist the feeling. I allowed myself to observe it as it progressed through its form and faded away. A few moments later, I was breathing easier, with a sense that something had opened up within me.

"Remember, I'm not asking you to buy anything I say," Adam added, as we walked back to the cabin, "only that you be open to what I'm saying. Think of all these new ideas as hypotheses which have yet to be proven to your satisfaction. I know that flies in the face of the way you and I were brought up. You are going to have to be bigger than your beliefs. Are you ready to go on?"

"Yes," I answered, before my doubts could be voiced.

A shadow crossed in a pulsing ripple on the sunlit patch of grass in front of me; a rhythmic whoosh of wings beat the air. The hair on the back of my neck stood up as I sensed something bearing down on me from behind. A loud rasping call close above startled me. Instinctively, I ducked to the right. Furiously flapping wings glided past into the shadows of the trees beyond.

Then silence, except for the quick, short gasps of my breathing.

"Do you see it?" asked Adam, pointing toward a deeply shaded area about twenty feet in front of us. I could not make out what he was pointing to. Its dark form merged with the background, safe from my detection. Gradually I glimpsed a still black form against the darkness, then a strutting movement into the light.

A shiny silhouette moved in stiff, jerking steps in our direction, alternately spreading and folding its wings like a grand opera cape, opening and closing its beak, strutting across the clearing toward us. Ten feet away it stopped, tilting its head slightly from side to side. Then stone still, it stared at me with bright sharp eyes.

A crow.

With a sudden shift of its head, it rose quickly into the air, circled around us once, and flew beyond the clearing.

"A shape shifter!" Adam exclaimed delightedly. "That's synchronicity for you! For the people who used to call these woods home a few hundred years ago, the crow was the guardian of the essential principles that design the universe."

"Why was it called a shape shifter?" I asked.

"Because it symbolized the ancient wisdom that said nothing in the universe was actually static or solid. Sound familiar? The crow represented the ability to create new realities, inwardly and outwardly."

Suddenly, Adam's face took on the wide-eyed, goofy-grinned look I remembered from our high school days when he was about to play the joker.

He began to poke my arm playfully with his index finger to make sure I was paying attention to his next point. "Creating new realities! That's what an effective leader does, isn't it, Dave?"

He took a step back and turned on his right heel in a counter-clockwise circle, his arms stretched wide, reaching upward. "Shape shifting! This could be our leit motif! Our theme!" He took his hat off and flung it into the air, catching it again as it came down in an almost perfect, spinning ellipse.

"The dynamic of The Tree of Life is the same as shape shifting isn't it?" I added.

"Yes, the eleven sefiroth — that's shape shifting, all right — bringing something forth from the infinite to the finite, from the formless to form. And it's all there in the first story in 'Genesis'! The same idea: the power to create something from nothing, to bring forth form from the formless."

Even though I'd known the stories from the book of Genesis for most of my life, I'd missed the very heart of them. "It's so easy to miss the shape shifting element when you listen to these texts only as myths or stories, and not for the deeper meaning," I said.

Adam nodded emphatically in agreement. "There's a reason these stories are still around. Take the Greek myths," he said. "Zeus is the consummate shape shifter! He takes the form of a swan, a cloud or rain to unite with a mortal woman who gives birth to a child — Spirit uniting with form to father a new creation imbued with both godliness and humanity. It's the transmutation of energy into matter.

"But people are not consciously aware that their emotional, mental and spiritual landscapes are shifting all the time, though unconsciously they can be very sensitive to the changes. Have you ever said to someone, 'You seem to be in great shape,' or conversely, 'You look like you're in terrible shape?'"

I saw what he meant. Somehow we can sense a mood or emotional state of another person, but we're not so aware of each little factor. We sum them up as an overall 'shape.'

"Maybe the reason we talk so much about shape is that we live in a culture that has an aversion to the abstract and tries to make everything concrete," I suggested.

"The mind can't grasp the idea of shapelessness," Adam offered. "If we speak about shifting shapes, it gives the mind something to latch onto. It can understand transition, evolution, even transformation. But...no static shapes at all in the universe?...everything in a constant flow? That's almost impossible for the mind to grasp. Yet it's absolutely true. We live in a shape shifting universe.

"What we call a solid form is a perceptual 'snapshot' taken from our narrow point of view that seems to capture the energy flow as a frozen moment in time and space. Consider a building, for example. It starts out as a collection of materials that may originally be spread all over the world: lumber from Oregon, marble from Italy, tile from Portugal. Then these are gradually gathered together and the structure emerges over several weeks or months until finally it becomes a house. After that the finishing touches are put on, it's filled with furniture and people move around inside it, fiddling with the details so that the house becomes a home. After a long time its existence comes to an end. Maybe it burns down, blows up, rots or is demolished. In any case, the materials that made it up are now scattered again; turned into junk, smoke, and dust. If you operate on a large enough time scale, all you ever see is the flow of beginning, middle and end, over and over again reorganizing into different shapes and forms of reality. Nothing is ever static or concrete, and nothing holds its shape for more than a fleeting instant.

"The truth is, the range of available shapes is infinite. We've got this palette of emotional colors, of physical expressions, of mental constructs, all potentially available to us. But each of us samples very little of that potential, because we get stuck identifying ourselves with a particular shape, believing that's who we are. 'I'm a very serious person,' we might say, or 'I'm just not a city person.' Then we are stuck in our own dim assessment, thinking that it is static and 'the truth.' We don't give ourselves permission to shift shapes. We have no room to experience anybody else's point of view. Why?"

"We're afraid we'll lose who we are?" I offered.

"Of course. We're afraid we'll be co-opted and lose our identity as an individual."

I remembered an argument I'd recently had with Janet. I couldn't even remember what it was about. I'd been vehemently defending some position or other when it had suddenly occurred to me that what I was saying was nonsense. At that point it would have been honorable to stop and say, "You know, I just realized that I'm mistaken."

But I couldn't do that. Even though continuing the argument was infantile, I kept going with the lie. Why? Passionate commitment in the service of the wrong master. I had been willing to inflict more damage to our relationship in order to avoid giving in to my wife. I'd been willing to kill off love in order not to look like a fool. I had thrown away a chance to be authentic and generous, insisting instead on defending a reality that I already knew in my heart to be wrong. What a waste of a life!

"A creator is not concerned with being co-opted," I said quietly to Adam. "He knows that there are an infinite number of life forms, all energy in motion, and they are all expressions of Spirit."

Adam nodded. "Now you're getting it."

124

SIXTEEN

THE GRACE OF DISCERNMENT

The ignorant reject what they see,
not what they think;
the wise reject what they think,
not what they see.
— Huang-po

"You know Dave, I've been thinking. Our work here can't be all talk. It's got to be experiential, if it's going to matter at all." Then he shook his head, correcting himself. "Even that's not good enough. It's got to be trans-formational. I'm not interested in having you leave here a few days from now with merely some added information or a nice experience that will wear off in a couple of weeks. What we're after is a state change in your being. Under-stand?"

I nodded, though I had no idea what he had in mind. The prospect seemed daunting.

"Our work together has to be tailored for you, not something generic," he added.

"Don't we have that already?" I asked, puzzled. "I thought you were going to teach me The Genesis Principle."

"Yes, but what are the most powerful ways for you to get at that princi-ple?"

He was silent, his arms crossed over his chest, his head slightly bowed, as though listening for something. Thirty seconds elapsed, then a minute. Puzzled, I watched him. Then it occurred to me that he was waiting for the answer to come to him.

His face lit up and he suddenly looked satisfied. He smiled to himself, his eyelids half closed, nodding his head slightly as though he were listening to some whispered instructions. Then he grunted, opened his eyes, and gave me a big, mischievous grin.

"All right, what is it?" I asked, with an equal mixture of anticipation and trepidation. "Am I going to like this?"

He ignored my second question, as though the matter of liking it was profoundly irrelevant.

"Can you think of a time when you experienced yourself as creative and effective?" he asked.

I nodded.

"Allow yourself right now to close your eyes and recall that state. Observe what your body sensations are, what your emotions and feelings are, and what your thoughts are when you are in that creative state."

I took a couple of minutes to do as Adam requested, immersing myself in the memory of such a creative moment. Then he asked me to come up with a word that could trigger that state whenever I wanted to be creative. I picked the obvious, the word 'create', practiced it as he instructed me to do and then opened my eyes.

"We're going to be trying some experiments together and each time we try something, I want you to put yourself in this state before we begin. Understand?"

"Yes."

"There is *Grace* and there is *Discernment*," he continued. "Both these sefiroth are a function of your Field of Being. We can't really experiment too much with Grace right now. First of all, Grace is not something that you *do*; it is something you are open to receive."

"Like when you noticed the staircase in that book store you told me about, and knew to go up there."

"Right. If you're not open to it, you may not even recognize it when it does occur. Endurers, for instance, are rarely aware of the Grace in their lives, unless it hits them on the head. Strivers are usually too busy trying to make Grace happen to notice when it does arrive. A large part of creating is trust, letting things unfold rather than forcing them. Grace isn't one of those experiences you can force.

"And the flow is not one way, either. You can receive to the extent that you are open to give. Grace is a deep appreciation of the creative unfolding of Infinite Source, not a strategy for grasping spiritual and material blessings. To be open, to express loving-kindness, to be unconditionally accepting and inclusive of others and open to the gifts of Spirit in each moment — these are the hallmarks of one who lives with Grace.

"When we trust in Grace we become sensitive to synchronicities and the flow of new possibilities that are often unexpected, unpredictable, and even miraculous. Since Grace flows from the origins of your being, your life principle has a lot to do with the kinds of possibilities that can come down the cosmic chute."

"So, it's intuitive, you just know when you've met with an act of Grace. Is that what you're saying?"

"Yes. Often Grace comes in a symbolic form."

"The way Einstein experienced himself riding on a beam of light?"

"You've got the idea," he said. "How an answer comes is less important than that it comes. In certain cultures it might be expressed as a totemic animal or plant; in others a magical or mathematical symbol."

"That crow's sudden appearance, would you say that was an act of Grace?"

"That's yours to answer," Adam shot back.

I paused, undecided.

Adam continued. "And Grace can also be expressed as an insight, a thought, a body sensation, a vision, or something someone says. It could appear as a line in a book or just a knowing. In the bookshop, a book was the perfect vehicle for Grace. We're in the woods now, and I trust in Spirit; it's very inventive, far more capable than you and I at showing you what you need to know, if you're open to seeing."

"Then this intuitive way of knowing isn't a limitation. It's not something rigid."

"Right. What's important is that you be open to what you need to experience."

"Well, one thing is certain," I mused, "this is a new wrinkle on the art of information gathering. What do I do to tune into this intuitive capacity?"

"Nothing. That is, there's nothing to do. I know that I've already told you how I open up to my intuitive sense, but don't get stuck with any techniques. How you are *being* is what's important. Trust. Give up all doubt and be willing to receive with reverence, anticipation and appreciation for whatever insight appears. Expectations only muddy the connection. As much as possible, let go of all your mental chatter and stay present and aware. This kind of thing needs to be simple. There's nothing to figure out.

"Trust Spirit to give you what you need in just the right amount. Of course, what your conscious mind thinks you can deal with and what you can actually deal with may not be the same," he added with a mischievous grin, immediately removing the blanket of comfort I was beginning to wrap around myself.

Trust Spirit, Adam had said. Maybe it was time for me to actually do that.

"Grace is the flow of abundance and possibility," Adam continued. "Discernment is the mental mold into which Grace flows."

"What do you mean by mental mold? Is it our perception of reality?"

"No, perception comes later, but Discernment does determine what you can and cannot perceive. It provides the boundaries, parameters and priorities by which Grace is observed, organized and takes form."

"I don't quite get it yet," I said, pursing my lips. "I thought I understood from you that my life principle organizes my reality."

"You're accurate," Adam replied patiently, "but the way your reality begins to arrange itself in the world of Formation is a function of Discernment."

"Maybe I'm just dense, but..."

Adam shook his head and waved his hand back and forth as if wiping a sentence from a chalkboard. "You're not dense. You're legitimately struggling to understand an aspect of creating that most people are unaware of. It's like learning a new language.

"Perhaps an analogy would help. Let's use film making as a metaphor. Let's say, 'I am a film director' is my life principle. From there, all kinds of ideas and possibilities for expressing myself in the world begin to flow. What sorts them out? Discernment. As more and more I experience being a film director, the world appears before me as an expression of a filmmaker's vocabulary, a vocabulary that precedes and gives rise to my perceptions, a vocabulary of storytelling, drama, light, sound and visual design. I begin to finely discern the unfolding world as the source of my material, and discover all kinds of things I can use in my films. I start noticing the dramatic and powerful ways that human emotions expose themselves. I begin to see how universal meaning can be revealed in small, particular moments. I become aware of the emotional effects of light and shade, of color and sound. I begin to discern the subtleties of these elements with more and more sensitivity. My art discerns my reality, determining not only what I can and cannot perceive, but how I perceive it.

"Now it could be said that a film has a life principle too, and each film's Life Principle is a specific theme which runs like an invisible spine through the center of each particular film, be it comedy or tragedy. It's the field in which the plot, the characters, their motivations and their lines are going to be developed and organized."

"Adam, I need an example."

"Sure. Let's say the producer says, 'Let's make a war movie.' Now that may sound like it's pretty specific and limiting, but it isn't. The producer puts out a call for a war story and receives two radically different treatments on his desk the following morning. One is called 'The Heroic Patriot.' The other is titled 'All War is Insane.' Both are war stories, but with vastly different themes. Because they start with different premises — different life principles

— their subsequent steps will be organized in quite different directions."

"Let me see if I can add the next part," I said, connecting now with where he was going. "Then Grace is the flow of ideas and expression that begins to occur once the theme or Life Principle of the film is determined."

"Good. And then what?" Adam asked.

He waited patiently as I worked this out for myself. "Discernment must be what selects those ideas and possibilities that seem most consistent with the theme or Life Principle, and it downplays, ignores or discards those that are not."

"You got it!" said Adam, slapping me on the shoulder. "Discernment is like the director of the film, and one with all the talent and genius of an Orson Welles, where you have director, lighting designer, set designer and editor all rolled into one. Discernment's job is to operate consistently with the integrity of the theme, to create a reality based on that intention.

"You could have the same set of elements and circumstances as someone else, yet the way you discern the world will be distinct, because your life principle, the underlying theme, will shape and determine how those circumstances and elements are organized."

The more I thought about Discernment, the more I could see how it was always in complete harmony with the life principle. I thought about a colleague at work, whose life principle was probably something like: "Don't ever trust anyone." No matter what the circumstances around him, he seemed to be attuned only to catching the mistakes, the negative comments, and the suspicious expressions. When we'd come out of a meeting, I'd be flabbergasted by the wide gap between his assessment of what had happened and mine. I couldn't understand how our worlds could be so different. Now I knew. His inner director discerned his dark world with dim, narrow spotlights focused only on things he would then afterwards interpret as insufficient or injurious — real or imagined. I, in contrast, seemed to be able to view life with a few more "lights on," able to be aware of possibilities and successes that never appeared in his world. I realized my perception was given by what I could discern, not the other way around. In other words, it was Grace that enabled me to see life in a more positive way, and Discernment that filled in the details, so I could convince myself that life was, at least occasionally, a positive experience.

"Adam, it seems as if I put on some sort of a filter that evaluates everything that happens and accepts those things which fit into the mold of life as the kind of Grace I have experienced allows me to see it. Is this an aspect of Discernment?

"It depends on what you mean when you say 'evaluate.' If you mean judging, no, judging relative values is irrelevant in the Sefiroth. Discernment itself is free of value judgments like good and bad, right and wrong. But remember, the parameters it forms to shape reality are in harmony with your life principle. If, like most people, your life principle is one you are unconscious of and are operating from by default, it may contain judgments that color your discernment. But good and bad, right and wrong, true and false, profitable and costly, those comparisons are the tools of your ego, your identity, which tends to evaluate everything from its own point of view.

"True observation is not based on value comparisons. If you identify yourself as your essence — your I AM Awareness — your life principle is a self expression instead of your identity's reaction to the circumstances of life. Then you'll find that you have the freedom, when discerning, to be the non-attached witness or observer of what is appearing, able to accept and embrace whatever presents itself, with nothing added, taken away or resisted. You then will also know that the way you discern the world is one of an infinite number of possibilities."

"All right, I think I understand that," I replied. "If I'm comparing something to something else or to some standard I have, I may not see what it is as itself. You know, I do have the tendency to judge things quickly and label them as this way or that. But that sets up a dichotomy, doesn't it — an 'either/or' contrast, right?"

"Yes. And if you get stuck in dichotomy, it blocks the natural flow from Discernment into the next sefira, which is *Resonance*. If you and I are busy judging and evaluating everything as good and bad, right and wrong based on our beliefs and identities, we cut off one of the most profound experiences that Discernment allows for when it is in the service of I AM — the ability to resonate with another, to experience true understanding and compassion for what is shaping another's reality, no matter how distorted or lost from its Source that reality may seem to be.

"Real life situations are very seldom so black or white as our egos would have us believe. Good or bad, right or wrong, believable or unbelievable, sensible or nonsense — if you reduce situations to such simple comparisons, you miss a lot of subtleties and potential opportunities."

"Still," I said, "there have to be some rights and wrongs in the world."

Adam slowly cocked his head to the side, and squinted at me as if examining a specimen under a microscope. "Which world would that be?" he said.

"What do you mean?" I asked, confused by his response.

"You just said, 'there have to be some rights and wrongs in the world,' and I'm asking you, what world are you speaking of?"

I threw up my hands in bewilderment. "What am I missing?"

"Okay, okay," he chuckled. "I'll lay it out for you. Remember, there are four worlds of creation."

"Right. ...So?"

"Well, when you say, 'there have to be some rights and wrongs in the world,' you're only looking out from the world of Manifestation where people quickly judge things as right and wrong. That's too narrow a view. You're forgetting about the other three worlds of creation, where right and wrong do *not* exist. That limited view make's it impossible to live as a creator. That same confusion has caused so much suffering throughout history in the name of doing 'right' and punishing 'wrong.'"

"But if we didn't know right from wrong we would live in anarchy and chaos," I protested.

"Nonsense! The really dangerous folks are the ones who are absolutely certain how everyone ought to behave. Most of the horror inflicted in the 20th century was *not* done by people who had no sense of right and wrong. That is a profoundly mistaken notion. Most of the atrocities were carried out by people with a very strong sense of what was right and what was wrong, but who had no sense of Grace, loving kindness or compassion! I'd much rather deal with someone who wasn't so sure of right and wrong but who honestly investigated the best thing to do — the course that naturally worked best for everyone. There are ways of being that transcend the right and wrong distinctions from which most people live."

Adam was quiet for moment, patiently waiting for me to digest what he had said.

"Dave, do you know the Gospel story where Jesus stops a crowd from stoning a woman caught in adultery?"

"Sure."

"Well, Jesus's defense of that woman — in that day and age — was nothing short of revolutionary! The woman had broken one of the most important laws of the time. She was 'wrong', and according to that law it was 'right' to stone her to death. In fact, it was demanded! But Jesus took a stand for wisdom, grace, love and compassion. He transcended right and wrong and acted from the first three worlds of creation, not merely from the fourth world's moral judgments."

An insight glowed to life in me. "You know 'The Golden Rule' — 'Love thy neighbor as thyself'?

"Sure.

Well maybe that isn't a rule at all," I said. "Maybe it's a principle that transcends yet includes the realm of morals and judgments."

"And it's only got true power when you know who you are beyond your

131

personality, identity and history," Adam added. "'Right and wrong' exists in the domain of Identity and in the world of Manifestation — the world of dichotomy. While 'right' and 'wrong' are valid interpretations in the physical world, true transformation and healing is only possible when dichotomy is transcended."

I thought of history's great peacemakers who were able to put aside their differences to go forward into healing. I remembered my impression of Nelson Mandela when I saw him on television soon after his release from imprisonment. I was struck by his smile, which was not only in his mouth but in his eyes as well. It seemed to well up from the depths of his heart, resonating in his voice, and filling his every gesture. Somehow, the horror and tragedy of *apartheid* and of his own 29 years of imprisonment had not left him bitter and vengeful. On stepping into freedom, he had left behind all his prisons — his actual physical bondage and all inner prisons of self-pity and vengeance. He did not come out obsessed with being "right" about how "wronged" he'd been. Instead, he was living from a place beyond right and wrong, good and bad. He had wisdom and understanding of the fears that had driven his jailers — they who had wished to harden his heart as they had hardened their own. Perhaps his real war had been waged within himself — to not allow his spirit to be turned to dull, cold stone like those of his captors. He had the power to forgive, to heal, and to build a new future for his whole country.

The thought of this forgiving person made me question myself. If I could so easily wallow in self-pity when I thought about my marriage, if my soul could so quickly fill with resentment of Henderson, what would I have become had I been given a life of house arrest to bear? Perhaps Nelson Mandela was a practical example of Grace in action — of loving kindness expressing itself through humanity in the face of any circumstances. Maybe that is where we ultimately are tested. Even if we persevere physically, and "triumph over our enemies," what kind of victory do we gain if we become what we have conquered? What do we win if we lose our Selves in the process?

"I'm beginning to realize something else about Grace," I told Adam. "I've been thinking of Grace as merely some sort of mysterious cosmic chute that opens suddenly from time to time, down which all sorts of wonderful things fall into my life, and when they do, I call myself lucky or blessed. At those times, it's easy for me to think of life as an act of creating. But other times — when I'm not feeling particularly lucky or blessed — I behave as if there is no Grace in my life, and that who I am is nothing more than my identity, my story, my emotional state and my body. Then the thrust of my life is simple; to finally get myself to a place where nothing will ever trouble me again — a safe harbor. My strategy to accomplish this has been to become successful, rich, well liked, and appreciated. At best, I've held Grace as those moments of flow, inspiration or synchronicity that have helped me to arrive closer to my safe harbor.

"What I'm beginning to sense now is that what I've called Grace is only one half of the equation, as if I've only been describing the yang of it, and never noticed its yin side. This is the part where Discernment comes in, I guess."

Adam was clearly intrigued. "Go on, go on," he urged.

"If Grace is a gift of Spirit, is it only present when I get what I think I want? Does it only manifest itself when things go well, and the circumstances are to my liking? Maybe that's merely Grace 101."

"What do you mean?"

"You know the phrase, 'grace under fire'? What is that pointing to? Maybe that's the real test of Grace."

Adam nodded appreciatively and added, "Maybe we can only truly know Grace when we've moved beyond connecting it with good and bad, right and wrong, fair and unfair, and instead, see it as an expression of Spirit that is senior to the circumstances. That is always the biggest stumbling block for anyone who is trying to understand Grace. Ever read the Book of Job? It deals with this issue pretty powerfully. Here's a story about a human being whose life is just humming along; who is a good man; who honors his Creator, and all of a sudden his whole world is destroyed. And it seems capricious, arbitrary, unfair. He doesn't deserve this! His wealth, his possessions are stripped from him, his health fails, and hardest of all, he loses his family. The Book of Job is a problem for those who think that Grace has something to do with getting an insurance policy against tragedy or disaster. It's as if they believe the only purpose of life is to earn bonus rewards for good behavior! What does that tell you about our relationship with Spirit? Ever notice that when we're knocked off our keisters by a tornado, hurricane, earthquake, tidal wave or other natural disaster, it's called 'an act of God'?"

Adam tilted up the brim of his hat and arched his body backwards, allowing the sunlight to dance across his bare brow. He crinkled his eyes into slits, and laughed a deep throated staccato laugh spiked with irony.

"How come the stories of so many authentic spiritual transformations happen in 'the dark night of the Soul?'" he continued. "Job keeps being tested. Tested by what? For what? At some point in your life, that's the question you'll have to deal with Dave."

Like a soft breath in my ear, I heard again the phrase that had caressed my soul some nights before.

133

"...though I walk through the Valley of the Shadow of Death, I will fear no evil..."

What was evil? Perhaps it was too easy to lay it all on the sometimes brutal circumstances we are confronted with in our lives. Maybe evil doesn't just refer to some outside force that comes upon us. Maybe it's we who find the evil in our circumstances. If the carpenter from Nazareth wasn't kidding, if he was really onto something when he said that the Kingdom of Heaven is within me, then denying that I am an expression of the Creative Spirit is the ultimate in self-imposed darkness. Maybe it's evil when I harden my heart to Spirit simply because I perceive that things are not going my way. Maybe I discern evil when I act like a victim of circumstances, and give up all possibility to create a new relationship with the circumstances.

Maybe it was as Adam said. Maybe Job is all of us when our greatest fears come to pass. Then who are we?

Perhaps when I find within myself the capacity to stay open and to love even in the darkest times, that is Grace in action. Would I continue to reach out, to look for possibility, to be true to I AM when my world is collapsing around me? Would I have the courage and strength to stay open to Grace — if I were losing all that I held most precious in the world?

This inner inquiry was suddenly taking me to a place I didn't want to go. I tried to short-circuit the images that were forming in my mind: losing my job, destitution, becoming incapacitated — being paralyzed and trapped in the prison of my own body. I knew there were things that could happen to me that would harden psychic scabs on my heart, which I'd probably pick at over and over again, so they might never heal. When circumstances crushed my expectations for the future, when I received no satisfactory answer to my desperate cry of "why?", when I turned myself to stone to dull the ache in my heart, when I found myself wanting to shake my fist at God — then would I be able to stay open to Grace and hear the voice of Spirit speaking to me from out of the whirlwind as Job did?

With a trembling voice, I expressed my gravest doubts to Adam.

"Perhaps the true test of Grace is the ability to discern yourself as I AM Awareness in any situation," he said, "to actually embody the miracle of creation arising over and over again from the ashes of your burned out dreams, still going on, still giving and receiving love."

"That may be the biggest miracle of all," I agreed, "to have my losses in life become the pathway for my transformation to something else. That is something I've yet to embrace."

"Dave, a way to think about Grace is to look back over your own life and ask yourself, 'What things have happened to me that I would very much like to be able to go back and change?' If you are not in a state of Grace, you may rail against your lot for having suffered some of these things. If you are in a state of Grace, you will reflect that everything that was taken from you provided some sort of opportunity for growth that has made you the richer for it. You would never have willingly sought or asked for some of the things that have happened to you, but their end result has, in the long run, come out all right. This is because the Grace in your life allows you to discern meaning in what has happened in such a way that you feel in collaboration with God, or the universe, as far as your life is concerned.

"If you try to judge your own experiences when they happen, you will fail, since you cannot know how you will perceive them at a later point in time. Discernment is the awareness of something without judgment. You can't say that it's bad. But, then, neither can you say that it's good. You can only say that *it is*.

"That doesn't mean, though, that you can't reflect upon a situation in more practical ways that will guide you in how to proceed with your life. There's nothing wrong in asking if something is workable, unworkable, profitable, unprofitable, or otherwise useful in a practical sense. In fact, these are the kind of questions that as an executive you damn well better be asking. However, there's a limit to what you can learn from them. They're very useful in one context, but they can obscure your effectiveness in another."

"I think I see why that is," I replied. "I can't resolve the dichotomy — decide if something is good or bad — unless I refer to the past, to either my own personal experience, or to some conventional wisdom that says 'this is the way things are.'"

"Yes, and that's true in your personal life and in business too. It's fine to refer to the past if your business is merely carrying on a tradition, doing things the same way they've always been done," Adam interjected. "The problem is, things are changing so fast that none of the old rules seem to apply anymore. Now most people in your business think they know that, don't they?"

"Yes, they do."

"Yet, because they are not aware that the way they perceive the world is one of identity-based comparison, they are unconsciously trapped using the past to determine their present and their future."

"I'll admit we often cut off serious consideration of new ideas prematurely because we insist on knowing how the new ideas will be accomplished before any further discussion is tolerated," I said. "If a person can't immediately answer the question, 'How will you do that?' their idea will be nixed — it's as good as dead. Since no one wants to be in this position, many new ideas don't make it to the table. What we forget is that we have competitors, and if our competitors are good at listening for new possibilities... Ouch!"

"You're not going to foster innovation by having to square new proposals with the past," Adam added. "But that's what happens when you have rigid ideas about what's true and not true. In that case, do you know what your main game in life becomes? Being right about your view of the world. Then the rest of humanity is out of luck. They either have to come around to see it your way, or, depending on your identity and inclination, you have to dismiss them, pity them, reject them, or in extreme cases, eliminate them. Haven't you done some of that with Janet, with people at work, and even with yourself?"

Part of me was relieved that Adam's last question was rhetorical.

"Oh, and there is one other piece to that comparison game that I almost forgot to mention," he added. "When we do judge and evaluate others, we are usually damn self-righteous about it! Of course, if we want to disguise our self-righteousness, we can throw in a little guilt so no one will notice!

"So, Discernment, in the service of I AM, doesn't operate by the rules of the comparison game?" I said.

"Not at all. Discernment is not a function of identity or ego, but of the Self's intention. It's another game entirely — a game of creation. There are many ways to experience the world, and you needn't invalidate another's reality. In fact, quite the opposite. When freely discerning, you don't identify any view as 'the truth;' instead you appreciate the multiplicity of possible realities."

"But how can you organize what you discern and experience if you're not comparing?"

"You don't organize what you discern and experience. It organizes you," he laughed. "The life principle shapes what you discern and experience. Ultimately, it's all an expression of Awareness. Sometimes you're conscious of it and sometimes you're not. Either way your I AM Awareness is always operating. The majority of people are asleep to what is running their lives and live from deep-seated, unconscious intentions that shape who they are much more than what they consciously say they are up to.

"You want proof? Check out the statistics on the success of most people's New Year's resolutions. A disaster! And remember, if you can drive your car home and not even remember doing it because you were so in your head with fantasies, you know that you can be unconscious yet aware at the same time."

I laughed. I'd driven that way too often to count.

"And if you want more proof, notice how well all the organs and cells of

136

your body are doing at keeping things going and communicating with each other without much conscious awareness from you. Whether you're conscious of it or not, your Self is aware at a fundamental level."

"But are you implying I have no choice about how and what I discern?" I asked.

"Not exactly, but close," he chuckled. "At the dimension of Discernment, what you get to choose is to embrace and be present to what you are discerning."

"I have no power to alter what I discern?" I was worried now.

"I didn't say that. You have to go one level up in the Tree of Life for that leverage. When you become aware of your life principle, and you can embrace it as your own creation, then you have the choice to create it newly. If your life principle shifts, what you discern shifts also. That is what allows you to create and select those possibilities that are consistent with who you are, and to ignore those that are not. What you discern is always in harmony with your intention and life principle. You could say that Discernment itself is an act of Grace from the life principle.

"I'm still not sure that I understand," I persisted.

"When a composer creates a piece of music," he responded patiently, "if he's any good, he is not trying to copy someone else or measure up to other composers, or even to his own past works. That's an ego function, not a creative function. A composer's power to discern is shaped by his intention to express new possibilities. From there, he chooses.

For example, Mozart is supposed to have said, 'I do not know where this music comes from.' He may not actually have written the letter in which he is supposed to have stated this, but the basic idea is one all artists are familiar with. As you work on a piece of art (whether it's music, painting, literature or anything else) the work begins to take on its own life and seems to be creating itself. You feel as if you're just putting down what comes to you without your awareness of where it comes from. Even in the secondary arts, like interpretation, this is true. Leonard Bernstein, for example, said that as he conducted a piece of music he felt as if he had composed it himself, which meant that the music came out of his own sense of being, not someone else's.

"In this state of Discernment, the creator and what is created become one. The sense of 'I am making this happen' dissolves and the creator feels that he or she is witness to the thing creating itself. Mozart, for example, could write down a piece of music while engaged in other activities, since the music was already complete in his head as if it had been put there by someone else. All he had to do was write it down. Walter Piston, when asked by a colleague how his symphony was coming along once said, 'It's almost done. All that's missing is the notes.'

"If Grace gave Mozart his music, Discernment gave him the form it took. He made the decision about what instruments and themes to use, but the genius that we value, the ability to shape something that we find breathtakingly beautiful, was done in some way that he himself could not understand and that no one else can replicate exactly.

"All of life can be like this, though it seldom is. You can have the sense of your direction in life and then come very close to watching yourself unfolding all that happens in it as if you were observing a movie in which it was all happening to someone else.

The whole personality is so united with itself that there is nothing blocking contact with the purity of the Self. Then the ego disappears and everything flows so perfectly that there is no sense of an individual working against something else. In a sense, the whole universe is cooperating with itself at that moment and during that experience."

"So then," I replied, "there really is no choice at all. It just happens. At least, that's how you make it sound."

"On the contrary, choice is essential. But choice is not always made consciously. Suppose, for example, you have a choice, when you are standing in front of the teller at a bank. You could reach in, pick up the stack of bills that's sitting there within your reach, and run from the bank. Or you could just continue making the deposit you are there to make. That's a choice, but not a conscious one, because even though it's obvious you could take the money, it's so against your nature to do so that you will not perceive it as a choice, and will simply go about your business as planned. Most of life is lived in this way, making choices that do not appear to be choices at all. Yet if you did not make them, almost moment by moment, you could not proceed with your life at all.

"So in writing a piece of music, the composer must make choices.

In the process, the notes he leaves out of the composition are as important as the notes he puts in. If all notes are left in, you have chaos. Grace without Discernment, without limitations and choices, devolves into confusion and disorder. Discernment without Grace turns into rigidity and predictability. Grace and Discernment balance and complement each other. When that occurs, Discernment allows for both simplicity and elegance. It selects and defines the shape that both your inner and outer reality can take to have integrity with your life principle. In a sense, Discernment guards the integrity of your life principle."

The guardian of integrity. I laughed at the image that sprang to mind.

"What's so amusing?"

"Nothing really, I just thought of something funny. Did you ever see the Kurasawa film, *Yojimbo*? When you mentioned integrity, that's what I thought of, Toshiro Mifune as the ronin samurai. I can still see him — walking down the dusty street, a warrior who could tell the phony from the genuine, the one person who was not impressed by rank or station, only by authenticity — the guardian of integrity, rubbing his whiskers, scratching his neck, his mouth partly open, his eyes piercing."

"Very good, Dave! Very good!" exclaimed Adam, much amused. "It's perfect, you know. In the Kabbalah, Discernment is often represented by a chariot or a warrior, ready to defend its lord's domain. The lord in this case is Origination — I AM THAT I AM.

SEVENTEEN

DISCERNMENT 101

There is no longer any need to believe, when one sees the truth.
— Al-Alawi

"Now, it's time to get started on our experiments! I want you to trigger your creative state the same way you did it before. Let me know when you've done that."

Adam had me sit in a relaxed position on a large log, with my arms and legs uncrossed. Then he paused while I brought forth the experience "I AM a creator" for myself. When I was ready, I signaled him with a nod of my head.

"Dave, we're going to begin with a very simple experiment in discerning different states in your body. A creator can be aware of any of his internal states and shift those states at will. As much as you may resist that statement, it's been proven in biofeedback laboratories as well as in yoga ashrams. In fact, we'll demonstrate this together."

As a reference point, Adam had me take my pulse. Then he asked me to close my eyes. "This is a simple exercise in shifting awareness and relaxation throughout your body," he said.

He had me take three deep breaths and feel my body relax as I did so. Then, starting with the top of my head, he led me through the different parts of my body, asking me to place my awareness in each part he mentioned, while letting that part relax.

I was surprised at how easily my awareness was able to shift from place to place, and how just the intention to relax each muscle group seemed sufficient. I was aware of my heart beat, sensations in other parts of my body, and warm and cool feelings as I journeyed through my body with my awareness, sensing its inner and outer shape. Finally, he had me slowly become aware again of sitting on the log near the cabin and told me to open my eyes.

"Take your pulse," he said. I was surprised and impressed. It was fifteen beats slower than before we began.

"Discernment is also good for your health," he said, grinning. "As you can see, it's not difficult to move your awareness to different locations in your

140

body. As you practice, you'll become aware of more and more subtleties at the different levels. Notice that you not only shifted from one shape to another with your observation, but you also altered the physical reality with nothing more than your awareness. When is the last time you ever consciously lowered your heart rate and relaxed your muscles with your awareness alone?"

"I've never done that before."

"That's our first experiment in shifting levels of awareness," he said. "It's basic Discernment 101. A creator can shift levels, depths and states without getting attached or identifying with any specific state. When you can shape shift, the question of who or what you are is not fixed or static."

We stopped for a lunch of cold cuts washed down with ale and followed that with a thirty minute walk to stretch our legs and clear our minds for the next step. By this time I knew that I was after the big prize: to get my hands around what it took to be a creator, a shape shifter.

Adam laid out our immediate plans in a few sentences.

"In your first experiment, Dave, you opened up your ability to discern your inner world. In the next experiment, you're going to expand your awareness of your outer world."

My first reaction was mild surprise. I didn't think that I had much to learn in that department.

"Pick up something in your fingers," Adam said, "and look at it."

I shrugged, then pulled up a blade of grass. A little soil clung to its roots.

"What do you see?"

"A blade of grass."

"That's not what you see, that's what you *think*," he said. "That's the name you give it. What do you *see*?"

This was hard. I wasn't sure exactly what he meant. "Okay, it's green."

"What else do you see?"

There we were, back in high school, me in front of the class. Could I do any better this time?

"I've often speculated," I said, "on whether there's any relationship between the green I think I see and the green you think you see. I mean, suppose I could put on your brain and look through your eyes. Might I see something so different from what I'm used to that I wouldn't recognize it?"

"Okay, okay," said Adam. "look at what you just did."

"What I just did?"

"I asked you what you saw, and you started exploring a possible relationship between my awareness and your awareness."

"What are you getting at?"

"You looked at the blade of grass — just an ordinary blade of grass — and you launched into a tangential, irrelevant discussion. But now we want to inquire into your direct experience."

He held the blade of grass up in front of my eyes. "You're blind and don't know it. This object in my hand can only be known by letting go of your associated mental musings, and seeing it directly."

I began to reply, but Adam put his index finger on his lips, requesting silence.

"Okay, now you're going to get a lesson in Discernment," he said, handing me his sketch pad and a pen. "And the first thing we're going to do is let you shift your perception of the world from conceptual generalities to direct experiences."

"What the hell does that mean?" I asked.

"In simple terms, it means that in the future, when you are in a meeting with employees or clients, or when you are at home with your wife, instead of perceiving them mainly through your ideas about them, which are all past-based, you will be able to experience them directly in the moment. That will allow you to relate to *what is* instead of the way you think it *should be*. This is an exercise in getting you out of your head."

"Why didn't you say so in the first place?" I replied with a smirk.

"Well, you wouldn't have understood me and then I would have had to say all that other stuff afterwards. Okay, you're right-handed, correct?"

"Yes."

"Okay, see that birch tree over there? I want you to make a drawing of it."

"Adam I've already told you..."

"Yes, I know, you can't draw a straight line. Great, no problem. I'm going to take a walk and you draw it, and let me know when you are through."

I uttered an expletive under my breath and began the assignment.

"I'm done," I called out ten minutes later. I was displeased with my attempt, as I expected I would be.

Adam came back and looked at my handiwork. It resembled something a proficient first grader might draw. The trunk was two straight lines with a bush of sticks on top.

"It doesn't resemble that tree in any way," said Adam matter-of-factly.

"I told you I can't draw," I said defensively.

"Your problem isn't that you can't draw," said Adam. "Your problem is that you don't look and you don't see. You drew some schema in your head that you learned when you were in first grade. You didn't experience the tree in front of you."

"Well I don't see the relevance of this to..."

"This isn't about a tree, Dave," Adam interrupted. "It's about your relationships, whether with Henderson or Janet or anybody else. And it starts with you finding out that you rarely experience anyone or anything directly."

"That's a bit harsh, don't you think?"

"Maybe, maybe not. I told you we were going to play hardball, so I want to know, are you going to allow me to coach you? All I'm asking is that you follow the instructions I give you and see what you get with no presupposition, with no long explanations for why we are doing it."

"I just want to understand all aspects of it before proceeding. Is that asking too much?"

"Do you want me to explain the meal to you instead of letting you taste it?" he asked with a laugh. "Just taste it! Then the explanations will be irrelevant. If you don't want to do that, hey, we can just hang out the rest of the afternoon and I'll drive back to the city this evening."

It was my turn to laugh. I knew I was being difficult, but it was hard to let him just control everything.

"Okay, Adam, let's start from scratch."

"Good man. Now let's look at that tree. When you were drawing, how much time do you think you actually spent looking at the tree?"

"Well, uh, I don't know."

"I'd like you to consider the possibility that it was very little time."

"On what basis?"

"Well, I'm sure you looked up and saw there was a tree there. But how much time did you spend looking at the tree?"

"Well, the majority of time, I guess, I was looking at the pad."

"Were you really seeing the tree?"

"Well I thought I was."

"Okay, let's test it out. See that lowest limb on the right? The one that twists up and then down again with a slight curve at the end?"

"Uh, yes."

"Good, where is that on your tree?"

"Well...."

"And how about that other one? See the one on the left? The one that forks in two? I don't see that one on your tree."

"Well I told you, I can't draw. Is there a tune I can put this to?"

"And I'm saying drawing is not the problem. Dave, it's not possible to draw the tree if you don't experience the tree. To draw the tree, you have to be over there where the roots are, over there where the bark is, over there where the leaves twist and turn. You have to feel all of that."

143

"You're making this sound positively sensual."

"It is. To draw something is to see it, and to see it is to be in communion with it. It is actually being in non-verbal communication with the tree. If you can do that with a tree, you might even be able to do it with the people you spend time with and hopefully care about."

"Okay Mr. Smartass, how do I do this? I'll take your word for it for the moment that it's not that I can't draw — though I'm absolutely convinced I can't — it is simply that I can't see, and I'll withhold judgment on that as much as I can. So what do I do?"

"I thought you'd never ask. I'm going to ask you to do a contour drawing of that tree, and the way to do that is very simple. First, pick up the pencil in your left hand."

"But I'm right handed."

"I know that. I was watching you draw as I came back from my walk and I noticed that what your hand did bore no relationship to what your eye did. It is as if your right hand has a life of its own, it knows what to do, it doesn't wait patiently for your sight to direct it."

I picked up the pencil in my left hand. "It feels awkward."

"Yes, it doesn't have an automatic way of operating. It will wait to be guided by your eyes and your conscious awareness. What I'm asking you to do is very simple. I want you to allow your left hand and pencil to be nothing more than an extension of your eyes. I want you to get the idea that they are fused to your eyes and as your eyes move, the pencil moves. If you see what is in front of you accurately, the pencil will move accordingly.

"Pick a starting point on the tree. Now decide where to start on the paper and place the point of your pencil there."

"Okay, I've done that."

"Good. Now, look up at the tree again. That's right. Now from this point on you do not look at the pencil or your paper again until the experiment is over."

"What?"

"You heard me. You don't get to check out how you're doing. Just totally surrender to the movement of your eye and record it accurately. Got that?"

"I... I think so."

"Go ahead, do it."

I began slowly. I found that if my eye moved too quickly, my hand would not keep up. Gradually, I fell into a certain pace that allowed for the complete coordination of eye and hand. My attention was entirely focused on the tree. I had no thoughts of myself. The experience was both visual and kinesthetic. I was acutely aware of the color, the tones, and the shapes of the

144

branches, twigs and leaves, as my eyes moved along and caressed their boundaries. It was as if I was physically touching what I was looking at. There was no sense of division or separation in space. It was as though I was at the tree and in the point of that pencil simultaneously. I experienced more internal silence during this experiment than I ever had in my few attempts at standard meditation practices. At some point — I had no sense of time as I did the experiment — I heard Adam walk up close to me. I saw his shadow on the paper and he said, in a quiet voice, "Okay, stop."

I took my time releasing my gaze from the contour it had clung to so tenaciously.

"Now look down at your drawing," said Adam.

When I looked down, I had two responses. The first was a critical evaluation. I could see places where the line was shorter than what I imagined it should be, or where the contour of one limb moved across and intersected another branch prematurely. At the same time, I was stunned by the sensitivity of the drawing. For there, from my own hand, delicate twigs branched off from the main limb. The limbs curved, the leaves were visible. What was in front of me was a representation of that tree. Not the schema of a tree, not some general tree, but an experience.

"Well?" asked Adam.

"That's pretty amazing," I said with a mixture of surprise and delight. "First of all, it actually resembles that tree limb. Second, I realize that I never even saw the tree the first time. I was, as you said, in my head. Third, I don't think I've ever experienced so much awareness of the structure of a tree. I almost want to say 'treeness.' I actually experienced being over there where the tree is." I laughed. "You know, this is the first time I've ever been intimate with a tree.

"I've very rarely given this kind of attention to other people," I confessed, "though it's not that I've never done it. When I first meet someone, I think I experience them directly. But in pretty short order I've got them pigeonholed. To be honest with you, I don't know if I've ever gone for this many continuous minutes without having an opinion about what was happening. It's so easy for me to make everything mean something, to do a mental riff about it, rather than fully experiencing things as they are."

I had a sudden urge to touch the tree. I got up and slowly walked toward it. I put my left hand out and touched the bark, then ran my hand across the tree limb. I turned and smiled at Adam. "This feels just like I knew it would."

"Yes, to see something fully is not just a visual experience. When we use the term, 'I see what you mean,' it includes the integration of all the senses."

"You know," I acknowledged, "if I put as much intention into my looking and listening as I do into my speaking, I might experience the world a whole new way. I had the experience of being the tree. I suspect that this may be the only way one ever really knows another person or thing."

"Yes," said Adam. "This isn't a drawing exercise, as much as it is an awareness exercise."

Adam's words rang true. In drawing the tree, my intention had allowed me to perceive the tree in a way I never had before. I had stopped identifying with my persona and had allowed myself to identify with the tree itself. Intention and Being. Maybe true understanding and wisdom is possible only in the domain of Being.

"Maybe what I've called being awake is actually being asleep," I said ruefully.

"Now pick up a blade of grass again," Adam said. "Don't say what it is like, or what it reminds you of, or your preconceived notions about leaves. Let go of your internal commentator. Don't just look this time. See it! Take your time."

I looked at the blade of grass. As I concentrated, I became aware of textures, creases, striations on its surface. I was aware of its temperature and smell in my hand. What I had called "green" a moment before revealed itself as a range of hues: tones of greens, purples, browns and yellow. Maybe Monet did something similar to this when he looked at a cathedral or a pond of water lilies.

I described what I saw, fully aware that even my more detailed verbal description barely scratched the surface of its amazing form.

"What we have to do is plumb the depths, turn what we don't know into what we know," Adam said. "That's the creative response to change. Change looks like chaotic flow until we give it meaning, and we can always give it meaning.

"In our interactions with the outside world, we are able to take chaos and turn it into fields and patterns and flows of meaning and substance. When a mind looks at it, the meaning emerges from the background and is distinguished. It's a function of our minds to create stability even where there is none. Or perhaps because without it, there is none. Nothing around us means anything until we bring it into focus and attend to it. That's the role of the observer in quantum mechanics, the observer who "causes" a probability wave in an electron to collapse and the electron to define itself. And that's my role as an artist looking at the world. My job is to distinguish elements from the background so others can see them, recognize them and learn what they didn't know, and didn't know they didn't know. I create images that thereby become known for the first time."

He was silent for some minutes.

"Congratulations," he said finally, "you've passed the first part of this experiment."

"The first part? There's more?"

"Here's where we see if you can translate what you just experienced to the practical level. It's too good an opportunity to miss. How do these perceptual experiences apply to your work?"

I gave this some thought. All sorts of applications occurred to me. I realized that the way I minimized the differences between people was to *know about* them, to label and categorize them. The way to maximize the differences and celebrate the diversity of experience is to *know* them.

"*Knowing about* someone or something is easier than *knowing* them," I said. "In order to *know about* something I gather the relevant facts from the past and analyze and sort them into a logical, consistent pattern. But *knowing* requires an openness on my part to each moment's experience and a suspension of judgment from past-based beliefs.

"Adam, if I understand the implications of the experiment I just did, it looks to me that when I can resist the seduction of living in a pre-concluded world, then it's literally possible to see the world newly and differently every time I look at it.

"*Knowing* gives the power to distinguish the magic unfolding before me. *Knowing about*, on the other hand, is an act of control. It reduces things to their lowest common denominator, and I end up associating things in a general, schematic way, like saying, 'This is a maple leaf. It looks like the picture of the maple leaf in the book. It has certain characteristics of leaves that I've studied in biology.'"

I stood up and paced back and forth with excitement, gesticulating as I spoke. "*Knowing* doesn't reject conceptual knowledge, but it goes beyond it. It means seeing the leaf with the eye of an artist, who knows that this particular leaf has never occurred before in the history of the universe and will never come again. *Knowing* sees things in the leaf that are unique to a particular moment of observation. This doesn't mean that you have to see everything about the leaf, but that you are open to receive whatever that moment has to give."

I *knew about* my wife and children, but I did not know them. In some way, they were abstractions to me. They were the wife and children a respectable corporate man is "supposed" to have. I got married because, once I fell in love, it was the "right" thing to do. I had brought up my children in the "right" ways.

To do everything the way you're supposed to is ultimately to fail.

147

Inevitably, the rule books fall short and fail to describe what's really true. And in this way I was failing my family. But, if I could succeed in knowing a tree, maybe I could do the same thing with Janet, Sarah, and Stephen. Maybe I could even know myself.

EIGHTEEN

HAT TRICKS

Become seeing, seeing, seeing!
— *Rumi*

"Are you ready to try something else?" Adam asked.

"Sure. A creator is always ready for something new, right?"

"Right," Adam said, seeming a bit aloof in his response.

He tore some paper into narrow strips and wrote on several of them. Then he put the notes into his hat and stirred them around.

Next he had me stand in front of the tree I'd just drawn, part of a small grove in front of the cabin, surrounded by underbrush and rocks.

"In this experiment you'll see the relationship between Discernment and intention," he announced with a flourish.

"You're going to reach into the hat, pick one of the notes, read what it says and then take a good long look at what's in front of you. I want you to describe what's out there from the point of view suggested on the paper."

"Okay. I'm game."

Putting the hat between us, he situated himself among the trees so as to be part of my view. "First, before we deal with the hat, I want you to look up here and tell me what you observe."

I described the scene in great detail without any self-consciousness, pointing out the individual trees, their shapes and colors, the sky, Adam, everything I could take in. It all happened so easily. I had a sense of being a conduit for all the features around me. There was no need to insert myself in the process or search for things to say. Afterward, I was feeling very pleased with the job I'd done. My comfort and enjoyment during the exercise were eye-opening; the number and subtlety of details I'd described were pretty impressive, I thought.

"Okay," said Adam. "We'll use that dry run as the control group."

Adam's evident lack of enthusiasm for my performance disappointed me, but I took it in stride, realizing I should have learned by now not to try to predict his reactions.

"Okay, let's open this up a little," he suggested. "I want you to pick a slip from the little hat there and imagine yourself in the position of whatever type of person is named in writing. I want you to be that person. Then describe the scene before you from that person's point of view."

I drew out one of the slips. "Oh, shit!" I groaned. It said "fashion designer."

I spread my hands with a helpless glance at Adam.

"Just be it!" Adam said, his hand extended to stop me, like a traffic cop.

"I don't know where to begin."

"You don't have to know anything. Just do it."

I looked at the scene in front of me, forcing myself to be aware of Adam's clothes in much greater detail than I had paid attention to the last time I looked. I described the patterns and fabrics, the drape of the cloth, the aesthetics of styling. I used technical terms and jargon that I'd hardly been aware I knew, terms I'd picked up from who knows where — probably TV. At first I was kidding around, so it was kind of fun. It was damned weird, though. After a while it took no effort at all. It seemed as if the intention to be a fashion designer was in some mysterious way shaping my perception. When I paused for a breath Adam gave me a slightly approving nod and pointed to the hat.

I pulled out a second note, which read "botanist." This time the plants that a moment before had been nothing more than a blurred background took center stage. I was aware of shapes and colors in the leaves, textures of bark, the relationships of various plants to each other, the spacing and stacking of foliage to maximize light filtration. I noted signs of insect damage, darkened patches in the leaves caused by nesting or feeding parasites.

I chose another slip of paper, then another. Each new persona I drew from the hat became my way of being for the time, as my perceptions metamorphosed from perspective to perspective. Each time I assumed a new persona I felt a new set of attitudes. I was amazed at the ease with which I did this. I had always assumed that attitudes were accumulated through experience, bitter or otherwise; but I was discovering to my amazement that I could, if I wished, select them for myself, like helpings from a dinner buffet. Whatever I was for the moment I committed myself to, so that anything irrelevant to that way of being was subsumed in the background, folded into the undifferentiated noise of the scene.

When I pulled out a slip with "entomologist" on it, all manner of bugs, and other creatures swarmed to the forefront of this ever-changing tapestry that shifted its color, design and texture on the fulcrum of a word. I noted over twenty specimens in my immediate view. I exulted in the vitality of the insect world, their sheer numbers, their vigorous activity. They wore their bones on the outside of their bodies, giving them incredible strength. They were an engineering miracle that I had to admire.

Despite having first sided with the populace of the plant world as a botanist, and subsequently with their friends and enemies in the insect world, my inconstancy harbored no contradiction for me. We may pity the mouse that is stalked by the cat, but the cat and the mouse are partnered in an age-old bargain, for neither could exist without the other. An equilibrium of numbers assured that both could survive. So, in the greater scheme of things, it was all right. I was struck by the way I was suddenly sensing how it all fit together. I was surprised by this ability to see things in so many different ways, and I wondered how it could have developed so quickly. Then I reflected that I had done this very thing all my life, but had never been conscious of it before. Whenever I read a book I became the main character, whether a pirate, or a little girl, or the president of a large corporation. When I saw a film or heard of a news event, the same thing happened.

It didn't happen, though, in real life, when I felt myself in conflict with someone else. Then this flexibility to grasp others' points of view would shut down and I would become rooted in my own small mind, unable to glimpse even the smallest glimmer through the eyes of my opponent.

The key was to have a larger mind, a grand mind. Each view was a self-contained reality with its own internal logic. When I was stuck in any one view, the others seemed distant, irrelevant. But when I experienced life as a creator, rather than as a fixed position or identity, I had the freedom to shift the focus of my discernment and allow reality to take a shape consistent with that shift.

It struck me that if I could learn to live all the time with this much flexibility, there'd be no end to the possibilities and relationships I could give birth to in my life.

After ten or so dips into the hat, I was finally down to the last slip of paper. I read it and smiled, because what it asked me to do I had already done — at least to a certain extent. I had anticipated Adam, had done the assignment before it was given to me. "Ecologist" the paper said.

Yet I was to learn even more about the ecologist's point of view than I had already noticed, for my perception now was not at all what it had been before. As a botanist I had ventured beyond the call enough to sense interactions, symbioses, inter-species communications. Now, however, there was no such specificity. The word ecology was too abstract for that, it demanded a larger scale.

Sunlight, smells, a gentle wind from the south, the experience of interlacing, moving energy in an integrated union of astonishing complexity, and I was immersed in it all. Imperceptibly, like a championship sports car smoothly shifting gears, my awareness expanded. I felt as if I were seeing with new eyes. I experienced the world dancing and changing before me as a play of consciousness, a flow of energy unfolding into structure and then folding back into energy. In that moment, the universe seemed to be shimmering forms of light and dark that were not random, but expressions of a design I could not pretend to fathom. And it was complete and whole and perfect, and always had been.

Only my awareness of this transience had been insufficient. Everything in the universe seemed in a state of vibration. I stood up and walked around the clearing, luxuriating in these new sensations. I extended my arms as far as they would reach, while drawing the air deeply into my lungs. I felt transcendental and transcendent and ventured to take in the whole of it.

I'd been describing my observations out loud with each change of character, but I hadn't really been aware of Adam for quite a while. Suddenly against the soothing sound of rustling leaves I heard jarring, exaggerated applause. Adam was clapping in a drawn-out rhythm and sardonically shouting, "Bravo! Bravo!" It startled me. And the slow realization that he was actually mocking me left me confused.

"What's wrong?" I asked. "What did I do?"

"Oh, not much. You just disgust me, Dave," he said, point blank.

Disgust! I swallowed hard. He couldn't have shocked me more if he had punched me in the stomach.

"I don't understand. What did I do?" I asked, shamefacedly.

"You're a phony. I asked you to describe this simple and genuine place and all you could manage was fakery." He shoved his face right up to mine and shouted at me, "You have to be authentic, Dave," and he just stood there glaring.

I was even more shocked. I felt the hot flush of insistent emotions rising to my face: bewilderment, humiliation, and finally the sting of injustice. I had not, as he'd accused me, been faking it. I didn't know how I had come across — at the time I hadn't been thinking about my performance — but my feelings had been real and deeply reverent. I knew that with every ounce of my being. So what was with Adam? I wondered about him. Was he so shallow that he couldn't sense the spirit of this place, couldn't see that I had been genuine? I felt nothing but contempt for him. And finally, I became angry, so angry my body seized up, until finally I could do nothing but vent my anger.

"How dare you!" I exploded. "You don't know anything about me! You had no right to mock me! You're the phony here. You must be really shallow... and... and... vapid... and... shallow." I couldn't get the words out and kept repeating myself. All the energy in my body was channeled to my rigid limbs, which were just aching to strike him.

Adam moved away in silence, and with unstudied nonchalance he walked down to the lake and calmly sat down. I followed him fuming, continuing the harangue, more frustrated and less coherent with every passing minute. I kept calling him a fatuous asshole and whatever else I could think to say.

"Hey Asshole, I'm talking to you!" I shouted, banging my fist on a nearby tree. "Answer me!" Who do you think you are?" I demanded.

"Wow!" Adam said. "Did you see that?" He stood up to gain a better view of the water.

"Answer me," I shouted.

"Look, there it is again," he said excitedly. The look on his face took me aback. He was goofily grinning and completely happy about whatever was going on out there on the lake. The effect drained some of the energy from my anger.

"Dave, get a grip on yourself and come look at this," he called to me.

With great difficulty, I peeled my eyes off Adam and looked over to the lake. A magnificent osprey, successful at his game, was majestically winging toward the mountain, a large bass dangling limply from his talons.

"You don't see that every day," Adam said joyfully. "I've been watching it fish for quite a while now," he laughed.

"And what have you been doing?" he teased, turning in my direction and grinning mischievously.

And then I felt really stupid, and Adam knew it. He looked me in the eyes sympathetically to make sure I was okay.

"I was yanking your chain, Dave. But you didn't even realize that. I set up the trap and you fell right into it. It was way too easy."

He paused to let that sink in.

"You need greater mastery of your emotions," he said kindly. "You can't discern anything clearly when you've lost yourself in an emotional storm. You didn't read anything in the situation correctly. Any third party watching us would have known in a minute that I was putting you on. But you were so caught up in your anger, you couldn't see a thing. And what was all that anger about? Absolutely nothing. A minute before the storm, you were in the throes of pastoral ecstasy. What happened? Nothing. I said something. That's all. And what I said wasn't even true. And you must have known it wasn't true.

"Actually, you were great during the exercise. I've never seen anyone do it better. You should have known I was lying, that I was setting you up. You should have been able to discern that much."

I felt like an idiot and apologized to Adam.

"Forget it," he said. "Let's banish embarrassment here. Okay? It's over. Besides, it was my responsibility, I knew you were gonna lose it."

"Losing it, losing my Self, that's the problem, isn't it," I reflected, chagrined, "like the cork floating back and forth on the waves," I recalled. "I identified with the anger and it took over. We've already talked about emotions, but obviously I still don't know how to control them, or even how to think about them."

I was drained from all the shouting, getting worked up, as it had turned out, over nothing. What a contrast to the brilliant day that surrounded me. I'd been so caught up with my own emotional state that, even though I had given my surroundings an almost microscopic examination, I hadn't let myself be drawn into this idyllic scene. Damn Adam and his tricks, anyway!

"All right, let's talk about it," said Adam, "let's say you get up in the morning on the wrong side of the bed. Everything seems to go badly for you. Are you just going to let that happen, let external events determine how the day is going to unfold for you?"

"That's what usually happens."

"Have you ever tried anything else?"

"No."

"Why not?"

"I've always assumed that's just the way things are."

"Well, it isn't," said Adam. "You can feel any way you want to. All you have to do is learn to shift your emotional state."

"Well, then, show me."

"You got pretty pissed off at me, didn't you?"

"Yes."

"Why?"

"You insulted me, accused me of something that wasn't true."

"Why did you let me?"

"I didn't let you. You just did it."

"No, you let me. You could have told me I was mistaken. You could have stayed in the euphoric mood you were in. I don't have that much control over you. You let me deeply affect you in a way you didn't like. Do you let everyone push you around like that, taking seriously any comment that happens to come your way, whether it makes any sense or not? What determines when you make the decision on your own about how things are going to be understood?"

I was taken aback by this. It sounded like pop-psychology to me, nothing real. Still, on some level, I supposed, I had made the decision to be angry. But in another way I hadn't.

"It seems to me," I told him, "that emotions are not such conscious acts. You can't simply will yourself not to be emotional, like deciding not to watch TV, or not to slouch anymore. Emotions are stronger than that."

"I'm not suggesting you be unemotional," he countered. "Who would want to live in a world without emotions? What a flat, dull existence that would be — a kind of hell. No! Emotions are wonderful! But do you have your emotions or do they have you? What if your emotions are making you blind? Making you hurt your wife? Your children? Silencing your colleagues and staff?"

I got the point and nodded slowly in agreement.

"Emotions are a real problem if you can't be non-attached from them," he continued. "So *have* the emotions, but don't *be* them."

"Practically speaking, what does that mean?" I asked.

"It means that the full range of human emotions is available to you at any moment and you don't have to stick with any particular feeling. You can choose however you wish to feel."

"Well I certainly can't summon up feelings and emotions all by myself with no reason, no stimulus."

"How were you feeling as an ecologist before I interrupted you?" Adam asked.

I tried to get back to what that was like. I couldn't at first, but then it began to come back to me. After all, nothing real had happened to get me all bent out of shape. Adam had just been playing with my mind. I had been enjoying the beauties of nature and I ought to have been able to do it again.

I tried and sure enough, I was soon feeling once again the joy of my surroundings. Once again I was sensing the interwoven patterns of nature. I started to describe this, but he put his hand up to stop me.

"You told me you couldn't do this," he said.

"What?"

"You told me you couldn't decide to feel something and then actually feel it."

"All I did was go back to what I had been feeling earlier."

"Don't you see? That's exactly the point. You can always go back to some earlier feeling and recreate it for yourself. Any feeling that you've ever had you can have again, summoning it up at will. As Stanislavsky, the great Russian actor trainer, used to say, if you've ever wanted to kill a fly, you can express the fury of Othello about to strangle Desdemona."

155

"I can see that," I said. "I can imagine that might be true. It would certainly take a lot of practice, though."

"Oh, not much practice," said Adam. "You remember how angry you were a few minutes ago?"

"Yes," I laughed. "That was pretty stupid, wasn't it."

"Anger is usually stupid. But not always. It's not stupid to get angry about child abuse, or rape, but it is stupid to get angry if someone looks at you the wrong way."

I had to spend some time with that one. What he seemed to be telling me was that all my life I'd had choices about how to feel and hadn't known it.

How could this be?

I looked up at the sky. It was blue. It was a perfect day. Adam seemed to be telling me that I could use the sky as a cue for a feeling. I could put aside whatever I might be feeling at the moment and just look at the sky and imagine feeling some sort of elation. Then I would actually feel it.

There was some great truth here, but I didn't quite have it yet. Whenever I'd been really angry about something, I'd always felt supremely rational, as if defending the temple of reason against the contrary forces of delusion. That's how I usually reacted to opposition. I could very easily dismiss Janet as illogical, Henderson as a madman. In a state of anger I was absolutely certain that my position was the only possible one to have.

Could I really learn how to just step out of that kind of anger and see the other person's point of view? If I could, it would make the most incredible difference, because then I'd be able to do what I was always pretending to do — not be angry.

But how could one learn to do this? I asked Adam about it.

"Did you ever have the same tune playing over and over in your head until it drove you crazy, and still it wouldn't go away?" he asked.

"Of course," I nodded.

"Emotions can do the same thing, particularly negative ones. What happens is that your mind creates a series of circuits functioning as feedback loops. The more you try to stop feeling that way, the more intense the feeling becomes. You get angrier and angrier as you recycle the same thoughts over and over again."

"So what can a person do about it?"

"In the case of the tune, you can usually get it to go away if you sing a few other songs."

"That's true," I thought.

"The same is true of emotions. If you can get your attention off what's caught in a feedback loop and start to feel something else for a while, the original feeling will dissolve. That's why a mother will offer a new toy to her crying child. Get your attention off the emotion, and sometimes it will go away."

"That's kind of a Band-Aid approach," I said.

"You're right," said Adam. "But if you can learn to regard the world from a number of different points of view, you can also learn to shift your emotions at will, going from a negative to a positive fairly quickly. When you find a new way to understand an upsetting situation, a more appropriate emotional response will naturally arise. But as you point out, these are intermediate measures to take. They require a certain effort.

"Then.... of course, there is the way of the Creator. It is the way of nondoing, of no effort... the way of mastery," he said quietly.

"What is that?" I asked, my curiosity at full throttle.

"You'll understand it more fully later as you experience other aspects of the Tree of Life, but for now, I will say only this: when you're fully aware of your emotions — when you can discern them and embrace them completely from I AM, with no resistance — they dissolve. Do you understand what I'm saying? You don't need to cover your experience over with an emotional band-aid, you don't need to avoid it, deflect it or change it in any way. When you experience being Awareness itself, you have the capacity and power to shift your emotional state from *something* back to *nothing*; from form back to energy.

Then, from nothing you can create newly in the next moment.

"But how...." I began.

"Patience," he said firmly, "all in good time. For now, let's practice creating some emotions. See if you can call them up at will. I'll name an emotion and you try to feel that way, right now, right here among these surroundings. All you have to do to experience a particular emotion is remember a time when you actually felt that way, and then go to town on how that emotion feels to you right now. You should be able to do this experiment just fine."

Adam's first suggestion was 'cynicism.'

"That's an odd choice," I said skeptically.

"Why?"

"Because in order to really do this experiment, I have to be completely earnest, don't I?"

"That would help," he said.

"You expect me to be earnest and cynical at the same time?"

"That's pretty close to cynical. Now get on with it," he said, sighing in mock exasperation.

I collected my thoughts, trying to recall what it felt like to be cynical. I remembered our meeting in the museum. I'd had plenty of moments of cynicism in that conversation. I took a breath and began.

"There's Adam, standing before a grove of trees waiting for me to respond. What does he think I am, some laboratory rat he can play with to test out his weird theories? Does he really think I am stupid enough to submit to this voodoo — hook, line and sinker? Sure, it's interesting, but — give me a break — this stuff has about as much practical use as a discussion of how the eventual landing of UFOs might affect Wall Street.

"And even if these exercises do work, they will just wear off eventually, leaving me right back where I started. Nothing's really worked before, why should I believe him? I'm wasting my time, so I might as well drive home right now.

"This guy is nothing but a con man, and I'm sick of him. I'm so fed up with everything, the way everyone's out to con you and make you vulnerable to their lies and schemes!

"Look at him standing there so self-satisfied and smug, thinking he has all the answers! Look at that asshole. He can't even help laughing at me while I vent my spleen at him!"

Adam was still laughing when I finished.

"You did very well," he said. "You spoke of what you saw from a cynical perspective very well indeed."

He had me practice several different emotions. Fear juxtaposed with elation, compassion butted up against embarrassment. I practiced silliness and envy and sadness and apathy. I did so awkwardly at first, for the feeling itself was often embarrassing — not that I was afraid to express it in front of Adam. Oddly enough, some of these feelings I was terrified to express to myself.

This experiment was more difficult than the earlier exercise with the hat. I found it much more of a challenge to feel like myself as I tried on different emotions. This exercise threatened me more deeply than the other. In entertaining an emotion that I habitually rejected, I felt a kind of disloyalty to my own emotional history. It was a little like moving into a commune after occupying a penthouse condominium for a couple of decades. I couldn't get through this one just by changing my point of view.

Then I realized that this very reaction showed I was beginning to control my feelings. For the first time in my life I could toy with an emotion and actually turn it into a real experience. At first it seemed unreal and real at the same time. It seemed unreal because it was not a reaction to anything in particular, but real because I felt the way I would have felt if some real event had caused me to feel that way. It was weird, a sort of double vision, and I found I could objectively watch myself feeling something, knowing what I was feeling and at the

158

same time remaining aware that I could change the feeling any time I wanted to.

This must be how great actors do it, I thought. There they are in front of a director and a whole lot of other people, and they have to feel something really personal and be objective about it at the same time, ready to change it for a different feeling at a word from the director.

Then I noticed something else that made me aware of a facet of emotion I'd never thought about before. Different feelings were associated with different visceral sensations. Fear always came with a knot in my stomach, embarrassment with a hot sensation in my face.

I realized that these visceral sensations were not symptoms or effects of the emotion. The emotion and the physical sensation arose together. I tried focusing on the knot in my stomach, and sure enough, I instantly felt a flood of fear. Then I focused on my face and tried to sense the hot prickly feeling and slight loss of muscular control you get when you're embarrassed, and embarrassment was the immediate result. It was odd, because the embarrassment wasn't attached to anything. I was embarrassed about absolutely nothing whatsoever.

I thought back to what Adam had done that had made me so angry. He had not respected my integrity. That was it. I'd had a genuinely reverent experience that was important to me, and he had made fun of it.

Somewhere in me there was a sense that I was not being listened to, not respected. So I had felt in a certain way as if I'd been fragmented, and that I had to defend myself.

The more I thought about it, the more I realized that the way I'd responded to Adam's slight was not new; it was an old, familiar pattern. I'd reacted exactly that way in the past whenever I felt that I was misunderstood in some way. I could see a track of similar scenarios reaching far back into my past. I realized that at some time in the past, I must have learned to associate certain feelings with certain situations, and that I had developed a set of stimulus-response reactions, put together unconsciously and unwittingly over time, that were triggered when something in my present circumstances reminded me in any way of one of those past situations. If what Adam had said about dissolving my experience by embracing it was accurate, it might be possible for me to reorganize my inner wiring so that the same situations would arouse in me completely different feelings.

I wanted to ask Adam about this, but was afraid to. Something very deep in me wanted out, and yet I felt if it ever did come out, I would die. I couldn't risk it at that point. Not at all.

So instead I became theoretical, almost academic, to protect myself from what I really wanted to ask.

"One thing troubles me," I confessed. "I found it much easier to slip into the negative emotions than the positive ones. I had to struggle with 'joy' and 'enthusiasm.' Something within me seemed to want to suppress those more expansive states."

"Interesting observation," he replied, nodding his head. But he said nothing more.

"Is the point of this exercise to learn to experience positive emotional states and avoid negative or constricting ones?" I ventured.

"Absolutely NOT!" Adam replied vehemently. "That's more of the same comparison crap of good and bad, right and wrong! Now you're going to have good and bad feelings! Give me a break! You still don't get it! I'm not offering you a right way of being, I'm offering you the *freedom to be!*

"Well, it just seems to me that some emotional states are better than others..."

"I know you do! That's the problem!"

Suddenly, he lowered his voice.

"Dave, that's like saying there are certain colors on a painter's palette that are better than others, and we should only use the right colors! Well, to be a creator is to have the freedom to play with the full spectrum of experiences. The emotions themselves are not the problem. You're only in trouble when you identify yourself as any of them."

"I think I understand," I said. "So, you're saying that I should just vent whatever emotion is there?"

"No, no, not that either. Dramatizing doesn't equal experiencing. That's just more identification. When you can embrace the whole range of expression, you actually end up with joy as the baseline. By giving yourself permission to feel whatever you are feeling, you stop feeling bad about feeling bad. Let the emotion carry you into some new realization. Once you do that, once you just go with whatever emotion you're experiencing, you'll begin to trust the process of *being* itself. There's nothing bad that can happen, only a set of experiences, which have whatever meaning you can find in them. You are free from having to be a certain way, and can be true to I AM at each moment."

Adam put his hat back on and moved a half step closer to me.

"Here is the most important aspect of all of this. If I can't tolerate something in myself, I can't tolerate it in anyone else. But if I have compassion for my own humanity I have room to embrace the humanity of others. And let's face it, humanity exhibits some pretty disagreeable traits now and then. I may not like some of those traits, but I can understand them deeply. Sometimes you can really help people, just by being there for them, because they know

160

you understand what they're going through. But if I'm too busy avoiding those feelings in myself, all that will be left for me to do is try to make others deny their own experience. I will say stupid and useless things like, 'There, there, it will be all right', and 'Don't be sad' or 'Big boys don't cry'."

Adam stepped back, his arms outstretched, his legs spread apart. He tilted his head upward as if toward some imaginary spotlight. "Ladeeees and Gen-tle-men! Presenting, for your diminished enjoyment and personal enslavement, the most deadening, 'one size-fits-all' phrase ever uttered in the resistance causes persistence follies of humankind! Please join me in welcoming — straight from its world tour — the infamous, life-annihilating phrase, 'DON'T FEEL THAT WAY!'"

A chill went through me. How many times had I said that to Janet, to my children, to my staff?

Adam stopped and slowly shook his head from side to side. "I'll also be unable to tolerate your joy, if I can't allow that experience for myself. The first freedom is to be able to acknowledge what's so. Everything else is built from there."

Adam's gaze drifted upward for a moment and then alighted back on me. He obviously had something in mind. "I want you to create one more emotion," he declared.

I hesitated, reluctant to take up the suggestion and feeling disgruntled about it, though there was no logical reason to feel this way. I followed his advice, however, and didn't resist the feeling of resistance, allowing it to flow through me. He waited patiently for me to agree.

"How bad could this be?" I thought, and then said, "All right what emotion do you want me to do?"

"Love," he said.

At the word, my chest tightened up. I suddenly shut down, as though something was running through my body in a panic, flipping all the 'off' switches in my nervous system. My mind seemed duller, grayer and more confused.

"I... I... don't think I can do this," I stammered. I was perplexed and bewildered by my reaction.

"Relax. I think we just hit pay dirt, Dave. I know you can experience love. I watched you become an ecologist an hour or so ago. That was love you described, and you responded to it in the world around you. But do you notice what happens when I ask you to create the experience of love itself? It is as though you're paralyzed. What does that tell you?"

"That there's something wrong with me?" I ventured, still confused.

"No, no, wrong answer! There is nothing wrong with you. You are not

161

the problem. The problem is your life principle. It can't tolerate 'love.' For some reason, that's too threatening."

"Why was I able to create the other emotions without too much problem?"

"For some reason your default principle allowed you to, but this love business set off the survival alarms."

"I guess I failed the last part of the experiment," I said, in danger of slipping into self-pity.

He gripped my shoulder and grinned.

"On the contrary! You can't mess the experiment up; it simply reveals what is present or missing. Believe it or not, this is good news! It means we're on the scent of what's suppressing your Self-expression. Now remember, I've known you for a lot of years, and you're going to have to trust me on this one when I say I've observed that you are a guy who does love people, but your ability to express love freely is pretty shut down."

"I know that," I said, staring at my shoes, unable to look him in the face.

He moved in closer. "And more than that," he continued, "your ability to love yourself and allow other people to express love for you, is even more shut down."

I reacted violently to this suggestion, backing away from him in anger, my right arm swinging in a wide arc to free my shoulder from his grip. In that instant, something within me truly hated Adam. But there was something else too. I felt split in two; angry, yet at the same time detached from the drama.

Adam looked at me intently. "Good. Very good," he said, "you are holding onto your awareness even though you're threatened. You are beginning to separate your original Self from your identity and default principle."

"What the hell is going on?" I asked, as much bewildered by my ambivalence as by my anger.

"Your life principle is panicking. We may not know its name yet, but all your reactions are expressing it. Remember, whatever it is, you've considered it to be yourself. It has shaped your fundamental point of view about everything. It also thinks that it's you. It doesn't know any other you but itself."

I stood facing him with my arms crossed, protecting myself. But from what? What was I upset about? At first I thought it was with Adam. Then I realized that the sensations I was feeling were the ones that visited me whenever I felt out of control. I was afraid, afraid that what Adam was saying might be so, and that I would always fail to experience love. Then where would I be?

It was much safer to ignore love.

Adam was facing me, no more than two feet away. He placed his hands firmly and gently on my shoulders, then looked at me for a moment. When he spoke, his words went directly to my heart.

"Dave, this is the most practical conversation we could be having, and it is the absence of this conversation in life that has you feeling there is no way out. If you can't create a new reality, you'll be left by default with a reactive life at all levels: a reactive family, a reactive organization and a reactive society."

"I don't want that," I said, my voice choking.

"I know you don't. But that is all your default life principle can give you. To be a creator is to know — not know about, but know — that the way the world appears is not a function of a fixed objective reality on which you are reporting. You can transform your life principle. After all, you were its author in the first place, even if you don't yet recall that.

"Someone once said 'God is Love.' Give some thought to what would be true if that's actually so. Not love as the greeting card sentiment, but the real thing. What if the awareness of love begins with acceptance and inclusion? What if you could unconditionally accept the world and everyone in it, warts and all?"

He paused and seemed to look not at me but into me, his eyes penetrating my being in a way that ought to have made me feel uncomfortable, but this time did not. And in a flash I realized why. Adam was looking into me with the very love he was talking about.

"Remember, everyone has got to include yourself," he added gently.

Then the mood shifted as he stepped back a couple of feet.

"Do you know what one of the dictionary definitions for Grace is?" he asked, regarding the landscape as if searching for the definition there.

"It says that Grace is 'the unmerited love of God toward man.'

"Do you understand the power of that? Love is not a merit award. It's not meted out by a heavenly scribe tallying up the debits and credits on a ledger sheet of your earthly deeds. Whether I like you or not is a function of my identity's calculations about you, but love is not a function of identity, it's an expression of Self. Love is not something that is deserved. It's an unconditional gift and function of being, with no strings attached."

"So what do we do about this?" I asked almost plaintively.

"We keep doing what we're doing. You're creating a critical mass of experience to build a new way of living, and this process will unmask your current life principle. Then you'll be able to put an end to the fragmentation that you experience in yourself."

That got my attention. "To tell you the truth," I muttered, "I suspect that I've always felt fragmented, only now I'm more aware of it."

163

"The experience of your essential Self is one of wholeness. Without that, fragmentation is inevitable. Unfortunately, most of us spend our lives searching for someone or something outside of ourselves to mend or heal this incompleteness. Given that the creation of wholeness can happen only from within, that's a pretty tough road to travel, filled with frustration and disappointment."

I was feeling confused and a little drowsy. At that moment, all I wanted to do was lie down and shut my eyes for a while. The part of me that felt threatened (whatever it was) was doing one hell of a job to distract my attention from the conversation.

"Here is what I want you to do for now," Adam said. "Keep operating from 'I AM a creator' in everything that we do today, and recognize your doubts and uncertainties, knowing they're only a function of your default principle.

"You'll be receiving powerful ideas and insights. Embrace these unconditionally as gifts of Grace. Grant yourself the power of Discernment. Allow yourself to distinguish, choose and shape your world consciously. Be open to the gift of Resonance, the ability to be attuned to any level, direction or flow of reality. Resonance will give you direct access to the interrelatedness of everything, and will enable you to have true understanding and compassion for others and for yourself. Then you'll know directly what love is."

NINETEEN
UP AND DOWN,
IN AND OUT

Physical concepts are the creations of the human mind,
and are not, however it may seem,
determined by the external world.
— Albert Einstein

It was late in the afternoon. Adam and I decided to take an hour's break from our work. I opted for a walk and meandered slowly along the dirt path that bordered the lake, breathing deeply, taking pleasure in my body's sensations, and the tread of my feet on the pliant ground. So much had happened that day, I welcomed some time for private reflection.

I was thinking about love. Sarah and Stephen had often accused me of not being there for them. It had always been difficult for me to express my love to them wholeheartedly, and many times I'd been overbearing and exacting in my relations with them. All that said, and though I had no solid evidence other than my financial support for them to back me up, I knew that I loved them deeply and would do whatever it took to protect them from harm.

If I were to ask other parents whether they loved their children, the majority would look at me askance, as though I'd asked an obvious, superfluous question. But what if I asked them if they liked everything their children did? There's not much chance I'd get an unqualified "yes."

When it comes to loving our children, most of us enter a different realm. We cross a threshold where love arises as an unconditional field of acceptance within which our children appear. It is a field that remains unshaken by the circumstances of the world, no matter how disconcerting, disappointing or brutal they may be.

I'd confused the conditional world with the unconditional world. Adam was inviting me to see that my real power comes from tapping into the unconditional realm.

It was a tougher problem to find this unconditional love in the workplace. The corporate culture had always been uncomfortable putting the words, "love" and "organization" together in the same sentence. But I remembered Diane's fierce commitment to the people in our company. Maybe executives who provide a nurturing environment for creativity and leadership in their charges can be said to love their employees in some fundamental way. The majority of managers might be uncomfortable hearing that, but if they relate to their people with honor, integrity and an authentic appreciation for who they are, whatever they call it, it's tinged with love.

Yet too many of the managers I'd known related to their people as if their sole purpose for existence were to carry out the company's wishes.

Unfortunately, I could recall many times when one of those managers had been me. I'd arrogantly assumed that the people were the problem, that others had gotten it wrong, and that my job was to point it out to them. I'd left completely out of the equation the possibility that they had personal histories, unique values and agendas for life that might be seeking to enrich the company culture beyond just getting through a particular day's work.

I headed back towards the cabin feeling refreshed, ready to venture down new avenues of discovery.

Adam's voice shot down the path like a bugle call. "Okay, we're going to do another experiment," he shouted with a clap of his hands. He reminded me of the social director on the cruise that Janet and I had taken some years ago — the man we could hardly escape unless we hid in our cabin, and even then, there could always be the intrusion of his gratingly cheerful voice outside our door inviting us to a round of volleyball. But that social director's enthusiasm was forced and annoying. Adam's was naturally dynamic.

We sat down in a clearing on the west side of the cabin to soak up the warmth of the afternoon sun. Adam began.

"We're going to continue with Discernment," he said. "As I trust you are beginning to realize, Discernment shapes your perception of the world around you at many different levels. The first thing I want you to do is to sit up, look at the environment in front of you, and just describe whatever you see. Be as specific and detailed as possible."

I did as he asked, amazed at my growing sensitivity to the landscape. It was as if I had replaced a grainy, slightly out-of-focus black and white print with a high-resolution color transparency. After ten minutes I was still going strong.

"Can you relate what you've just done with your way of working in the office?" he asked.

"I think so. Usually, just to deal with what I believe to be my priorities, I filter an enormous amount of detail out of my awareness. It now might be possible to allow everything to flow through my awareness, rather than blocking things out, and allow my selections to be determined by my intentions."

He nodded. "Now let's try something else. The view that you've just taken in describing the scene to me is a pretty standard eye-level view. Now I'm going to ask you to shift your view. If you were in one of my drawing classes I'd actually have you draw it, too. I'm going to ask you to shift your scale of view to that of an ant. So, if somebody shrank you to ant size, how would the world appear to you?"

I sat there at first trying to imagine it, but Adam interrupted. "Don't just think about it, you can do that later. I want you actually to do it. I'd like you to lie down on the grass."

I got down on the ground, lying on my right side with my arm cradling my head.

"Look around the same way you were doing before, but from this point of view, as though you were an ant on the ground. Describe what you see, but imagine you're an ant. Let yourself *be* an ant."

I didn't say anything right away, but just looked, intently. A whole new reality sprang up from the ground on which I had so often walked, oblivious to its existence.

The blades of grass took on the dimensions of large trees, and what I'd thought of as 'just grass' was really a plethora of different species. I wondered how many kinds I could count. There were clovers and dandelions, of course, but also many other types I couldn't identify, with particular leaf forms and varied stems.

An ant was playing tug of war with some other kind of insect for a piece of dark, spongy matter much bigger than itself. Peripherally, I saw the sudden, spastic leaps of a grasshopper. It was a busy little intersection. There were subtle rhythms in the movements of the insects, and a geometric rhythm to the spacing of the plants. I'd never paid attention to any of this before, and I wondered how Adam, with his practiced, artist's eye would view it. There were whole worlds on the underside of a log near my head. Green molds nestled in the shadows amid ever present dampness. Long, shiny shapes moved slowly across the bark, leaving glistening trails on its moist, rotting surface. And then there were the smells: the subtle blending of aromas for which I had no names. I had never thought of associating smells with temperature and light before, but that is the way they presented themselves to me. There were cool smells and dry smells, dank smells and bright smells.

I looked up at Adam. From this angle his shoes appeared immense. I could make out a whole range of scuff marks on their leather. His head, by contrast, was far away, a kind of inconsequential appendage consisting primarily of two nostril holes and the underside of a jaw, out of which sound emitted from time to time, seeming only inconsequentially attached to the shoes and legs that filled so much of my visual field.

Adam's voice interrupted these reflections. "Ready for another view?" he asked.

With difficulty I raised myself from the ground, my knees cracking as I rose. I followed Adam to the trail that zigzagged up the hill behind the cabin. In twenty minutes we stood at the top of the ninety foot cliff.

From our vantage point we could see the whole lake from shore to shore. Below were the cabin and the clearing from which we had started our climb. The details in the clearing, so prominent up close, now disappeared within the larger landscape of hills, lake and clouds.

"What does this view do for you?" asked Adam.

As before, I described what I saw, heard, smelled and felt with as much detail as possible, though the view was wider and more general in nature.

"If you are the CEO of a company, a large part of your job is to look ahead with exactly the scale you are seeing now," said Adam, pointing out to the horizon. "Now let me ask you something. You've been observing at three different scales, a normal one, an ant's eye view and a bird's eye view. What analogies from this exercise can you form for the workplace?"

At first I drew a blank. Then I started to talk, telling Adam that the top of this cliff was like the view of upper management. While I had an overall view from my position, there were myriad details going on below me and beyond me that I could no longer see. Yet, I was the one who made decisions affecting all that detail out there — with no notion, really, of when I might be snuffing out the dreams of someone who had spent months working on a project that I, with a stroke of a pen might be terminating.

"If you're upper management at the top of the cliff, where do you place Henderson?" asked Adam.

"In a hot air balloon floating about one hundred feet above my head! He sees upper management the same way I see the ant's world from where I'm now standing."

That world below me had seemed like a chess board, with pieces to be moved around as needed. I'd often forgotten that those working below were the agents of the changes I'd planned, and were also those most affected by the changes. They were the ones working the lathe, building the machines, moving finished products onto the loading dock.

"The people below see things that management doesn't see. And we look like tiny disconnected life forms to them when they look up here. Probably what they're saying has nothing to do with what I'm thinking and vice versa. If I think the employees know what management is up to, or if I assume

168

that my communications are understood, I'm probably deluding myself. Do they understand even a little the plans I have for the company, the reasons for the changes I make in their patterns of doing things?"

I thought of managers I'd read about who were always out there on the shop floor, hob-nobbing with their employees. That had always seemed a little beside the point to me. But with a flash of understanding I realized that in the same way I'd insulated myself from the lives of my children, I had also distanced myself from my employees. I'd always thought my work was too important to sully itself with the trivial details that concerned them, never considering that the infrastructure on which my work was based was all supplied by them.

Without a clear understanding of the workings at these different levels, the choices we make from only one scale of view are bound to be flawed. So how had I gathered information? Mostly from printed memos supplied to me by managers who worked for me, or from meetings, conversations, general impressions that people had given me.

I knew from experience how easy it was to get disconnected from the other levels. I could spend all my time on the executive floor, and only really know about the company through someone else's report. Almost all the information on which I based my decisions was filtered through someone else's perceptions. What I knew was all hearsay, but I treated it as reality. I knew about what was going on, but I didn't know it directly. I was like an organizational mind, giving directives while being disconnected from the corporate body; driving the corporate organism with no clear idea of the eventual physical or mental consequences of my actions. I drove my own body in the same way, avoiding its needs with no mercy or awareness of the long range cost. It's like reading medical reports on the health statistics for people in your age bracket, but never bothering to take your own pulse.

It suddenly appeared so unnecessary. If only those of us in management would walk down the hillside and understand the reality and thinking on the ground for a few moments, we'd know a lot more about what life is like in other parts of the corporation.

I peered over the edge of the cliff to the clearing below.

"The day to day activities on the shop floor and the machinations of management often seem distant and unrelated to one another," I said. "We rarely ever shift to the other person's view, yet we assume that they see the world and our priorities as we do. In fact, they not only don't see it our way, they can't. No wonder we experience so much misunderstanding and so many adversarial relationships."

"Yet, these days, if you're at the top of a company, you had better be aware of all these different realities," Adam warned. "Seeing how everything fits within a larger view is a crucial part of your job. But if you're stuck in your own view, you sure as heck don't see what they're seeing from the other levels. If you're talking to me, and I'm a shop foreman, and you're telling me what things are like from management's perspective, you'd better translate it into something related to my concerns."

"Every single level in the company is a different reality, and none of the people who work there know that," I mused. "No one values the working of the company as an organic whole. The value is placed at the top, and from that perspective it's simply not possible to create a company that works."

"Effective leadership in the next century will have to include the ability to discern reality from every level of the company, and to invite and acknowledge everyone's contribution to the success of the enterprise," he replied. "Just producing results is not enough in the long run. I've seen too many results bought at too great a cost to the company in human terms. Success in the long run is going to require a commitment to support and develop people so that they grow and flourish rather than merely get used up. Then you can create an environment where each person in the system feels responsibility for the health of the whole. Corporate actions will have integrity when they resonate at all levels of the company. The view from the cliff, from the ground, and from the places in between — all resonating together as one interrelated organic system."

"Of course, that's what an organization is supposed to be, whether the different parts acknowledge it or not," I added with just a hint of irony, hoping I was listening to myself and that I would remember this lesson when the rest of the conversation had been forgotten.

We had been walking as we talked, and had reached the bottom of the cliff.

"What's the next step?" I asked, stumbling on a rock, my mind, as so often happened, on what I was saying, not what I was doing.

Adam, smiling knowingly at the irony, said nothing, but walked with his hands clasped behind his back, absorbed in his own thinking as he looked at a point on the trail about a body length in front of him. When he finally looked up, he seemed to have come to some important resolution.

He grinned and rubbed his stomach. "Dinner is next."

"You know, I brought fishing gear and not much food," I said apologetically. "Our dinner is in that lake. We haven't fished it out yet."

"I brought along some burgers when I packed the ice chest this morning," replied Adam. "They should still be good. We can have them tonight and catch some fish tomorrow, if we still want to."

"Nothing like planning ahead," I said. "You did it, and I didn't."

The temperature during the day had been warm enough for shorts and T-shirts. By dinner time there was a chill in the air. Adam and I changed into long pants and sweaters and searched for some firewood for the barbecue pit.

My dad had built this pit years before from field stones he'd dug up around the property. The barbecue was a little unkempt but still functional. I cleaned off the debris from the rust-covered grill. Adam arranged the kindling to maximize the draft. He had a good sense of design even for something like this, and the fire was blazing away in short order.

While he went to get the food from the ice chest, I fiddled with the fire, stirring it and blowing on it now and then. But mostly I just watched it, fascinated by its progress, chaotic but orderly at the same time.

Fire and water. Water and rocks. Fire and water both flow. Everything in nature has flow to it. The glass in windows is a slow-moving liquid, and you can see this in the rippled window glass in very old buildings. The crust of the earth flows in very slow motion, as does the magnetic iron core of this planet. Nothing doesn't have flow. You can build structures that take flow into account. You can have simple rules for directing the flow and focusing the energy.

Adam came back and tore some portions off a big roll of ground meat, shaped them into patties, and placed them on the grill. We watched crackling sparks spit upward toward the meat as drops of grease fell into the fire. When they were cooked through, Adam popped the burgers onto hamburger buns. Like millions of other people, we both required the same finishing touches of relish, ketchup and mustard. The aesthetics taken care of, we quickly and hungrily devoured two burgers each.

We were again old school pals around a campfire. There is something about the ritual of preparing and eating food that has bound human beings together for as long as our kind has existed. In this simple act we were prototypically human and uniquely individual at the same time.

When darkness arrived we moved inside and made a fire in the fireplace. I asked Adam about the next day's schedule, but he only said, "More practice. Deeper, more intense."

At the end of the evening he asked me to do two more experiments in shifting scale. He directed me through a body relaxation process similar to the one we'd done earlier in the afternoon, but this time it was deeper and more detailed. After I'd relaxed all the muscles in my body, he gently guided my focus inward, opening up my awareness of my internal organs, bones and physiological processes. I listened to the beat of my heart, felt the movement of my lungs and diaphragm as I breathed, sensed the processes of digestion throughout the length of my intestinal track, and became conscious of different temperatures in various parts of my limbs. I noticed subtle sensations and pressure changes in my ligaments, muscles and tendons, and I delightedly discovered three distinct tastes and textures on my tongue alone. I felt as though I were a traveler who, returning home after many years, walks slowly from room to room, turning on the lights and taking stock of my possessions.

Almost irrelevantly I remembered something I'd once heard about prayer. There are certain times in many religious traditions when prayer is highly recommended. One of them comes when you return from a long voyage. What is it about revisiting a place left behind a long time ago that requires such reverence? It is as if when we return to what we call home, something in us becomes whole again.

How far had I traveled from my own body, and my own Self? How much had I let the Odyssey of my career struggles distance me from the very foundations on which my existence was built? It was reassuring to find that all of me that had been there so long ago still existed, but it was saddening to think I'd been away for so long.

In the last part of my inner voyage, I was asked to observe the feelings, images and thoughts in my house of being. Some of them disturbed me, but I could no longer deny their existence. I was shocked at my self-delusion, at how much I had concealed from myself. Sometimes during the experiment I wondered whether I was just imagining all of it. At other moments I had a sense of being in touch with myself at a very deep level. Mostly, it seemed to be a mixture of both. When I suspended judgment, the experiment worked best. When I allowed my analytical mind to question the experience, the flow was muddied. If I resisted my own direct experience, what chance did I have to be in tune with another human being? I knew I should give myself the freedom to trust my own inner awareness.

The second experiment required more imagination. I lay on my bunk with my eyes closed in the relaxed state that Adam had taught me to enter. First he asked me to allow my awareness to follow his voice to wherever he suggested that it go, and to begin by expanding my awareness throughout my entire body. So far, so good. I'd done that before. "Now," he added, "expand your awareness to include the whole room and bring each of your senses into play — sight, hearing, touch, and whatever else you can think of."

I found I could easily imagine the grain of the wood in the ceiling above my head, and mentally I felt its texture. I visualized the inside of the room, noting the familiar surfaces, shapes, and lighting. I was feeling pretty pleased with my ability to conjure up the room, when I heard his voice ask me to expand my awareness to include the whole cabin, inside and out, and then the land around it.

I imagined floating above the roof of the cabin, circling it, aware of the light from the cabin casting a beam onto the dark grass of the clearing. As I did so, I felt as if I were turning in the air and looking beyond the cabin to the moon reflected in the lake.

"Now include all of the woods and the lake."

By this time, I was struggling. My analytical mind was in rebellion, questioning the validity of the experiment. Then I heard Adam say, "If you feel yourself getting stuck anywhere, allow yourself to relax by letting go and expanding your awareness even more."

I realized there was no way I could be analytical while doing this exercise and still hold all the pieces, much less myself, together. I heard myself say "shut up" to the stream of chatter, and suddenly there was silence. A deep sigh escaped my lungs; I no longer attempted to control the process. I let my body and mind go and visualized the land around the cabin.

"Expand your awareness even more. Now to the size of the state; now to encompass the whole country."

I set my mind free to fly unfettered on the wings of imagination. Cities lay below me, spread upon the ground like trinkets at a flea market. Smoke and soot, miles of roadways clogged with cars, millions of people. To the west, I could see the jagged Rockies; to the east, the undulating spine of the Appalachians peeking through the heat and haze. And water. Still water. Churning water. Lakes, bays, rivers. And sand. The sand and dirt of the desolate and wind-whipped desserts and badlands. And my awareness filled with life forms beyond count, above and below ground, crawling, slithering and soaring — each a brushstroke filling the expanding canvas of my imagination. But now it was easy. I was not trying to do it right, I accepted whatever appeared.

"Expand your awareness to the size of the earth."

A shift occurred.

I was circling the planet, orbiting like a satellite, gazing down at the lights twinkling on the dark side of our world, and then suddenly, illuminated against the light of the sun, the rolling, marshmallow folds of mile-high cloud banks sailing over brilliant blue oceans whose foaming edges lapped at the shores of continents, green and yellow, gray and brown.

He asked me to expand my awareness again.

Another shift and I ventured to the galaxies. Dwarf stars, red stars, white stars, planets, comets, nebulae gas, black holes, anti-matter, dark matter, infinite glitter, unending radiance, chaos, birth and awe — I AM... the universe, and now... it is all blacker than velvet black... Silence.

From far away I hear Adam's voice guiding me back, pulling me toward the finite, constricting my awareness toward my starting point. I am in the wood and stone room and aware of the crackling fire, and Adam sitting in the chair, and my body lying on the bunk. And I can feel my body's weight pressing against the mattress and feel my diaphragm moving slowly up and down and hear the sound of my breathing.

Through closed lids I could see the light in the room extinguished. I heard Adam's voice say softly, "Goodnight, Dave."

"Goodnight," I responded, unsure that I'd said it aloud. That question was the last one I posed to myself before sliding off to sleep.

TWENTY

RESONANCE

Above all that you hold dear,
watch over your heart,
for from it comes life.
— Proverbs 4:23

Adam was not in the cabin when I woke up the following morning. I quickly threw on my clothes and hiking boots and stepped outside. It was still early and the brisk chill in the air raised goose bumps under my flannel shirt. I rubbed my arms vigorously to warm myself, slowly walking around the perimeter of the cabin looking for him. The morning mist was rising from the lake like cold steam.

I heard a muffled splash and then an excited "Yes!" coming from an area slightly off shore. This was disorienting to say the least. I hadn't brought a boat with me and didn't think there were any around.

I heard creaking and splashing sounds within the silver mist and strained my eyes to peer through the vaporous curtain. Gradually I discerned the faintest elliptical shadow which slowly became a smudge, like an oblong stroke of the finest charcoal dust smeared lightly across the opaque fog, growing in thickness and weight with each passing moment until it emerged fully formed as a dark inflatable dinghy and passenger floating toward shore. Adam jumped out of the dinghy just as its bow scraped the sand. I stepped forward and helped him drag it to higher ground.

"Where the hell did this come from?" I asked, pulling the dinghy up onto grass.

"Surprised? This packs up into quite a tight little bundle. It fits in the container on my four-wheeler's roof. I inflated it while you were still sleeping.

"What do you think of this?" he said, reaching back into the boat and pulling out a string of four freshly caught fish. "This is our breakfast and dinner!" he proclaimed proudly. I felt like a slacker by comparison.

We fixed ourselves a breakfast of fried fish, instant oatmeal and slightly burned toast, washed down with some barely palatable coffee I'd made.

Then our morning's work began. Adam opened his sketchbook, and began reviewing the four worlds of The Genesis Principle.

"Have as your intention today to keep embracing Origination, to operate as if you are I AM Awareness, the always present witness."

Then he moved on to the second world of Creation, and the dual sefiroth of Wisdom and Being; emphasizing again that Being was a matter of intention, rather than a function of doing.

I thought I knew what he meant by intention.

"I'm clear that I want to have 'I will be a creator' as my Life Principle."

"Evidently you're not clear enough," he shot back. "Will be? What's that? It's something that hasn't happened yet. You spoke from 'not that'. You are not yet acting from the I AM state. Please understand, this is not a criticism but an observation. And it is not a matter of just changing the tenses of your sentences, though that's a start. When you're fully expressing your I AM state of being, your words will be in perfect resonance with it."

I didn't like to admit it, but I could see he was right. I was still a striver attempting to become a creator rather than being one. My clarity about the situation made it no less disappointing.

"What do you think is displacing 'I AM a creator' so I can only experience it intermittently?"

"Your default life principle is getting in the way. We haven't yet distinguished it and dismantled its power over you. So it keeps sneaking up from the shadows to shape your reality. But we've been shaking it up these past few days. It's worried. I suspect that our work today will flush it out into the open."

"You make it sound like a wild animal that we need to search and destroy."

He seemed amused. "That's pretty much the way it is, because at present you have no control over it. We do need to find it and identify it, but destroying it isn't necessary. We need merely to de-fang it."

"And how can we possibly do that?"

"Because it's not real. It is an illusion that you've created, and it's driven by fear. When you realize that and know yourself as its author, it will lose its power over you. In that moment of discovery you will have a choice about your life principle."

I was perplexed. "Why don't I know what my life principle is yet? Why haven't I been able to figure it out?" I asked.

"I don't know, Dave. Many people are able to discover their life principle very quickly. They simply look for the primary phrase repeatedly looping through their mind whenever they are upset or feel threatened, or when they honestly think about themselves. It usually turns out to be their most fundamental belief, the design from which all the rest of the mental chatter follows. Even though they're aware of their default life principle, however, it still has power over them, because it's not held as a life principle that they created; it's held as a statement about themselves which they deem true, and which they believe with every fiber of their being, all the way down to the molecular level. In such cases, the light of awareness needs to be focused on the structure that keeps the lie in place in order to dissolve its grip on themselves.

"Now every once in a while there is a default life principle whose very design includes keeping you, its author, unconscious of it. You may have one of those."

Adam reached over and put his hand on my shoulder to reassure me, adding with a smile, "But don't worry. There is no way that it will stay hidden from us today, and when it first shows its head we will pounce!"

"Is it my ego?" I asked.

"Well, that's Dr. Freud's term isn't it? I'll go with that word if you understand it in the context in which I'm using it. The organizing life principle is a specific point of view, a way of organizing reality. Its purpose is to be the Self's prime vehicle of expression.

"That is what ego is, as I would use it. It's the default life principle functioning for its own continuity and persistence, oblivious to its original purpose and design as a vehicle for creating and expressing the Infinite I."

"So what do we do about this?"

"We?" he said with a quizzical expression, then chuckled softly, shaking his head slowly from side to side. When within a few seconds it was obvious to him that my sense of humor wasn't rising to the occasion, he dropped the kidding around and answered my question straight.

"As I've said before, we keep doing what we're doing. We're up to *Resonance*, the sixth sefira."

"Okay coach, tell me about Resonance," I said, pointing out the circle directly in the center of the diagram, right in the middle of the world of Formation.

Adam nodded. "The Hebrew word is *Tifereth*; usually translated as 'beauty' or 'harmony.' But we've got to dig deeply to understand its real nature. Beauty and harmony show up when the world and the things in it are in resonance.

"Let me offer an analogy. If you take a tuning fork tuned to the key of C and strike it with a mallet, it will vibrate at that pitch. Now suppose you have another tuning fork in the room, some distance from the first one, and it's also tuned to the key of C. Even if the second tuning fork is several feet away, when you strike the first tuning fork, the second will begin to vibrate and give off a tone of C when it 'hears' the vibrations of the first tuning fork. That's resonance."

I had a good mental picture of what he was talking about.

"The first tuning fork could be said to initiate the vibration of the second one over a distance, without touching it, by the power of resonance alone," he continued. "The first one initiates the communication, which calls forth the same vibration in another that's on the same wave length."

Resonance. It seemed fundamental, but I wasn't sure why. I decided not to be concerned if my analytical self was a few steps behind the rest of me. Adam walked over and sat down with me on the steps of the porch, facing the woods.

"Notice where Resonance is located in the Tree of Life. It's right in the center between Origination at one end and Manifestation at the other. Resonance is the sefira that connects the way of Spirit with the way of the world. It's the point of balance, where your expression, thoughts and actions in the world are perfectly harmonized with your original Self. As the Bible says, 'as above, so below.'

"Remember how you felt yesterday when you were being an ecologist. You were able to sense the flowing, vibrational nature of your surroundings. I was watching you, it didn't seem like it was a conceptual experience for you at all."

"No, it wasn't conceptual. Somehow I transcended my limited point of view and was in resonance with everything around me. I understand what you mean."

"Now, I realize that I spoiled things a bit for you afterward, but still, there must have been some effect of that resonance in the world of manifestation. That is, there must have been some effect in you.

"Well I think there was. I think I'll be able to sense the flow of life better in other settings too, because, in a way, I resonated with Resonance."

"Good. When you are regularly drawing inspiration from some creative force that transcends your ego, you continually experience this type of resonance. To live in resonance is to live an authentic life without pretense, without phoniness, without fragmentation. When you're in resonance, life is experienced as an ongoing flow." He pointed to the three lower sefiroth that hovered above Manifestation. "And that flow embodies itself as Passionate Commitment. This is the sefira of imagination, emotional strength and endurance. Across from it lies Articulation, its indivisible twin, the sefira of expression, through which you honor your commitment — giving it shape as imagery, symbols, words, or sounds. Through Articulation the glory of creation takes form. And then, of course, is Identity through which all the sefiroth vibrate in harmony with yourself as the creator."

I looked at the diagram and pointed to Resonance. "I see. When you're a creator, your capacity to be in resonance expands. It's like the difference between a diatonic harmonica, which is tuned to only one key, and a piano, which can play in many keys. As a creator, I can shift from that one fixed key — who I believe myself to be — to modulated keys, moving up and down the keyboard at will, resonating with complexly varied music. It's like shifting from the point of view of the man looking out from the cliff to the point of view of the ant."

"Exactly," said Adam, leaning back on his elbows and watching me think.

Yesterday *Articulation* had meant nothing to me. Now I was starting to understand it. Articulation was the point where intellect and passion combined in the service of creation. I searched for an experience that could make it clearer to me.

I thought of a pianist articulating the notes of a piece of music, or a speaker clearly articulating his spoken words. In the well played music or the well spoken speech, passion is shaped and given precision by intellect. The long hours practicing scales or diction pays off in the moment of passionate performance when the expression simultaneously soars with the spirit and falls precisely on the ear in its tiniest detail.

Similarly, a large structure might be imagined with all its precise details, fully formed in every aspect, waiting to be realized in the form of a symphony, a building, a new form of government, or a birthday party.

In a more general sense, one could articulate a business plan, showing what in general was supposed to happen, the passion that drove the new company or the new product, and then laying out step by step, detail by detail, how it would happen. Anything well articulated is made clear and credible in its details at the same time that it inspires in its drive towards something new.

"And take a look at this," he said, pointing to the diagram again. "Articulation is directly below Discernment. Resonance assures harmony between what is discerned and what is articulated. Articulation, like all of the sefiroth, flows in two directions at once. It is not only my expression outward that is articulated, it is also the way the world appears to me, how it gets organized and articulated in my perception.

"Articulation sings the glory of creation," he continued. "It is the sefira from which *Don Giovanni* arose within Mozart as a cascading flow of heavenly sound only he could hear before he touched a pen to paper. It is the sefira in which Michelangelo's sculpture of *David* took form before chisel ever touched marble.

"When it's all 'in synch' throughout all the sefiroth of the Tree, you have a sense of wholeness."

"What are some ways in which Resonance shows up in day to day life?" I asked. It's one thing to resonate with the natural world. There's grandeur and glory here. Nature invites. But what about at home or at work? I can't imagine experiencing the same degree of resonance in those settings.

"Would it be of any use for you to be able to step into your wife's shoes and understand her world so fully that she feels you are really there with her?

"Would it be practical at all for you to be able to know the reality of your co-workers? Do you think that might be of some use to a person who wants to be a brilliant leader? Would it be of any practical use for someone like yourself, who states that you are attempting to discover how best to deal with the owner of your company, to be able to see the world through his eyes? Is that practical enough?"

"Well, sure, I guess it's all very practical, but..." I was floored by the obviousness of Adam's questions and the incredible unawareness it revealed, stretching back over the hills and valleys of my own life. I found myself groping for something to say in my defense, as if I needed to defend myself from the help he was trying to give me.

Once again Adam had shown me up. In thinking of Resonance I'd been willing to resonate with the scenery, but it had never occurred to me that I might resonate just as well with another human being. This showed me how very isolated from others I had been. The creative force obviously existed in nature. But so it did in every human being, even the meanest and most confused of them. If there was a God force in the mighty typhoon, the rolling hills and fields on an October afternoon or the opening up of a rose, there was certainly a God force everywhere a human nervous system could be found, for the human nervous system was the most complex structure so far discovered in the universe.

And yet to me, what is this quintessence of dust? Man delights not me.

Hamlet had spoken those words, and I had lived them. I had lived as if no human being could really inspire me, could be a source of origination for me. I had to think of everything myself, do everything myself. I had no sense of true collaboration, no sense of the give and take of minds working together in such harmony that no one could remember who had thought of what as a new idea took shape. Why was I so blind to these treasures that surrounded me everywhere and often tried so hard and so unsuccessfully to get through to me?

"From what you've told me," Adam continued, "you've had particular points of view about your wife, your boss, your company and yourself, and you've been stuck in them. None of what you perceived seemed to be working; and up until two days ago, you lived as if reality was fixed and finite, and that you had to work your ass off to convince, cajole, manipulate and dominate other people into bending to your view of the truth — because you believed that the truth was what you perceived it to be. But it's been okay, because the people around you have been doing the same thing to you."

Adam poked his finger at my chest for emphasis. "You haven't been a creator, and you need to be. Without it you have no leverage, no power and no freedom to create."

Adam paused, looking at me with his head cocked to the side and his lips pursed.

"Does this all ring true for you?"

"Yes, of course. Except that I think you're going a bit overboard about my being stuck in my own point of view. I think that I've tried to include the point of view of others as much as possible." I spoke like a drowning man thrashing to save himself. I hated the direction the conversation was taking, and I didn't even know why I hated it.

"From your point of view," Adam interrupted.

"What else can I do? It seems to me that you are simply describing human nature," I said.

"We'll see," he said. "Everything you are up against in your life right now is stuck in your relationship with who and what you think you are and what reality actually is — that includes everything and everyone else. If you could look from their view of reality to understand what it is like over there, you might be able to come up with a new view that would bridge the gap and be satisfactory to everyone."

"I *do* look at their view of reality..."

"Yes," Adam interrupted, "from *your* view."

"Well, yes, but..."

Adam waited patiently. "There's a Native American saying that you can never know another human being until you've walked in his moccasins. It starts when you open yourself up to another with the intention to perceive from that person's point of view. But to do that, you have to be unstuck from your own view. You have to suspend your own interpretation of everything, at least for a while.

"I'm starting to understand what that might actually mean," I said quietly. "You're saying that it's possible to tune into someone else's experience of being without having had the same experience, simply by listening."

"Have you ever done that?" asked Adam.

"I think so," I said. "But it's not something I've done consciously or knew that I could just decide to do. I think it must be something I do occasionally, though. If I'm not distracted I can open up and listen when someone comes to me with a problem. In those circumstances, I think I really do experience knowing directly."

"It's not just sympathy?"

"No, there's a difference, I know that. With empathy there's power. With empathy I can know what it's like for them. I can see the world from their position. I'm guessing that with sympathy I stay over where I am, listen to what they have to say, but I don't experience it for myself. Yeah, that's the difference. Sympathy feels like agreement, while empathy feels like being known." I could see the shore now and I was swimming towards it.

"Being agreed with versus being known. Interesting distinction," said Adam thoughtfully.

Adam was describing what a great negotiator, or a great listener, has to do: become the other. If my shape is rigid, if it is unbending, if it is positional, the other person will never experience me knowing their world, knowing what it is like for them. They will never think, 'He understands me.'

And if I did understand, what then? For some inexplicable reason I felt that I might be annihilated. If I knew their point of view, if I stepped into their shoes... I was afraid it would be the end of me. I imagined myself looking into the eyes of someone who had total power over me. What would happen if I allowed myself to resonate completely with their point of view? The prospect was disturbing to me.

I forced the image out of my mind enough to wonder if what happens with the tuning forks isn't also what happens with great leadership. Maybe true leadership is communicating an idea or vision so powerfully that it's experienced by those listening as being in resonance with their own hopes and desires for the future. A leader's voice is like the mallet striking, and his or her vision reverberates in a way that awakens others to that vision within themselves, reinforcing the resonance with the leader who initiated it. Pretty soon the whole organizational field is vibrating with the vision and an escalating spiral of mutual empowerment and self-generation is set into motion. A structure and strategy can then be designed that is consistent with and reinforces that resonance — just as the shape of the tuning fork supports a consistent vibration at the physical level.

I felt easier now. I could think about it this way without the feverish feeling all over my body. I liked the leader's role, being the one who looks into someone else's eyes and gives them hope, gives them a sense of who they are, of their own power.

Over the years, I'd met lots of people who called themselves leaders, yet who knew nothing about leadership. Instead, they knew a hell of a lot about manipulating and threatening people. On the other hand, I'd also had the privilege to know a few inspirational and effective human beings who elicited and nurtured leadership in others. I knew from my experience of them that they didn't try to make people do what they didn't want to do. Dictators do that. Dictators don't lead, they control and dominate, using the fear tactics of threats and rewards. That's not power, it's force — and force brings out dissonance. Instead of harmony you get conflict and subjugation. That's a different game. Calling it leadership doesn't make it so.

"What people call reality is all made up," Adam offered with a wide grin. "Everything's an illusion, but it can be a valuable illusion if it creates a better future for everyone — one that others agree is doable, feasible and worth playing for. A leader develops that reality with others — the field of meaning, the organizing principle — and then designs the structures that will bring it to fruition. It's like designing the composition of a painting or a piece of music, or a poem. It is a creation, a game. You play it not because it is the 'only true reality', but because it is the reality you envision and which you are committed to bringing into being. To be able to do this successfully and not have everyone resist you, it helps to be able to understand others' points of view and include them in a vision which is broad enough to encompass a wide range of perspectives, not just the one you happen to be hanging onto at the moment."

"I understand," I said simply. I was at peace.

"You're ready for the next experiment," he replied. "This one focuses on your ability to experience to the fullest extent what it's like to walk in another's shoes. Let it flow, intend to discern that world, and allow yourself to resonate with it. The outcome takes care of itself."

"You're going to tell me what to do, right?" I asked, grinning, already knowing the answer.

"Of course. This one couldn't be simpler."

And that was the truth. It involved very little motion, but after it was over, I realized I'd communicated with Adam in a way I hadn't done before.

All we did was sit facing one another on the porch. We didn't speak, we didn't make faces. We simply looked at one another.

The first couple of minutes I felt very awkward. I was embarrassed to experience my existence in that way — without doing something, or having to do something. I had no clever things I could say to cover the awkwardness of just having to sit across from him, doing nothing but looking at him. My mind engaged in an explosion of activity, mostly about how I was doing. I was aware that on some level I was trying to impress Adam. When I focused on actually looking at him, I became aware that his whole attention was concentrated on being with me — just being, totally without judgment, obligation or agenda. It flashed on me that I had spent my entire professional life trying to avoid this very state, always trying to look busy, even if I wasn't, always "doing something." Not doing something seemed unnatural to me, and it was driving me a little crazy.

So I was sitting there analyzing what was going on and what it meant. That, too, was a way of keeping busy, of copping out of the exercise.

Finally I calmed down and was able just to be with him as he was being with me. I abandoned all efforts to make something happen and quieted my mind. I felt my body relax. I felt my breathing entrain to the same steady rhythm of Adam's respiration. I felt I was drawing closer to him, and my heart responded with a gladness and warmth. My perceptions changed. My eyes softened and my visual field seemed to tingle with vibrations. It was as if I were seeing more of each moment of time.

And then I sensed the Adam beyond the face of Adam and knew he sensed me too. And I heard the thought behind the thought: 'I am you, Dave.' And wordlessly, I answered him: 'Yes, Adam, I am you.' I don't know how we communicated this sense of union. It was a subtle but deep exchange, deeper than the grasp of our eyes and ears.

I was filled with a feeling of equanimity, wholeness and peace. And we sat there together for a while, united in a field of resonating hearts, breaths and minds.

Gradually the intensity of the experience faded and we both began to move again. I stood up and smiled gratefully to Adam. He nodded his head and smiled in return, but that was all that happened. We didn't need to talk about it. Neither of us wished to demean the experience by reducing it to words.

I left Adam on the porch and walked around the lake until I reached a large rock that protruded out into the water. I climbed up onto it and looked out. The surface of the lake was still, the reflections deep and glassy. A line of T. S. Eliot came to mind: "The still point at the center of the turning world." I had glimpsed that stillness in my encounter with Adam. It seemed to be a kind of connecting to something else and thereby going beyond oneself. It made me feel intensely humble, and I could almost see myself as a very tiny part of something immense, something so miraculously immense that every part of it was wonderful, even joyful in some very basic way.

And I understood why Adam was doing all this work with me, why he had shortchanged his painting to spend his time among the stressed-out, misguided strivers of the world. He loved them, and he didn't think of them as misguided, or wrong or stupid. He saw something else in them, something we all are. And I, as one of those strivers, was profoundly grateful he had taken on this mission.

I realized how powerful the experience had been. It was the kind of escape from my own rigidities I had unconsciously sought all my life, and here it was, achieved in the presence of a person who was willing to try to know me exactly as I was and accept me totally without judgment.

At that thought tears welled into my eyes, and I felt that I had at last been accepted in a way I had never known before. Adam stood there for the mother and father who hadn't been able to allow themselves to shine through completely in my parents. The shock of recognition came then, that I had spent my life looking for the unconditional acceptance my parents had never been willing or able to give me.

Does everyone do that? I wondered. Is that the endless search that drives so many people to do again and again and again the things that never satisfy them, never work for them?

And here, in such a simple way, I'd sensed a piece of myself I'd never appreciated before; and implicitly, through Adam's acceptance, I accepted myself too.

But what kind of a parent had I been to my own children? The thought tore into me like a knife to the heart. Over the years, the stuff of my communication with them had mostly been all the striver stuff: worry about their grades in school, about their goals (which usually happened to be my goals for them.) How often had I looked at them and simply seen them as the beautiful spirits they are? Why had I criticized them so much? Why had I worried so much? I surely had scarred them as my parents had scarred me.

I could remember some happy times when I had responded to them purely, as free and tender spirits, especially when they had been little and I could simply play spontaneously with them, knowing that what they really wanted was to be tickled or wrestled or carried off into flights of fancy with a good impromptu story.

But as they grew older, I'd thought I should get more serious about them, and fix them when they seemed off course to me. I hadn't trusted them. I hadn't believed that with a little gentle guidance they could steer themselves, because they were a great deal more than the flesh on their bones or the ideas I'd tried to insert into their brains. I hadn't really seen who they were. As a result, all I'd done in the last fifteen years was guarantee that they become strivers. Now, feeling sad for what I'd done, I wished my efforts had been less successful. But unfortunately, they had worked. My children were strivers.

And right there, in the presence of the whole world that surrounded me, the world that I had begun to feel a new kind of oneness with, I silently vowed to be different with them: to accept them completely, to trust them to be and do what they needed to be and do, to see them as who they were. After that I thought about Janet. This was harder, because I could feel a much stronger wall between us. But I wanted to tear down the wall by accepting her in exactly the same way. It wouldn't be easy. My various rejections of her had become reflexes in me. But I wanted all that to be different. I hoped it wasn't too late.

Resonance: it wasn't just a concept. I could feel it vibrating within me, connecting me with my surroundings. I saw an image of two tuning forks, the tops of their u-shapes almost touching, connected by a vibrating field. For a few moments, sitting across from Adam, the tuning forks had become one. I knew somehow it could also happen with Janet and my children, because I loved them so much. But could I do that with others, all the people that thwarted me and opposed me? I didn't think I could. If I let go that much, how could I keep control of the situation?

I was standing on a threshold of *being*. If I stepped through I might have the opportunity to live as a creator. But it would mean giving up the person I had always known myself to be.

What was the trade-off? To love and to resonate, were they the same? Could I allow myself to resonate with the people I worked with, to achieve deep understanding of their concerns, their hopes and fears? And what about Henderson? Was I willing to understand and know his world from his perspective?

Sitting there I acknowledged the power of Resonance. To be interrelated. To experience another without the distorting walls of one's own identified view. To contribute to another, to do no harm, to support another to expand their reality, I would have to understand their world, and they must know that I understood. Then, from that understanding, I might be able to support their struggle to see the world through new eyes, from new principles.

I was up against the very thing that I would have to ask from others if I expected them to shift their fundamental ways of being. Was I up to it? Could I cross the threshold? The partition was made of only one thing — fear. I knew I couldn't avoid it. Was I willing to experience it and pass through it? Did I have the passionate commitment necessary? Was my commitment to being a creator greater than the fear?

"To be or not to be," that really was the question, for until now I had lived a kind of death and if I wanted to end that, I would have to die, in a sense, into a new kind of living. The result, I suspected, would probably not feel very different, but it might be suffused now and again with "the peace that passeth understanding." For the paradox of what I had just been through was that I had felt myself coming to experience something about life that I knew I could never fully understand.

TWENTY-ONE

THE MYTHS OF THE CAVE

The solution to your problem is to see who has it.
— Ramana Maharshi

I walked back to the cabin. Adam wasn't out front or inside. I strolled back down to the lake, where I found him sitting cross-legged in his dinghy, sketching the rock across the lake that I'd been sitting on a few minutes before.

I felt a little surprised that he hadn't come to join me, even though I knew it would have been unnecessary. Besides, I'd had to think by myself for awhile. Only I could take the next step. No one can cajole you into change. You have to want it as badly as your next breath.

Adam looked up, and seeing me, asked for no explanations; he simply said, "What do you want to know?"

"I want to know how to resonate with people all the time. I want to experience for a lifetime the possibility I tasted for just a few seconds in that exercise."

"Yes, that's a good desire," he said. "Climb in." He watched me closely as I nervously moved forward to get into the boat. Then he waved me off, seeming to change his mind, saying we would take the boat out later.

"Let's walk instead." He pointed to a path through the woods.

"You're familiar with Plato's allegory of the cave?" he asked.

"I read it while I was in college. But I hardly remember it, so I doubt that I really got it."

"That's probably true," he replied. "If you'd understood it deeply, you'd be living differently. Then you and I might never have had to meet. You're like the ones in the cave who stayed behind."

"Maybe you'd better refresh my memory," I told him.

"It's the story of a group of people who live their lives chained in a cave and facing a wall. Behind them is the opening of the cave, with the light streaming in, but they can't see it. They see only the shadows of their own forms upon the wall. They are bound, trapped, suffering one day after the next in this terrible world.

"One day a man breaks free. He turns from the wall and sees the light and the entrance. He sees that the forms on the wall are merely shadows. He walks to the entrance of the cave, about to enter the light and freedom. He calls back to the others, telling them that they are looking at an illusion, that they don't have to live that way any longer. He tells them that what is real is behind them if they will only break free, turn and look.

"But they're deaf to his assurances. They don't see anything other than his shadow on the wall. His words are ridiculed. He speaks of a world that is invisible, unreal. They laugh at his stupidity, though it's bitter, resigned laughter. So they continue to stare at the wall, living their lives within a prison secured by the myths they believe. They soon forget the man who has turned and walked out of the cave, into the light, into freedom."

We continued our walk in silence for a few minutes, wending our way through deeper woods. Adam turned and looked at me. "Have you decided whether you're going to leave the cave?" His easy tone contradicted the import of his question. I knew that my answer to this question would shape the rest of my life.

Was I ready to take the leap? I wanted to, but something was holding me back. I was about to discuss my ambivalence with Adam when I realized he wouldn't be interested in such matters. That was just chatter. He wanted to know only who I was being. I was either committed or I was not. Yes or no. It was a clear choice: the cave or the light.

The moment is quiet. A butterfly hovers against a green-blue leaf. There's no other movement. No cloud shades the sun Silence, as if all of nature is hushed, and listening to my breath.
I choose.
The butterfly flaps its wings and soars upwards, disappearing into the trees. The light brightens without evident cause.

"I'm out of there," I said with a grin.

I was surprised by the firmness in my voice as I spoke those words.

In the instant of choosing I had crossed the threshold. Choosing had been effortless. Indecision had created all the struggle.

"Good," Adam said with a broad smile, taking my hand and shaking it. "Good for you!" He seemed genuinely pleased. We walked along in silence for a while, enjoying the simple beauty of the forest.

We reached a small clearing. The light came through in filtered beams, dancing in mutable patterns on the decaying leaves at our feet. There were a couple of old stumps and logs among the trees. We picked a spot and sat down to talk.

"You have to understand that we all have myths," Adam began. "However, most human beings know them only from the inside. They live their lives embedded in the myths and thus they construct their reality to conform to them. A creator, however, can observe the myths from the outside as well, because he knows he's the author of his myths.

"Here is the myth I have consciously created for myself to live from: *Each of us is an expression of the Creative Spirit. We are all co-creators of our reality, and being human is the opportunity to express our creativity in infinite play.*"

"A sense of being human as an expression of God at play?"

"Yes, and the play is the act of fulfillment," he added, his hands gesticulating gracefully as if plucking the ideas out of the air as he spoke. "An idea that takes form fulfills creation. Then it starts to move in the other direction, dissolving back into formless energy. There's a constant cycle of creation and destruction."

Adam came to a stop and began to chant: "*Om Namah Shivaya, Om Namah Shivaya, Om Namah Shivaya, Om Namah Shivaya,*" repeating the words in rapid succession.

"What was that?" I asked.

"It's a sacred Hindu mantra to Shiva; that aspect of Spirit that is the destroyer of form and illusion. It releases form back to the state of nothing so that creation can keep flowing. The mantra means something like 'I bow to Shiva." It honors that aspect of Spirit that gives you the freedom to dissolve your stuck energy, to complete the past so you can create your future anew."

"If you're fortunate, you'll experience the workings of Shiva very directly today."

My body clutched at this suggestion, my chest and throat tightening. I allowed myself to observe the sensations, not resist them.

"Remember," he said, "no form of reality is permanent, only the cycle of creation itself continues. That fundamental axiom of science, 'energy cannot be created nor destroyed,' captures it in modern terms."

"It sounds like another version of the four worlds, moving up and down through the principles of creation. Who had the copyright first?" I asked, laughing. I marveled about our human compulsion to take what is given us by the gift of grace and call it "mine."

"The consistency from one tradition to another is remarkable," he replied. "The universe is the game board where the infinite play of the game

190

is fulfilled. Each of us gets our very own playing piece." Adam pointed to his body. "See the piece I got?" He laughed loudly at his own joke. For a few seconds, the sound seemed to hang in the leaves overhead.

"The real master game is: how close can my creations match my original intentions?"

This last question set me wondering. What if my company operated this way? What if we focused our energies to bring forth realities that were expressions of our intentions, in an infinite game of building and learning? Then our bottom line would be a measure of our success at creating, not merely the end in itself. What if we operated as if creating reality were an ongoing process, rather than resigning ourselves to the frantic search for certainty — embalming our successes into a fiction called 'the answer,' and denigrating ourselves for our shortfalls and mistakes?

Adam leaned forward and casually doodled on the ground with a pointed stick.

"It's interesting the number of traditions that have myths which include some version of 'the fall' where we sever our connection with the divine and assume that we are separate entities, forgetting who we really are.

"In Plato's story, one man leaves the cave and recovers himself. That is what I want to accomplish with you. To do that, you need to expose these myths because right now you're chained to them. But don't feel too bad, most of us are. They're so much a part of us that we don't even see them."

"I'm ready. Where do we look for them?"

"Well, they come with being human. We inherit them through the experiences of our earliest existence.

"Imagine the process of being born," he reflected. "You come into being to express your Self in a particular form. Before birth you are one with your mother. Suddenly you're thrust from a warm, soothing environment where all of your needs are met, into a tight tunnel, where you're pressed, and twisted for hours. Then you enter a world of blinding light, blaring sounds, and shocking temperatures. You're helpless. For the rest of your life you're forced to find an outer source to alleviate your hunger, thirst and discomfort."

"Welcome to the world," I muttered, feeling vaguely ill at ease after his description.

"At first," Adam went on, "you don't even distinguish yourself from the rest of the universe. You're simply aware. You don't perceive the world as divided into 'me' and 'not me' or 'mine' and 'not mine.' The hand that moves before your eyes is a source of wonder and fascination. Only later do you identify it as yours. Meanwhile, you're being vigorously trained in the first myth."

"You're taught?"

"Yeah, you get a lot of instructions. And guess who your instructors are?"

"The people, who in your perception, make your existence possible."

"Bingo! And the instructions you receive tell you who and what you are and who and what you're not. You're the baby, I'm the daddy. You are there and I am here. You're shy, you're pretty, you're smart, you're stupid, you're good, you're bad, and on and on and on, you're indoctrinated in who and what to be. As you grow up, an ever expanding group of people tell you about yourself: first your family, then your friends, then society."

"Then you go to school, and what is one of the main things you learn?" he asked.

"Well, a major thing I learned was that who I am is defined by who I 'should be.' I think that a major purpose for school, whether it's verbalized or not, is to teach us to yield to authority," I said.

"And we either buy it or resist it," Adam added. "Either way, it shapes who we are. Then we go to church, synagogue, mosque or temple and again we're told who we are, and what is right, and what is wrong. And then we go to work and it's the same thing. Over and over again, our society defines us. Over the years, you're successfully indoctrinated with all of the aspects of your inherited identity — your name, your family history, their perception of your place in the world, and what you can and cannot accomplish."

He stopped his doodling and put down his stick, sitting quietly for a few minutes. When he spoke again, it was with a solemnity I had rarely heard from him before. "Most of the messages and instructions we absorb are based on the same underlying lie. Each of us designs our life around attempting to recover from that lie. We feel a longing and we don't know why. We try to fill it up, but rarely find our way home."

"I think I know what the first myth is," I said quietly.

"What?"

"*I am separate.*"

"Yes, you understand." He smiled warmly for a moment, his eyes meeting mine, then returned to his doodling. "'I am separate.' It's the first myth of the cave, and it firmly slams your door to freedom. What else do you see there?"

I sat there among the lengthening shadows, reflecting aloud on his question.

"When I live as if I am separate, I can no longer know myself as the Infinite I. I've become a finite me. There now exists a dichotomy: me, and others. If I'm separate, who must you be? You're 'the other'. But not just you, of course — everyone's 'the other.' I'm surrounded by 'not-I's.' How do I experience the world when there is one finite me and over six billion 'not-I's?' It's a very scary, very threatening place."

"But what about your friends and family?" asked Adam, testing my conclusions. "Certainly they're on your side. How do they fit in?"

I took a few minutes to consider this question.

"I think that the myth plays a very sick joke here," I finally said. "Inside of 'I am separate' there is no middle ground. There is my 'I' of identity, which I think is all I am, and everyone and everything else is some version of 'not-I.' But there's a spectrum of 'not-I's.' On the far end are the people who completely disagree with my point of view — my enemies. They're the ones whose vote I would cancel if I could.

"On the other end of the spectrum — and this is the insidious part of it — are those people I call my friends and my loved ones. These are the people I am close to, who agree, at least partly, with my view of the world, and who know, most of the time, that I'm all right. They are the people I want to have around me. But no matter what, they're not going to make it with me unconditionally. My relationship with them will always be conditional to some extent, predicated on how much they continue to validate me."

The more we spoke, the more I saw how 'I am separate' shaped the very nature of my being. The moment I say 'I am separate' I'm a subject in a world of objects. I become a thing, bounded by space and time. If 'I am separate' I can never fully allow myself to step into another's shoes, or allow them to step into mine, because if they became me or I them, I might lose myself!"

I shook my head slowly at the irony. Fearing to lose myself as a separate identity, I lose myself as I AM. If I were to remain aware of my true nature, I'd know myself to be inclusive of all the rest of the universe.

"You know, there's a contradiction I can't resolve," I said. "I don't see how I can remain in touch with my original Self and fully become an individual. Isn't it true that to be an individual is to be separate?"

"Your confusion is understandable," Adam replied, "but it is not because there's a contradiction between being your original Self and being an individual. It is because inside of the myth 'I am separate' they appear to be a contradiction, when, in fact, they are not. By dividing the world into 'I,' and 'not-I' we make individual mean separate. But that is not the way it works in the universe, only in the human mind.

"Let me offer you another interpretation. Individual doesn't equal separate, individual equals distinct."

"I don't know what you mean by that."

"Look at your fingers," he said, "they are each distinct, individual appendages, but they are not separate. They are interrelated aspects of your whole hand, but each has a distinct function. They are not some homogenized sameness; yet they are not separate, they work in harmony with the whole. I could expand this to include everything on the planet and in the solar system.

"It's the same with human beings. Each of us has a specific purpose or expression that is part of the whole. Our individuality allows us to fulfill our expression of creation. But it would be insane to think that we are not connected to everything else in the universe in a very real and direct way. Let's remove you from the air that surrounds you and see how long your individuality survives. Your separateness is only a mental construct, and not a very logical one, at that."

Adam leaned forward to underline his point. "Look, which is more important and which moves first, the back or the front of my hand? The back of the hand can be described, and so can the front. You can't remove one without removing the other. They are individual expressions of 'hand,' distinct, yet always one.

"Within the 'I am separate' myth we can distinguish two levels of the 'finite me.' The first is Identity — the ninth sefira. This is the level I recognize as the self I present to the world, the whole conjoining of thoughts, body sensations, judgments, beliefs, opinions, emotions, memories and sexual urges. But within 'I am separate,' I can misidentify Identity as the thing who I am, rather than as a vehicle for the expression of my Self. However there is another even more fundamental level at which who I consider myself to be is unconsciously formed, and it organizes my perception of myself and my reality. It exists in the world of Creation as my life principle.

"But what was my default life principle formed for? What is its purpose?" I asked. "Even though it is my creation, albeit unconsciously formed, its purpose can't be creating, since it stifles my ability to create."

"Let's think about that. If you believe that you're a separate 'I' surrounded by all of these billions of 'not-I's,'" Adam replied, "what immediately becomes the prime purpose of your life?"

"That's easy. Survival, preserving the 'finite me.'"

"And under the conditions you've described, what is this 'finite me' that you're attempting to preserve?"

"My point of view of who I am."

"And if you were to lose that precious point of view of yours, you'd feel like you were dying."

"Absolutely."

"So what you consider yourself to be could be any of those things we've talked about that make up an identity. For some people it's their body; for some, it's their job; for some, it's their reputation; for some it's their belief

194

system; for some it's their family, tribe, group or possessions. Whatever it is you say you are — that is what you are protecting.

"And that's the ego's role. Here's this body and personality which is a vehicle for the Self's expression in the world; but now it gets identified not as a vehicle anymore, but as yourself. It's as if you were to identify yourself as the car that carries you from place to place. If that were true, you'd stay in your car all the time. You'd live there, and you'd go around to drive-in restaurants, banks, pharmacies and movies and do everything from inside your car. If you were ever, God help you, forced to get out of your car, you'd be a turtle without a shell. You'd be naked and feel like you were dying. You'd have no idea that the car surrounding you was completely artificial and mechanical, and something that all the people around you were able to enter and leave at their slightest whim.

"In just this way, the default life principle operates for the protection of whatever you identify yourself to be, and it will do whatever is necessary to accomplish that."

Adam lowered his voice and leaned even closer, as though to impart an intimate secret. "The purpose of life, when you are your Self as an Infinite I, is simple and glorious. The purpose of life is creating. The myths of the cave conceal that purpose, except in fleeting moments of inspiration."

"I know I've experienced those moments of inspiration from time to time," I said. "I can be in a conversation with somebody and really hearing them, and it's as though I'm not there. If anything, I'm the energy floating between us. I'm getting into their mind, experiencing what they are experiencing."

"That, I think, is what excites people about romantic love, about physical passion that is deeply shared," said Adam. "When you're having the kind of sexual experience that is an expression of love, you can lose your sense of separateness and experience being completely with the other person."

"And that's what everybody is longing for, I guess," I added, "that union in which we lose our identity for a few seconds, even if we spend all the rest of our time holding onto that identity with a death grip. Yet, when I think about it, the experience of freedom occurs only when I lose myself into the nothing."

How rare that experience had been for me with Janet!

"Many people have had that experience," Adam said. "It can happen when you are completely engaged in something, whether it's a work situation or during an intimate conversation. You don't have to worry about what you are going to do, because you trust that your Self will know how to respond. Instead of sitting there thinking, 'what am I going to say?' and not really hearing the other person, you are completely hearing and spontaneously responding. Or you may be totally caught up in watching a good movie or reading a book or listening to music that you love, and you drop your identity for a moment. You experience you are no longer a thing here, in contrast to that thing over there. All boundaries dissolve, and you are suddenly the field in which everything around you is appearing. When you are really working on something, really into it, loving it, and being it, you don't have to eat, you don't have to go to the bathroom, you are not tired; it is then that you are simply the I AM Awareness of all these forms that are interrelating, whether it is a conversation, a meeting, or working by yourself in front of the computer. Those are the times when you are really your Self and there is a sense of freedom and endless room in which to stretch your wings.

"That's the sacred space of Resonance — where you're able to tune to other beings and know them directly. You feel compassion, the deep understanding of another's world. And with compassion comes humility and open-mindedness. Only then do you experience *agape* — the unconditional love and understanding of another."

"You say that our real purpose in life is creating. But isn't there lots of scientific evidence that all life forms operate out of survival?" I asked.

Adam grimaced and rolled his eyes. "You know what otters spend almost all of their time doing?"

"What?"

"Playing. It all goes back to the game of Creation, which is happening right now and all of the time — far more miraculous a phenomenon than the supposed creation of everything all at once. The otters are exquisitely expressive playing pieces in that game.

"Besides, if you take all the examples that have been used to show that survival is the purpose of life, and you look at them from the possibility that the purpose of life is creating, they'll work just as well. The conclusions tell you more about the view of the observer than they do about what is being viewed."

"This is another example of the thief seeing nothing but the saint's pockets, then?"

"Of course. When you make that first error and say 'I am separate,' it is like Kryptonite to Superman: you immediately remove your power to shape your life. You perceive yourself as separate and small: a thing, located somewhere, with a set of permanent characteristics, attempting to protect your turf. All this gets solidified. It's as if you are stopping the flow of the river and trying to turn the water into ice to hold it in place."

"But people seem to have two opposing desires. They want a sense of their own unique identity, but they also want to be part of something larger, part of a social group. How do you reconcile that contradiction? Why is the fear so strong that it overrides the desire to belong, but not completely?"

"At some level you never forget who you really are. But whatever you are stuck in muffles that awareness."

"So to regain some of this awareness I need to detach from my identity and all the things I think I am?"

"Yes, so you can understand others' points of view."

Adam stood up and began pacing as he spoke. "A good analogy is the hologram. If you take a conventional photograph and cut it up, all you have are fragments of a photograph. You have to put them together to see anything. If you take a holographic plate, you can cut it up into pieces, and every piece has the whole image on it. This remains true no matter how many pieces you cut it into. It will get fainter, but the whole image is always there. Every single point on the holographic plate responds to the field of the whole image. Now, imagine that a person's mind is like a hologram, and that the universe is like a hologram, and there are billions and billions of people on earth. Every point of view is a point of view about everything in the universe from that perspective. Each point of view implies the whole thing, which includes all points of view from that point of view."

"Don't you see?" said Adam, "it's not possible to resonate with another's point of view when you're feeling separated from them. You're right back there with all your little invented problems that stem from a misunderstanding of what life is all about in the first place. So you and Henderson don't agree about how to run the business, that's a given."

"I'm relieved to hear it," I said.

"But you and Henderson do agree on basic things like the need for food and water. You also are individually dueling with your separateness and seeking ways to reconcile yourselves with the universe and thereby with one another. The trouble is you have very little idea about what to do to achieve this, so many of the things you do only intensify the problem.

"Now let us say that the two of you were to overcome your separateness and become able to access each other's point of view and actually think together. Then there would be no conflict. Henderson, in his role as head honcho, and you in your role as executive manager, would work in perfect harmony to accomplish something that would be of service to the rest of humanity. You would be able to do this because you would agree on certain universal human principles that each of you saw from the distinct point of view of your special roles in life, free of the default life principles that are now confusing both of you."

"I see, you were being just a bit idealistic."

"Idealistic, yes, in the same way that the person who has exited Plato's cave is an idealist. As he leaves the cave he hears the scornful shouts of those who remain behind: 'You are an idealist.' But he goes out into the world of reality and drinks from the fount of divine inspiration, which is the creative source of all reality. In that sense, I'm an idealist, though as I'm about to show you that's really the last thing I am. Your problem is that it is you who are the idealist."

I was sure that he had it backwards. I prided myself on my practicality. I decided to ignore his last remark and move on. "So do you think that some magical process is going to get all of us over our default life principles so we can indeed become like this hologram you're talking about, a hologram that encompasses billions of unique and individual human beings?"

"I think that the struggles we go through can be defined as struggles to replace the default life principle with a life principle that reflects our true purposes in life," said Adam. "How quickly and how well we do that depends on the success of those who seek to change the rules of the game by which the culture operates. As long as the rules are primarily oriented towards dominating other people, it could take a long time. But each person has the option to refuse to play that game, and set up another game that is about the search for a true relationship to the universal structures that gave rise to us in the first place.

"Once you've put the default life principle behind you and become sensitive to the realities that shape the people around you, you become an invitation to them to join you in exiting the cave. That's because, in knowing yourself, you help them to know themselves. You are a creator, and you pave the way for them to be creators too.

"To be a creator is to have the ability to know yourself from many, many points of view. When you have a transformational experience, you know that you are not any of the points of view. You know your Self to be the awareness in which the points of view arise."

"And each individual is not just a distinct part, but an essential part?"

"Very good. Distinct and essential. It's not the bullshit everybody is worried about, which is, 'Oh god, I'm going to lose myself! I'm going to be one of the mindless horde!' No, because every drop, every cell, every molecule, every person, is the opportunity to celebrate the individual expression of the whole, and to celebrate the infinite ways of expressing it. Each wave in the ocean is distinct from every other wave, yet none are really separate from the others. There is no wave that is not the ocean; each one implies the ocean itself. An individual has a shape, but if you think you are separate, you relate to your shape differently than if you know you are an essential, integrated, distinct part of the whole."

"So I have to see my life as a particular expression of a much larger hologram of existence."

"Yes, and you have to accept everyone else as a particular and necessary expression too."

"But how do I do that?" I wondered aloud.

"You've already tasted that possibility. It's not so complicated. You make room in your heart for other people and shut off your criticizing, demonizing, opinionated brain to really see and hear them. It's a combination of your awareness of yourself as I AM and your intention to bring out the best in the situation."

I slowly and thoughtfully nodded my head.

Adam sat down again on a nearby log and looked at me for a few moments. When he spoke again, it was in an even quieter, more intimate tone. "Let's talk about the second myth," he said. "See if you can intuit what it is. If your driving concern is the survival, the continuity and security of your point of view — your separateness, so to speak, then what is your ultimate goal?"

"To get what I want?" I offered tentatively. But, after a moment's thought, I came up with another answer that seemed to fit every circumstance of my life. "Okay Adam, I can tell you what my ultimate goal has been: to reach that safe harbor, to never be threatened, questioned or invalidated by all the 'not-I's' out there."

"And that, Dave is the second myth of the cave," Adam confirmed. "The belief that we can live an undisturbed life. It is the great illusion, the ultimate goal that the mass of humanity is pursuing: *to be undisturbed.*"

"Oh yeah, ain't that the truth!" I had to laugh. "The myth of the 'impossible dream'! But boy, don't we all wish we could really be undisturbed," I added. "In that ultimate ideal, there are no problems, no upsets, no situations that seriously threaten the existence of my view of myself and my world, and no unexpected circumstances that I can't handle. When that state of being undisturbed is finally achieved, I think I will be happy and satisfied. And that ideal can only be accomplished if all the other people in the world — all those 'not-I's' out there — agree that my view of the world is correct, proper and justified. Short of that, I need to become either smart enough, rich enough, popular enough, invisible enough or strong enough to prevail over any adversaries."

This drive to be undisturbed shaped everyone I knew. From the basic desire to avoid bodily threat, such as hunger, cold, and injury, through the attempts to avoid fear, loneliness, and, ironically, the burden of separateness.

In that context, I could see that the whole purpose of my life was to protect and defend the point of view of the identity called Dave Carey. Everyone was seeking this invulnerability. Why should I be any different?

"An undisturbed state is called security," said Adam. "The form we give that security may be power, wealth, fame, approval, or even anonymity (if that's the way you avoid being disturbed.) Ironically, the harder we try to be undisturbed, the more we pursue security, the less likely we are to find it. Think about it. If we were completely secure, we wouldn't be happy. We'd just have more chances to think about our separateness and disconnection.

"The great irony of this is that the undisturbed state is the ultimate state of entropy. When the universe has completely 'run down' if that ever happens, then every part of it will have achieved a totally undisturbed state. You can get there quicker — at least the physical you. All that it takes is dying. That's no solution to the pursuit of happiness, though, because all around you the universe goes on changing, which is what the universe is meant to do.

"But since we can't achieve happiness or relatedness inside the myth 'I am separate', that leaves us walking around feeling isolated and sorry for ourselves — angry, resentful, regretful, fearful, righteous or guilty. Then the game is the 'blame game,' either blaming others or ourselves. That's what it's like in the cave. We believe we're separate. We think the point of life is to be undisturbed. And we've bought into the lie that it's just human nature to seek security. So we're prey to *four basic urges*."

"What are they?"

"They are what we organize our lives around when we believe we are separate and believe we can be undisturbed. We seek to gain pleasure, approval, attention and control — and of course avoid at all costs the lack of these comforts: pain, disapproval, being ignored and lack of control. They are four variations on a theme. Most of us seek all four variations. But we may have one or two that predominate, depending on what our default life principle is and our personal inclinations."

"I think I know what my primary urge is," I said. "To gain control. If I can gain control, all those 'not-I's' out there won't surprise me or dominate me, so I'll finally be able to relax and be undisturbed."

I suddenly understood why I had so little tolerance for ambiguity. My obsession for certainty stemmed from my need for control. I would tell my managers at work that I wanted them to swing out and make decisions on their own, yet I could never stop hovering over their shoulders to make certain things were going the way I wanted them to go.

"There's a twist on this urge, Dave! Sometimes the avoidance is not of

200

being controlled by others, but an avoidance of *being out of control* yourself or *avoiding the loss of control*."

It was as if Adam had flipped a switch in my mind with those last few words. I felt a sudden stirring of agitation. The idea of "going with the flow" had always sounded like b. s. to me. Now I could see why. In my need to control my world, "going with the flow" sounded like being swept away down river.

"I think you just hit a bull's-eye," I said hoarsely.

"I think we're getting closer to your default life principle," he said with excitement in his voice. "The four basic urges are the strategies it uses to protect itself. So these four urges: gaining pleasure, approval, attention and control are often the only motives for a person's actions. The trouble is, the integrity of the Self may be compromised in satisfying these urges. And they have nothing to do with creativity."

"But, Adam, I know that at certain times and in certain situations I have been creative in my life. How do you account for that?"

"Easy. Your life principle will give you permission and room to create, as long as what you create leaves you undisturbed and in control."

"You mean I create to remain undisturbed?"

"Exactly. Creating is allowed, but only in the service of that ultimate ideal. Remember, the default life principle is who you consider yourself to be. That is what is attempting to remain undisturbed."

We were both quiet for a while, reflecting on our own thoughts. There seemed to be few times in my life when I was not motivated by an urge to avoid pain or gain pleasure, to get approval and avoid disapproval, to get attention and avoid being rejected, to be in control and avoid being out of control. Those urges had propelled me through most of my life.

Every once in a while my purpose had been to create. Every so often I'd actually been able just to be with another human being without trying to satisfy one of these urges. But now I was even suspicious of my motivations in those moments. How many times had creating been not for the joy of it, but rather to win approval or pleasure or attention or control? Could I even count on one hand the number of times I had operated outside of this mechanical and conditioned way of living?

TWENTY-TWO

THE TYRANNY OF IDEALS

Others gain authority over you if you possess a will distinct from God's will.
— *Rabbi Bahman of Bratzlav*

We began walking back toward the cabin.

"Adam, you said there were four myths of the cave. The first two are very clearly forces in my life. I don't like to admit that, but it's true. So I guess I should know about the other two."

Adam's response made me think that he was avoiding my question. He asked me, "Are there ways you believe your life should be? Is there a way you think your wife should be? Are there ways that your company ought to be? Or society should be?"

"Of course. I have ideals in all of those areas."

"Where did you get those ideals?"

"Son, whatever you intend to do with your life, and I've given you my two cents worth in the matter already, I know, make sure that you aim high and strategize how to get there. And that includes planning to get good grades and doing it, starting now. Excellence can never come too soon. Always remember, 'There are men in the ranks who will always be in the ranks. Why? I'll tell you why! Simply because they haven't developed the ability to get things done!"

How many times had Dad said that to me?

Ideals. I hadn't realized that, as much as I thought I'd resisted my Dad's advice, I'd still bought into the ideal of a ladder of success. I'd operated my whole business life trying to reach the top, as if it were a real ladder that would get me to...what? Even near the top, striving seemed to be the only game in town.

Most of my ideals were hand-me-downs that I'd picked up from my parents, my schools, church, comic books, television, movies and advertising. My ideals about work I'd picked up from my Dad, college, the conventional wisdom of the marketplace and the culture of my company. All I had to do was follow the ideals of "the good life" and keep on striving — no creating necessary on my part! How little my accomplishments had meant to me if they hadn't met my ideals!

I had ideals for just about everything and everyone. I knew how Janet and my children should be, how the company should be run, how Henderson ought to be, and how I needed to be. I realized that in some part of my mind, achieving those ideals equaled victory and satisfaction, and that equaled comfort and security. Not meeting those "shoulds" and "should nots" wasn't an option in my formula for success.

I struggled to find a way to put a created life into the equation. "What if we were to say that life is about creating ideals that were never there before?" I proposed to Adam.

"I think I disagree more with that statement than anything else I've heard you say," Adam replied.

"Why?"

"What you've done is identify the third myth of the cave. *You live as if there are ideals.*"

"What's the big deal about that. What's wrong with having ideals?"

He shook his head. "You didn't hear what I said. I didn't say that the third myth is that you have ideals. I said the third myth is that you live as if there are ideals. You live as if there are, inherent in the universe, ways you are supposed to be, should be, ought to be, and shouldn't be."

I still didn't get it. "I shouldn't have ideals?"

"There'd be nothing wrong if you merely had ideals — that is, had some ideas or points of view about the way things should be, and knew that they were your own creations or preferences. Then they would not be a problem. But that's not the way you hold them.

"You hold them as if they're material facts as real and objective as a rock. Idealists all know they are right because they are the guardians of the truth. They act as if there are some universal 'shoulds' and 'should nots' and believe their job is to make sure others see the light."

I was perplexed. "Well, what's the difference between an ideal and a possibility?" I asked. "They both seem to be different words for what I'm striving for."

"Possibilities, unlike ideals, have no 'shoulds' and 'should nots' attached. Creating evokes possibilities, not ideals. Ideals are spawned by beliefs. Possibilities are flowing, inclusive and expansive. Ideals are rigid, exclusive, and confining.

"Millions have been slaughtered in the name of ideals. It's an age old method to become undisturbed. Eliminate the dissenters!" he proclaimed melodramatically. "Cleanse them from the face of the earth!

"But we can do this to other human beings only when we turn them into things, 'not-I's', and deny their humanity. Of course, to do this we have to become things ourselves and deny our own *beingness.*

"You do this with your personal relationships, and with yourself, too. You work on either changing yourself or attempting to change the people around you to fit your ideals. Only then can you love them. Only then can you love yourself. Only then will you be content and undisturbed. It's a cruel joke. Look at all the time, money and energy spent on cosmetic surgery, drastic diets, the fashion of the moment, the fad of the week, not to mention the never-ending attempt to get others to buy into your sacred set of ideals and beliefs. Do you think it ever really results in a permanent sense of well being?

"Do you want to guarantee for yourself a life of suffering? Easy! Just try to attain an ideal life. The results are always the same. Have your eye on ideals and you lose what's in front of you. You only see what's missing, how you or others have fallen short. The very nature of an ideal is that it is unattainable. It is the magic 'someday' that you are striving for. But does the striver ever get there?"

"But, wait!" I objected. "Without ideals, what's the point? I can't understand how I, or anyone else, would be motivated to get off our asses and do anything without ideals."

"You wouldn't *be* motivated," Adam said, throwing me for a loop. "Motivation is all 'management by carrot,' and operating without a motive is incomprehensible to a striver!"

He leaned forward as though he was about to whisper the secret of the universe in my ear.

"Did it ever occur to you that it may be possible to create something because of the pure joy of creating it?" he said. "That it may be possible to live life creatively with a sense of your soul's mission, and what you realize is your calling? When you have a calling you don't need to be motivated. When people experience themselves as creators they don't need external prodding. You have to get out of their way because they are passionate about expressing themselves and will create — whatever, however, wherever.

"Ideals are actually brakes on a company's innovative capacity. What most people call a vision, particularly in a company, is actually an ideal — something you are supposed to salute, something that should be done. But that has no power, no punch. In a company with creators, people are fueled by the passion to bring forth a world that never existed before.

"It's just possible that if you approach life that way, you may have an opportunity to make a difference. There is no 'should' in a vision, there is only 'shall be.' You don't expect what already exists to look like your vision. If it did, you wouldn't need a vision. The vision gives you the place to play the game of creation — between the present and the future that you have imagined.

"Of course," he added after a few moments, "ideals are all that is possible when you're chained in the cave."

I shuddered. Ideals are like coals of fire. They burn themselves out. They can *only* burn themselves out, and certainly they had burned me out. They made me depreciate the reality before me, demanding something better. In trying to live up to ideals I'd fallen from grace, proving that in the end I couldn't live up to them. Even the times I'd met my ideals had soon turned sour.

I had always measured reality in terms of its inadequacies. Maybe I really did form ideals in order to build my career; but if so, they weren't worth having.

But when I look at the stars I get a glimpse of the eternal. Starlight has no inherent meaning within its light. It becomes meaningful only when I look at it. It is in the field of my awareness that meaning exists, arising at that instant of awe and wonder when a creator celebrates creation.

We had almost arrived back at the cabin.

"Are you ready for the fourth myth?" he asked, seeming to divine my thoughts. "Can you guess? It's inevitable, given the other three. You believe you're separate, so you strive to be undisturbed. And to attain this comfortable position, you create ideal worlds within ideal worlds — 'shoulds', 'woulds', and 'ought-to's which you can't possibly reach, no matter how hard you try. So what's left? What does it all lead to?"

It was so obvious. All I had to do was look at my life. What was the one thing left to do? And I had done it, over and over again, never having the slightest clue of how hopeless it was. What were the majority of strivers attempting to do?

"Self Improvement," I uttered with an audible sigh. And with that insight I seemed to be looking at a whole new picture of myself. The voice of Adam seemed to have moved inside of me, speaking about my life from the perspective I was now entering, seeing it for what it was, as it looked from the outside, not from the point of view of the man with blinders on who clings desperately to the need never really to transform anything in his life because it is too risky to do that.

The fourth myth of the cave was *The Myth of Self Improvement* — the biggest joke of all, like a gerbil running in a cage, going nowhere. I was

Lewis Carroll's Red Queen, trying to run fast enough to keep up with the landscape. That urgency had powered all my ludicrous attempts to change my life, to alter my behavior inside a default life principle that didn't allow for change, that allowed for nothing inconsistent with itself to exist. That was my life. I was a master of the three main moves of the self-improvement myth: do *more*, do *better*, and do *different*. It was a play with a plot like a Mobius strip that kept returning me to where I started, no matter how many twists and turns I thought I had taken.

My relationship with Janet isn't working; so I try the first move of self improvement: I do more. I try to make her happy with gifts. When that doesn't work, I give her more gifts. When nothing really changes in our relationship, and she still seems unhappy, I take the next step. I do what I was doing before, only better — the new, improved, more expensive version: cars, houses, jewelry. I hope that will do it. Then one day, she says, "I don't want stuff, I want you."

Aha! I finally have the answer! She wants me to be different! The third step in the self improvement myth! But I can only perceive what she is saying from my point of view. I have no way of comprehending what she is talking about, but I go through the motions and try to be different. I can't be of course, since that would require a shift in *being*, and I am clueless about that.

Finally, I'm resigned that it will never work, and what do I do? I try the third step again and really do something different. I stay at the office longer and avoid talking to Janet and upsetting her when I am home. And nothing really changes. But I tried, so it must be someone else's fault.

That's where the other game comes in: the credit and blame game.

That was certainly the main game at the office. Credit and Blame. People flock to take credit for any successes not already nailed down. It's like a bidding pit on Wall Street. Me! Me! Me! And the one thing that can silence a roomful of loose-lipped and gesticulating executives is the question, "Who's responsible for this?" asked with even the slightest intimation of blame. Suddenly everyone finds something incredibly important to look at other than the person who asked the question. When it gets really desperate, the variations on the blame game become "Find the scapegoat" and "Who do we hang?"

Blame is the refuge of victims and cowards, and I had not been immune to its temptation. In fact I'd gone along with all of the myths. But I wouldn't be chained to them any longer. Nothing was really holding me in place. The chains were illusions, mere structures in the architecture of my mind, and my default life principle was the keystone. If that could be pried away and dissolved back to dust, I might have the opportunity to build a new Dave Carey. I knew that would be a large order.

We reached the cabin.

"Are you ready?" asked Adam. We both knew what was next, if I chose to go through with it.

"Yes," I said. A heavy sigh escaped from my lungs. The constriction in my chest and throat reappeared. This time, however, I didn't shy away. I didn't attempt to become undisturbed. Instead, I focused on the sensations and opened up to them. 'Hello, old friends,' I thought. 'Welcome. This time, I'm finally going to get to know you.'

TWENTY-THREE

TRANSMUTATION

Watch your thoughts, for they become words.
Watch your words, for they become actions.
Watch your actions, for they become your destiny.
— *Swami Chidvilasananda*

I think one must finally take one's life in one's arms.
— *Arthur Miller, After The Fall*

I entered the cabin, Adam following a few steps behind me. Without a word he motioned for me to sit down on the edge of my bunk. He smoothed the cover on the other bunk, and sat facing me.

"Dave, you're going to be taking an inner journey to experience your Default Life Principle. When you do this you'll be free. All you have to do is open up and allow your awareness to seek what it needs."

"What makes this work?" I wasn't sure if I really needed to know that, or whether some fear within me was just stalling for time.

Adam cocked his head to one side. "There are two principles at work here," he replied patiently. "The first is, *resistance causes persistence*. But let's begin with the second, *awareness allows for transmutation*. When you're aware of yourself as I AM, you are in the flow of life, embracing what is, and letting go of it in the next instant. Each moment is whole and complete as the cycle of creation continues unabated. You're free to create newly in each moment."

"I understand," I said. "But what does the word transmutation mean?"

"A transmutation is a change in form, shape, or function from a lower to a higher nature, as in alchemy."

"I thought alchemy was transmuting base metals like lead into gold or silver."

The glimmer of a grin flitted across his lips. "Yes, that's the story all right," he said. "That was a cover for the real work of the alchemical schools, which was to transmute human beings back to their essential nature. That's

208

what we're up to, returning to the essence of a form or experience. The energy is released from its static state as matter, and transmuted back to its original state as flowing energy. Only then can its seeming permanence be recognized as illusory. A creator transmutes stuck or stagnant forms back into energy to be used creatively again."

"But when you say forms," I interjected, "you're talking about behavior and emotions and ideas. It's hard for me to think of these things as forms. They seem pretty ephemeral."

"The hell they are!" he retorted. "Thinking makes imprints in matter. Thoughts become patterns embedded in your neural networks. And that's the trouble, they're like trains on tracks, traveling the same old routes."

Adam leaned forward on his bunk. "Answer this, Dave. Which sefira allows for blocked energy to dissolve?"

"I don't know. Resonance?"

"That's it, of course. You can say awareness allows for transmutation or resonance allows transmutation. Same thing. To transmute something, to dissolve a stuck experience from the past requires resonance, the ability to observe and experience something directly, unconditionally, with non-attachment. In other words, to transmute an experience, you have to perceive it from the perspective of its creative source. That depth of relatedness to your own experience creates a flow that dissolves a stuck, fixed state. When you resonate with what you observe, you are like a tuning fork, vibrating in the same frequency, creating the flow that dissolves its fixed state."

"I think I understand, at least as much as I can without experiencing it directly. What about the first operating principle you mentioned? That sounds like the one that causes all the mischief in the first place."

"On your last point, you're right, of course. Resistance causes persistence. If you resist or stop the flow of energy, you begin to build up a form, which takes more and more energy to hold in place."

"Like building a dam across a river?" I offered. "You have to build up a lot of bulwarks to hold back the flow of the river, and the pressure buildup is enormous."

"Yes. Look at all the energy people use when they try to hide what they are really feeling. The pressure buildup is called stress, which, if continued, devolves into disease. Dis-ease, get it? It occurs whenever you are out of balance, when you resist the flow of life energy, be it physical, emotional, mental or spiritual. Now if you identify yourself with any of your creations, if you become attached to them, you impede the flow. Identification is a form of resistance. It's an attempt to freeze the flowing and transitory into a permanent state."

"I think I understand," I said. "I haven't allowed myself to change. I've been repeating the same old problems over and over again. There have been slight variations on the theme, and a rotating cast of characters; but it has basically been the same plot. I attempt to show my competence and gain control of a situation only to have someone or something come in from the wings unexpectedly to take away my control, and then I don't know what to do. Then I struggle, persevere, and survive, and the story begins all over again."

I winced. "I've had other Hendersons in my life before Roger showed up."

"And that is the cost of giving up the possibility of creating for the certainty of persistence. What you get is no real change, only dead, conditioned repetition. What you're about to embark on is a process not of change, but of transmutation. You're going to observe and resonate with some of the past experiences stored in your mind so they will transmute back to their original state of energy."

"What will that leave me with?"

He laughed. "If all goes well, it will leave you with nothing. *No-thing*. In the Kabbalah, it's the Ain Sof, in other disciplines it's the Void. You've always been satisfied to get *some-thing*, which merely reinforced the old patterns. This time you won't be reinforcing the forms, you'll be dissolving them. All you have to do is stay aware and observe and experience what you get in this process without resisting in any way. Observe, embrace, experience whatever happens. Don't resist the flow. Don't attach to any form, whether it's an emotion, a sensation or a rule you've concocted.

"Remember, in this process, you are the witness; you are the awareness of what is appearing."

"But wait!" I said in sudden panic, "how will I know what to do when I still don't know what my life principle is?"

"Relax. That's one thing you don't have to worry about. You'll know what you need to do. While having a mind that's automatically associative is a pain in the ass when it's unconsciously replaying the same useless messages, it also works in your favor in this process. All of the elements associated with your default life principle are interrelated. They're woven together in a giant tapestry of physical sensations, emotions, thoughts, beliefs and images. It's holographic: each element can lead you to experience all the rest. As you experience and dissolve them back to energy, the forms that have imprisoned you will become dimmer, less substantial.

"You start with some element of the tapestry, pull one thread, and that memory will lead to all the rest."

"How do I pick the right thread?"

"Find something that frequently troubles you that you have no control over, something that closes down your flow of expression when you experience it. That will be your 'hook.' When you start to pull it, the rest will unravel. There is nothing to figure out. It's not a logical process. A word, a tone of voice, a facial expression, an aroma, the notes of a song, the sound of traffic outside — anything can start the associative process. Just observe, discern, and resonate with whatever you experience, knowing that you are transmuting it back to its original nature in the very act of becoming aware of it."

Suddenly Adam stood up. "Enough talk! Have you got a hook?"

"That's easy. The tight, full sensation I get in my upper chest and in my throat. They've been bothering me ever since we started this conversation."

"Good. It's visceral for you and you'll know very clearly whether it dissolves or not. Now the hook needs to be as specific as possible — not general or conceptual at all, but directly experienced. Which is more prominent right now, the feeling in your chest or the one in your throat?"

"The sensation in my upper chest."

"Good. Let's get started."

What happened next was an enigma too irrational for words. Words had about as much chance of capturing the experience as they do of evoking a Beethoven symphony. There are thresholds across which words, no matter how well crafted, cannot pass.

On the other hand, the result was ridiculously simple, and can be summarized in three simple words: *I am free.* That was the bottom line. I was free of the default life principle that had enslaved me for so long.

Adam asked me to lie down in a comfortable position, close my eyes, and simply follow his instructions. "Whatever you get, observe and don't resist," he reminded me.

He led me through the progressive body relaxation process he'd taught me the day before. I'd gotten better each time I'd done it, discovering bodily sensations I had been oblivious to earlier. This time I easily relaxed my muscle tension in response to his instructions. I was fully aware and listening. Adam's voice was inviting me to descend in a mental elevator down ten levels of consciousness. I heard him slowly count from ten to one. At each level of descent my awareness expanded. At the base I entered a level of awareness deeper than any I'd attained in our previous inner forays. It was new, and yet familiar.

Adam spoke again. "Recall the hook you've selected as your entry key."

The tightness in my upper chest was there, its grip unmistakable.

"Describe the sensation and its exact location."

I did as he asked. I realized this was a first for me. In the past, I'd

211

always resisted the sensation. Now, I allowed myself to feel it, know it. There were subtleties to the sensation — pressure, pulling, heat — that I'd been unaware of before.

"Imagine a large circular building in a great open field," Adam said. "Can you see it, Dave?"

I did.

He invited me to walk toward it. I approached it slowly and deliberately until I reached the looming entryway.

"Now feel the tightness in your chest and enter."

The door was a deep, glowing red. It opened at my touch and I walked through, entering a dimension of physical sensations, a world of aching tension, of throbbing pain and nausea. My awareness somehow moved within the energy field of my body as an observer, and yet at the same time I felt the actual sensations within my physical form. The feelings arose spontaneously, irrationally — the tightness in my chest, a throbbing sensation in my right knee, cramping in my lower back, nausea in my gut, a hot, dry sensation in the upper part of my mouth. One bodily sensation followed another, and I did as Adam had asked — experienced it without resistance, without analysis, describing my sensations to Adam as they occurred.

The simplicity of the process was staggering. Wherever I placed my awareness the energy discharged, flowing throughout my body like an electric current.

Adam must have sensed a change in me. He asked if I was ready to move on. "Is there another door, Dave?"

I described it to Adam. It was purple and round in shape, cold to the touch and hard as steel. I couldn't open it, no matter how much I struggled. So I surrendered. I stood at the threshold and opened myself to Grace.

"I AM."

At those words, the door rolled open like the diaphragm of a camera lens, and I was swept through the eye, into a world of flickering images.

"It's like dreaming," I murmured.

I heard Adam's response as if from a great distance. He was asking me to describe what I was witnessing. The images were as fully dimensional as dreams, and I was watching and experiencing them simultaneously. I was with Henderson. There was a heaviness to the scene. I was losing control of the situation and struggling with my feelings.

"The pressure in my chest is increasing," I told him.

"Allow an earlier image to surface that is associated with this feeling," Adam said.

"I'm with Janet in the family room. We're both upset. I'm trying to fig-

212

ure out how the hell to make her happy. I don't know what to do. I seem to be out of my depth. Struggling."

The feelings in my chest and throat were alarmingly strong.

I heard Adam's voice asking me to allow an earlier scene to emerge. I could barely keep from choking.

"I'm ten years old. My Dad is frowning at me, telling me how disappointed he is in my report card. I am trying to listen, trying to maintain control, but I'm having trouble breathing."

"Don't resist it," Adam instructed.

"The boy is here now," I suddenly said.

A small figure, wet, cold, and shivering had curled up next to me.

"Who is it?" asked Adam.

"I know who it is," I whispered, "It's David."

"How old is he?"

"Five years old."

"Can you go back with him?"

A pause. "Yes," I said softly.

An earlier image emerged. Slowly at first, then with a roar of heightened consciousness, it enveloped me. I was at Ground Zero.

I am five years old. I'm standing at the end of the wooden pier behind the cabin. Jimmy Greenfield is motioning for me to get into his rubber raft.

I tell him that I can't. I'm not allowed in the deep water by myself. I can't swim.

"Don't worry," Jimmy says. "I won't tell."

I hesitate.

"Carey, you're chicken!"

I'm climbing down the ladder into the raft, and now Jimmy is pushing away from the pier and I'm looking over the edge, and it's deep. I can't see the bottom. The raft is rocking in the water, and I'm scared. Jimmy is laughing and rocking the raft back and forth, and I'm holding onto the sides so tightly my hands hurt. I'm asking him to stop, but he just keeps laughing. He's rocking his body forward now, and the front of the raft is dipping under the water, and Jimmy falls forward into the lake holding the front of the raft with his hands. The back of the raft is tilting up. I'm trying to lean back to balance it, but it's too late. The raft is flipping over. There's a loud splash and then it's dark and cold all around me and I'm swallowing water, and it's filling my mouth and

213

*nose and I can't breathe. I can see my arms and legs furiously churn-
ing in the dim green light. Sounds are distant and muffled. I'm afraid,
and my voice is screaming, "Mommy, help me!" but the sound can't
get out. A pressure is building in my chest, and I'm gasping for air.
My feet touch the soft, slimy bottom of the lake. Now I'm pushing up.
My arms and legs are thrashing in terror, trying to go toward the light
above me, trying to regain some control... now my face breaks the surface, feeling the air.*

*I'm choking, coughing, gasping. I catch a blurred glimpse of the pier
through water-filled eyes, but I can't reach it. I'm sinking, watching
the bubbles escape from my mouth in a beautiful stream, upward
toward the light.*

I can't struggle anymore.

There's no one to help me.

I'm alone.

My body is sinking toward the bottom. I no longer care.

*And now there's a muffled splash and I see a white bathing cap and a
woman's body in a black bathing suit, and her arms are around me.
I'm choking, gagging... now I'm lying on the pier, and my body is shivering and I'm heaving up water and gulping for air. Hands are on me,
turning me on my stomach, the woman in the black bathing suit is
straddling me, pressing and pumping her hands on my back. She is
saying words I can't make out. All I can hear is my own sobbing,
"Mommy, I'm sorry. Mommy, I'm sorry."*

*I feel a towel wrapped around me, and the woman in black is asking
me if I live in the cabin at the end of this pier. I'm too scared to talk,
but I nod my head. I feel her hand on my shoulder as she leads me off
the pier towards my cabin.*

*I want my Mommy. I break away from the woman's grasp. I'm run-
ning, stumbling on the grass; and now I'm up the two steps and burst-
ing through the cabin door.*

*I rush up to Mommy in my wet towel. I'm crying, and I try to hold on
to her. My sobs are coming in waves now, all the terror and all the
shame coming to the surface.*

*Mommy is sitting up, holding me at arms length, her grip is tightening,
stopping me from coming closer, holding me at a distance.*

"Stop crying! Tell me what happened!" Her voice is strident, annoyed.

*And now the woman in the black bathing suit comes in and starts
explaining. I watch Mommy's face and I know she's frightened and
angry. I keep trying to snuggle up against her but her grip on my arms
is tighter, and she is thanking the woman.*

*Now she is yelling at me in front of the woman, saying how upset she is
that I didn't listen, that I didn't obey. And she is telling me to say
thank you to the woman and to say that I'm sorry for causing such
trouble. And I'm shivering and afraid and ashamed, and I'm stammer-
ing the words my mother wants me to say; but I'm still choking and
sobbing and the words don't come out right. The woman is saying it's
not important that I apologize and that she is just glad I'm all right,
and my mother is saying it's not okay.*

The woman in the black bathing suit leaves.

My world is breaking.

I don't know why my mommy doesn't love me.

And it is over.

I was quiet then, all imagery had dissolved into the light. With one
exception. He stood before me, slightly shivering, still wrapped in the lime
green towel.

"He's still here," I murmured hoarsely.

"Let him know that you are always there for him," Adam's voice offered
quietly.

I reached out and took the hand of my five year old self. He looked up
at me.

"I understand," I said. "I was with you the whole time."

I knelt down to his height.

"I am always here for you, and will always be here for you," I said, wiping his hair from his eyes. "I know what it was like for you."

I took him into my arms. "Let it all go," I whispered in his ear, kissing
his cheek. "Give it all to me." And he let it all go. All the fear, terror, grief
and loss that he had held for forty years, frozen in time and space. I took it
all without reservation and with unconditional love. I felt it flowing from him,
and embraced it as my own, enveloping it with my awareness, within the light
of I AM.

And as I held him, he too dissolved in the light.

"Have you reached the end of it?" Adam asked softly.

I nodded my head.

He gently asked me to run through the experience again from the beginning. This time, as I did so, I felt detached, as if observing a film. The energy

stored in the memory had dissolved; it was merely a story I was telling. As I described each moment, I noticed that the sensation in my chest and throat had disappeared.

I was lighter, full of space.

As I got to the end this second time around, I finally understood it — the organizer of my life, my default life principle. Obvious. Simple. Ridiculously simple. I began to chuckle, and then laughed out loud, even as I lay there in the cabin where I gave birth to the whole stupid idea in the first place — at the age of five.

I heard Adam's voice gently coaxing. "What is it?"

"My life's been a joke put together by the mind of a very stressed-out five year old. The other day, you said that it isn't what happened to you that makes the biggest difference in your life, it's what you decided it meant. I didn't fully understand that until this moment.

"The default life principle that I've lived my life from for over forty years has been, *'I'm not worth loving.'*

"The moment that I believed 'I'm not worth loving,' I became that idea, and I've been trying to prove my worth ever since."

I lay there, at peace for the first time in my life, watching the images of my life come together, finally making perfect sense.

I looked back at the memory of that long ago day with new eyes. I was filled with compassion and love for my mother. She had always loved me. I saw now that her behavior had been in reaction to her own shock and fear of losing me, an expression of her embarrassment and anger with herself for not being there when I almost drowned.

I could see the whole design now. If I'm not worth loving for who I am, but only for what I do or don't do, then I'll become very good at doing. If I do good work they may want to keep me around. But I can't get too close to anyone, because if I do, they will see me. And who "me" is, of course, is "I'm not worth loving."

All kinds of behavior had issued from this life principle: my need to control everything, my constant worry about how things were going, even when they were going well. I had to be concerned. *"I can't do the wrong thing or it may cost me my life."* That was the internal logic of the default life principle.

I could never enjoy any of my accomplishments, but I could easily find fault with what I did or with myself. No wonder I tried to micromanage everyone and everything! No wonder I had trouble cutting other people some slack. I cut myself none at all!

I could never give my family the one thing they'd been asking for all these years — myself. How could they possibly want me? Inside my life principle that desire didn't even compute. They couldn't really want me! Only what I did made me worth something, so I needed to stay busy.

My life principle had guaranteed a life of striving, organizing my life into a futile attempt never again to be taken by surprise. I had focused every waking moment on trying to prove my worth.

What a joke! Inside a life organized by "I'm not worth loving" how many successful projects, awards, promotions, and people saying "I love you" would it take before I finally felt worthy of love? It had cost me everything I really wanted from life — joy, the freedom to create and express myself freely, a sense of peace and satisfaction, gratitude, authentic relationships, even love itself.

Adam's voice calmly guided me back to the outer reality where my journey had begun: up the elevator of consciousness, back to the awareness of my physical body lying on the cabin bunk. I opened my eyes and slowly sat up. I looked around the room. I looked at Adam and silently stood up to embrace him in a bear hug. I walked outside. I noticed a difference in my movements. There was a lightness in my gait, a sense of ease and peace throughout my body, a sense that All Is Well. My breathing was easy. I looked for the old feeling of tightness, but it was nowhere to be found.

I felt tremendous relief, but some sadness too. I had squandered a lot of years and lost a lot of love in this life. My whole idea about love had been wrong. Worthiness is irrelevant to love. Love either happens or it doesn't. Worthiness is a game called "trade." Love itself is unconditional. It is an act of grace — an act of being, not an act of doing.

All my feeble attempts over the years to gain certainty were doomed to failure and distracted me from my real opportunity to express and experience love in each moment of existence.

Now I understood, and my awareness was not an occasion for sorrow, but for celebration. I felt finally released from my lifelong obsession with permanence — my pathetic, futile attempt to capture life's rainbows in a bottle. I could, for the first time, joyfully embrace life's transitory nature. From the evanescence of the present comes the actuality of the future, all mixture and manner of form; and that is the truth and the power of creation. I could sense it pulsating, flowing in the great world around me. I walked out of the cabin and stood looking at the lake for some minutes, filled with wonder and awe, observing the flow of it.

Grace, the fourth sefira, unconditionally offered the world to me. Finally I had discerned the gift. Finally I was awake.

I was free. Free to be.

Who was I? I AM Awareness.

What was my created life principle? I didn't know yet, but I was open to receive it.

I walked down to the water's edge. My whole life I'd disliked being in the water — hated even getting my face wet.

Now, there's no dread, no pulling back. It's just...water. I put my hand out and feel it, cool between my fingers. The coolness is pleasant, the reflections on its rippling surface, beautiful.

I kneel at the shoreline and bury my face below the surface of the water, opening my eyes without fear. The underwater plants, moving slowly in the water's flow, catch the late afternoon light. I feel happy and relaxed. I blow some bubbles into the water, watching them glisten and break at the surface.

I stand up and turn back to the cabin. Then I stop, and turn again to face the lake. Lit by a rising inner joy, I shed my clothes in a pile at the edge, and wade into the dark green water. Feeling the sudden, invigorating shock of cold water on warm skin, I submerge completely; swimming slowly, strongly and quietly below the surface, out beyond where a five year old boy once dared to go.

TWENTY-FOUR

LIFE IS BUT A DREAM

If one advances confidently in the direction of his dream,
and endeavors to live the life which he has imagined,
he will meet with a success unexpected in common hours.
— Henry David Thoreau

It was late afternoon when we pushed off from shore in the dinghy.

"I'm enjoying my new found relationship with water," I said, grasping the oars. I shot a downward glance at my paunchy abdomen. "And I think I'll take up swimming," I added with a laugh.

Adam flashed a smile and settled languidly back, his head cradled against the air cushioned stern, arms outstretched. "Not too shabby, eh?"

I rowed us out to a spot where we had a three hundred and sixty degree view of the lake. We got the anchor in place and leaned back in the cramped little boat to feel the sun's warmth as we talked.

"I can't thank you enough. It's hard to describe how different I feel. I'm a new person."

"New?" he replied with mock surprise. "Not new. Not old. Timeless."

"Yes, that's more like it. I stand corrected!"

We became silent, watching the light play upon the lake's surface, appreciating the shifting colors and shapes of each new moment. Nothing was fixed. Nothing was static. It was all always flowing. Adam moved his hand back and forth in the water, watching the small ripples radiate across the surface.

When he finally spoke, his voice was as soft as the sound of leaves skittering across a city sidewalk. "Most human beings have no appreciation for the way their minds create reality. In the service of I AM, the mind can unfold the world in novel, innovative ways. We really are shape shifting all the time."

I nodded. Finally I understood and was content. I closed my eyes, feeling the sun's warmth on my closed lids, reflecting on what I'd experienced over the past few days. It could not have been more practical. I had learned how to create my life from day to day.

What specific lessons had I learned?

Live from my original Self as a creator, and embrace my world.

Discern in each moment what is consistent with my Self and act accordingly.

Listen for the possibilities that others offer, open my heart to experience their worlds, and offer them the possibility of entering mine.

Listen from Spirit.

To listen from Spirit is to be faceless — to be an open field of awareness, able to put my ear to the ground and hear the great, timeless rhythm of life.

Resonate with Spirit, resonate with others, resonate with the world. Then I'll know what to say and do in any situation. Who I say I am gives shape to my world. Who I am being defines the course of my life.

What form will my future take? I don't know yet. The first step is welcoming and eliciting the personal creativity of everyone around me, affirming that each person has a stake in creating the future.

Perhaps this kind of leadership is more like coaching than managing. A great coach brings forth the creative powers, the greatness of his players.

Average coaches show what actions to take; they tell you what to do — rules, instructions, micro-management, riding herd.

Good coaches tell you where to look from — the vision, the operating principles, the values.

But great coaches create a new way of being so compelling that you take it on as your own and become it.

I opened my eyes, sat up and gripped the oars.

"Adam, this is perfect!" I said excitedly. "I have here in my hands a practical metaphor for leadership. I'm rowing the boat. Now let's say that you're the owner of the boat, and you've employed me to row you around. If I get paid by the hour to row, I don't really care how fast or slow I go, or in what direction. It's all the same to me. I row when you say start, and I stop when you say so. You pay me for that. I have no real interest or commitment in any outcome other than getting paid and doing my job sufficiently well to continue to get paid. Period. I couldn't care less about words like 'excellence' or 'proactive' or 'empower' that you might be silly enough to throw my way; and if you talk to me about them, you're wasting your time. I'm operating from a 'slave ship' mentality, which is 'Don't row unless told to.'

"If you want me to do anything specific you'll have to direct me at every step. 'Go faster, go slower, go left, go right.' It's the perfect example of what happens when you're trying to shape my behavior only at the level of action. All that's available at best is: You give instructions and I follow them."

Adam was paying close attention, nodding delightedly.

"And nothing is going to change at that level," I continued. "If you offer me a bonus, a vacation, or anything else, it might affect my performance in the short run, but alters nothing in my fundamental ground of being. It is stimulus-response all the way. Carrot and Stick.

"But, if you're able to get me personally interested in reaching this destination, it will shift the appearing world for me. Because now we've added a higher leverage to the game of creating reality, called vision. Now I've got my own vision for what rowing this boat can accomplish. I'm no longer just putting in time, carrying out your orders. I have a personal stake in the matter. All of a sudden I'll see opportunities for reaching our destination that are separate and distinct, and maybe even better than your instructions. I will be more aware of the weather and the wind and tides. You no longer have to micro-manage me. You have time to attend to other aspects of the journey. You know I will correct myself and row at the speed necessary to accomplish our goal, because rowing is no longer just one stroke after the other. Each stroke is a step toward fulfilling a future I am also committed to achieving.

"Let's say that one day I have an epiphany, a shift in who I am being. I realize that the purpose of my life is no longer to get by each day and earn a living. Nor is my purpose even to fulfill a particular vision. Now who I am being is beyond time. Who I am is a new field of meaning. Who I am is: *I am a master rower.*

"At that moment, I've created a life principle for myself that gives direction and meaning to my life. Now I look for opportunities to express my mastery. Each stroke of the oar into the water now counts, as does its angle of entry, speed and pull. I am constantly looking for opportunities to test myself, to go beyond my current level of performance. I become an expert on boats, oars, weather patterns, and currents. No one has to manage me in this. Soon I am not merely rowing, I am a successful teacher of rowers. New ideas flow to me through grace, as my life principle shapes my inner and outer world. I develop new, more effective oar strokes and design an innovative design for oars, oar locks, and boats, not because I have to or even want to, but because it is a naturally appearing expression of who I am in the world. I open my own rowing academy, and the first thing I teach my students is to ask themselves the question 'Who am I?' That's where the real leverage will be found."

Adam was beaming, but was not so enamored that he neglected to push me further.

"Anything else?" he asked.

"I thought you'd never ask," I laughed. "The life principle is the heart of it all. I AM is the soul of it all."

"And anything else?" he persisted with a smile.

"The Ain Sof," I said softly. "The unnamable sacred silence that gives."

I glanced over his shoulder at my tree floating in the lake, the light flickering on it and within it. Was it the reflection of another world or was the reverse also true? This time I saw it as one with its counterpart on land. There was no separation. The tree that lived on the lake's surface was only a dream until fulfilled in form. They were mirrors of each other: the tree of no form and the tree of form, in perfect resonance.

The Genesis Principle is the continuum of creation. It's a whole, complete package, simultaneous and multidimensional. The world of Creation is only a possibility until its counterpart is fulfilled at the physical dimension, the world of Manifestation. The fulfillment of creation is the flow from nothing to something; from No-thing to Be-ing. The ocean of Spirit at infinite play.

"Being a creator is knowing ultimately that I'm not any shape at all," I said. "I'm not even a life principle. Even that is interim. It is a field that gives direction to I AM' s purpose in the world — creating. I don't *be* a shape, I *have* them. That's the job: to bring forth being, and to embrace and love all aspects of creation.

I paused. "How'd I do, coach?" I wasn't really asking for approval. I was complete. It was a way of saying thank you. I smiled at Adam with love and appreciation.

He said nothing. He didn't have to and he knew it. But his face looked like a cross between a Buddha and the cat who ate the canary.

"So who's rowing back?" I asked.

Adam grabbed the oars, and as he started to row, he began to sing in a sweet, melodious voice.

Row, row, row your boat,
Gently down the stream,
Merrily, merrily, merrily, merrily,
Life is but a dream!

"What was that all about?" I asked incredulously. The song seemed a little silly given the mood we were both in.

He chuckled. "You don't get it, do you?" he said, without missing a beat of his rowing stroke. "You've known that song all your life, you've even sung it I'll bet, yet you don't really know it at all! Pearls before swine! If you are 'to enter the kingdom of heaven, you must again be as little children,' remember?"

"What do you mean? What's to get?"

Adam sang the round again. Louder this time. He was watching me, delighting in my puzzlement.

222

"Dave, I don't know where this song comes from, but it practically holds the secret of life in just four short lines! Think about it, my friend. To row your boat is to propel forward your vehicle of expression, your identity, on the river of life. The rower is I AM — Origination. The first row is the world of Creation. The second is the world of Formation. The third row is Manifestation. All three strokes of the oars are necessary for an intention to be fulfilled in the world.

"Gently means smoothly, without effort or struggle. Down the stream. Going with the flow of life, the way life unfolds itself with grace.

"It's the experience of being in charge and not in charge at the same time. Row your boat *gently* down the stream.

"Merrily, merrily, merrily, merrily is a joyous celebration of uninhibited enjoyment, delight, and sweetness. It's the state of being you attain when you live as a creator. And it's repeated four times — one for each world of creation."

"From I AM to IT IS!" I exclaimed.

"And finally, Dave, the last line, the truth that all enlightened beings directly know! Life is but a dream! And we are its dreamers. Life's a passing play of forms, sights and sounds, wins and losses, ups and downs — energy in motion, the medium for creating.

"We can surf the quantum waves of possibility, backwards and forwards in time, coming from an infinite void that is timeless, spaceless and characterless, but that holds within itself, waiting to be unfolded, all the possible pathways of being. *We are such stuff as dreams are made on.*

"Knowing that gives us the freedom to create.

"Even the structure of this simple song is revealing! It's a round. It can keep going indefinitely, and you can enter it or leave it at any point in its cycle."

For a moment I was at a loss for words, struck with admiration for this humble little song that I'd never thought much about before. As Adam rowed us back to shore, we sang the round over and over at the top of our voices, our hearts overflowing with thankfulness and joy. We were all too happy to be doing nothing more than singing together a small song, on a small boat, on a small lake, within a vast, unending universe.

TWENTY-FIVE

THE ELEVENTH SEFIRA

HEAR, O ISRAEL:
YHVH IS OUR GOD, YHVH IS ALL.
And you shall love the Lord your God
with all your heart, and with all your soul,
and with all your might.
— Deuteronomy VI, 4-5

Attain the Source, and the rest need not bother you.
— Yang-shan Hui-chi

We sat by the edge of the lake in silence, contentedly watching our portion of earth slowly turn away from its star. Stillness prevailed at this cusp of twilight; this brief intermission between day and night, when, for a moment, nature paused and held its breath, and all vibration seemed suspended.

The full moon, floating above the hills cast a glow that rescued the surrounding forms from oblivion. In its pale radiance, I could see Adam's face intently gazing at the lake.

There was no striving here, only being.

And stars.

I was not, and had never been, separate or alone. I was part and parcel of the universal flow. Aloneness was possible only in an imagination determined to isolate itself, determined to make itself miserable.

In my own way, I was one of those stars in a galaxy of billions of stars; a little pinpoint of flame in the natural expansion of the universe, a suddenly created reality with all eternity behind it.

I heard Adam get up. He stood silently for a full minute, looking at the hovering, pock-marked disc and its glowing twin on the lake's surface.

"Any final questions before we go back?" he asked quietly.

"You never did tell me the eleventh sefira of the Tree of Life."

"Ah, yes! Now we can talk about it," he replied.

224

He walked back to where I was sitting, crouched down next to me, and pulled a small pen light from his breast pocket. "Here," he said, giving it to me to hold. From another pocket, he took the diagram of the ten sefiroth, and spread it on the ground.

As I held the light on the paper, he drew a dotted circle on the diagram along the center line, right below the top triad. He located it directly in the space between the worlds of Creation and Formation.

"In Hebrew, the eleventh sefira is called Da'at. It's often translated into English as 'knowledge', but it has nothing to do with knowledge. It's intuitive knowing or *Faith*. It is the bridge over the abyss between Creation and Formation. It's essential for creating, because ultimately, Faith confirms the unprovable. You just *know*."

"Are you talking about being a true believer?" I asked with a momentary spasm of concern."

"No, no, no!" he said vehemently, wincing at the very notion. "I'm not talking about blind faith. When that happens, it's no longer Faith, it's been fossilized into belief. Beliefs are concepts. Dead concepts. Faith begins with an intention to bring forth from I AM. It's the background for all the other sefiroth of the Tree of Life.

"You can't be a creator without Faith. But with Faith you can say, 'This shall be,' even when no physical evidence is backing you up. Faith begins with trust in your Self as an expression of YHVH, allowing you to resonate with the world and with your original Self."

"So, you don't wait for proof?" I ventured.

"Proof does not exist in the first three worlds of The Genesis Principle, only in the world of Manifestation. Strivers demand proof before they are willing to act. They want guarantees, fall-backs, life-preservers. But proof is always a derivative of creation. A physicist named Popper demonstrated we can only prove something to be false; we can never ultimately prove anything to be true. Even the scientific method is a matter of Faith. It's as much a structure of interpretation as anything else. Everything finally reduces to Faith, which is always a matter of creation."

"Do I have enough Faith?" I wondered aloud. "In the face of inner resistance or outer adversity, can I trust myself to know and stand my ground as a creator?"

Adam let out a belly laugh. "Look at yourself!" he exclaimed. "You've proven the power of Faith for years, though in a very distorted, unconscious way!"

"What do you mean? I don't get it."

"Your default life principle. Remember? You created the view of yourself, 'I'm not worthy of love,' and lived from it with complete faith for forty odd years! In the face of all evidence to the contrary, and numerous attempts by the people in your life to express their love for you over the years, you successfully resisted everything that didn't fit with your default life principle!

I laughed. How right he was! I had been conning myself. I had always possessed the power of Faith, but had diverted it from serving I Am to serving false gods.

"You might be wiser in the future to have faith in a way of being more consistent with your Infinite I," Adam suggested with mock reproach.

He sat there in the moonlight, his head cocked to one side, grinning, slowly stroking his beard.

Later, in the cabin, just as I was about to turn out the light and retire for the night, Adam said, "Wait. I have something for you."

He reached into his backpack and pulled out a thick, blue notebook. He thumbed through it, and opened to a well-worn page. Smiling, he read it to himself.

Then slowly and carefully, he tore the page out and handed it to me.

"I want you to have this."

"What is it?" I asked, accepting the page.

"More questions of course!" Adam was chuckling as he answered. "But you'll like these," he added. My father quoted these lines to me often when I was growing up. They guided his life, the way he treated people: his family, friends and business associates. They mean a lot to me. They've become my compass, helping me find my way, even in the darkest of times."

"But it's the page from your notebook! Why don't you just send me a copy?"

"That is the copy," he chuckled. "The real one is here!" He pointed to his heart.

There were three lines on the page, three simple questions. I read and reread them. These questions were not to be answered, they were to be lived from. As I read them a third time, I knew instantly, with an instinct I could not really account for, that in the weeks and years to come these questions would return to me in moments of doubt, and renew my soul whenever I was in danger of losing faith with what Adam had been teaching me. Here was a guide to life that would forever renew itself:

If I am not for myself, who will be for me?
And if I am only for myself, what am I?
And if not now, when?
— Hillel

I reached out and took Adam's hand in both of mine.

"Thank you," I said simply.

Awakening to awareness.

That's the only way to describe my first experience that following morning. It was distinct from the thousands of previous mornings in my life. Eyelids opened and the world was present. The whole room filled the field of awareness at once: light, shapes, colors, textures and sounds. There was no sense that I was located anywhere, just an experience of inclusive awareness not bound to a particular point. Then, body sensations. Even these were included in the total fabric of experience, given no more weight than a pale yellow beam of light upon a wall or a high pitched chirping from outside the window. The visual awareness of wall, chair, ceiling, and floor was simultaneously accompanied by textures, weight, sounds, and smells — an impression of directly knowing the whole room at once. Then an awareness of being aware, an awareness of lack of mental noise.

That was the first thought. The second thought was surprise that I felt no aches and pains when I got out of bed. Instead was an effortless flow of energy throughout my body. The first appearance of identity soon followed. My sense of myself as a finite me, as a personality, was soon back in place; but somehow it was different, as though it were a suit of clothes I had put on for the day.

Almost simultaneously, the third thought arrived. And that was the realization that I knew my life principle. And right then and there I clarified my intentions for the future of my life and all the people in it.

I AM a creator. My role in life is to assist others to know and experience this principle for themselves.

I know when I return home there will be no guarantees, no certainty about the direction things will take in my relationships with Janet, my children, Diane or Henderson. Such uncertainty would have been a problem for me before. Not now. I am no longer stuck in preconceptions of Janet, Henderson or anyone else. I can relate to them as creators of their own worlds, whether they know they are or not.

I love Janet. That is the background for whatever form our relationship will take in the years ahead. I am going back to create a devoted partnership with her; one that is alive; one that means something. With Sarah and Stephen I have a chance to create a new relationship devoid of any suffocating ideals of how they should be or shouldn't be.

I expect it may take them a while to see me in a new way. That will be the challenge, to create a presence with others that sweeps the past aside — a presence that finds grace and harmony in the inspiration of the moment. Playing life as a finite game requires winners and losers. Life as infinite play, however, creates new kinds of relationships. I have a choice.

I can see business in a new light. Business, like everything else in the universe, is an expression of the holy. The philosopher, Martin Buber, divided the universe into two realms: the holy and the not-yet-holy. He said that the not-yet-holy was simply the holy that we had not yet perceived as itself. All that we encounter is an opportunity for us to recognize and reveal God's presence in the world, to reveal the sacred center pulsing at the heart of form.

Diane can count on me to be a partner in our company's resurrection. I trust myself to present our decisions powerfully to Henderson; appreciating his reality, while offering him another, more inclusive vision. My negotiations with him will take place in an altogether different framework than before. I am confident that I'll be able to see his point of view for what it is, even if we are in the most profound disagreement. Negotiation doesn't mean approval. It means creating and taking the next step together. If Henderson can sign on, we'll have a game. If not, another opportunity will present itself to me, maybe in another field of play entirely. I finally know: The Self has nothing to fear. The material world is the expression of our Spirit. There are material expressions, and there are spiritual expressions, but they are not separated; they are points in a universal continuum.

Why should I walk the earth at all if material life isn't an opportunity to express and fulfill Spirit in form? The Infinite I is either All of it, or it's not it Self. The earth is a material thing. It's the reality of God's dream, perhaps, but it's material. I can dig in it. I can live on it. I can destroy it. I have flesh, and walk this earth precisely so I can involve myself with material things, and if I don't do that well, I'm missing the point. If I give action to the essence of my life, then I'm being spiritual. What really matters is who I am being and how I affect other people's lives.

The Genesis Principle is real to me. I can look from the four worlds. I have faith that I can open up to receive the guidance I need from the universe, whether it takes the form of Adam, Janet, or anyone or anything else that might be its messenger. Yes, even Henderson.

I can embrace life as a flowing creation.

I am no longer "I'm not worth loving."

Nor am I "I'm worth loving" either.

They are two sides of the same coin in which love is conditional: my default life principle and my ideal I—the dual faces of my mistaken identity; the two lies I told myself that reinforced each other, forcing me to live in the airless, confining gap between them. Together they denied my true nature. Together they kept me trapped in enduring and striving. Both positions deny love as itself. Love is the unconditional expression of Self.

Thanks to Adam, I now know who I am.

It was just sunrise. I decided to drive back early. I wanted to talk with Janet, even if I had to drive to Boston to reach her.

Adam wanted to get in one last round of fishing before driving back, so I left him the key to lock up the cabin. I didn't know where he and I would go after this. I was interested in working with him further. I wanted to integrate these principles into my daily life, to design my future goals from my created life principle. Adam suggested that I wait two weeks and give myself a chance to digest what I'd learned.

"Call me if and when it's appropriate," he had said. "You'll know when."

We left it open like that. I knew that even if I never saw him again Adam would always be in my heart. That may be the greatest gift of all, to hold others in our hearts.

I finished loading my gear into the car and strolled down to the lake. Fifty yards out, Adam was sitting contentedly in his boat, his fishing rod curving in a graceful arc over the side. In the rising mist the boat seemed to be floating, not on water, but on a cloud. I waved good-bye. He looked up at my motion and waved back. Then he put down his rod, and grasping his oars, began to row away from me toward the center of the lake.

One, two, three strokes, and his form evaporated into a field of silvery white.

About the Authors of The Genesis Principle

Hal Isen and Peter Kline have been associates and colleagues in various enterprises for almost forty years, as educators, consultants, workshop leaders, thespians and fellow travelers on the path of transformation. They have been both student and teacher for each other and feel privileged to call one another, "my friend."

Hal Isen, MFA, CHT, is the creator of Core Wisdom® and LifeCoaching®, the methodologies that are the foundation for The Genesis Principle. As an educator, organizational consultant, executive coach, clinical hypnotherapist, and artist, he has 30 years experience designing and conducting transformational programs in personal effectiveness, creativity, communication, and leadership for thousands of people nationally and internationally. His company, Hal Isen & Associates, Inc., located in Mill Valley, California, provides a synthesis of timeless principles and innovative practices to individuals, groups, small businesses and Fortune 500 organizations. He has illustrated three books, and done drawings for magazines, newspapers, and television. His drawings, prints and sculpture have been exhibited nationally, including at the Baltimore Museum of Art and the Corcoran Gallery in Washington, D.C. His artwork is included in the collections of the National Library of Medicine, The Smithsonian Institution and the Library of Congress. The Genesis Principle is his first book. He may be reached by e-mail at hal@halisen.com. His web site is www.corewisdom.com

Peter Kline is Chairman of the Board of Integra Learning Systems of South Bend, Indiana. Over the past twenty years he has been introducing the dynamics of learning to an ever-growing audience of business, government and educational institutions. An exponent of innovative, highly successful educational and organizational practices, Kline has pioneered methods that accelerate learning and bring involvement and creativity to the classroom and the workplace. He is the author of several books on the theater and several books on education, including two widely popular titles, *The Everyday Genius* and *Ten Steps To A Learning Organization*. His previous novel, *The Butterfly Dreams* is a visionary look at the common ground between Science and Religion. His books have been published in seven languages. Mr. Kline has appeared on numerous TV and radio programs, and has been the subject of a variety of profiles and studies.

In *The Genesis Principle* he joins his friend and colleague in helping to explicate Hal Isen's Core Wisdom® and LifeCoaching® methodologies. Currently, Mr. Kline is working on a book on Shakespeare. He may be reached by e-mail at peterkline@aol.com.